"Dr White has written ... *tical basis* this clearly written and useful book ... n formulating cases at a macro and micro level and ... London n therapy and select interventions for patients with various chronic medical problems. Excellent case examples, transcripts, and assessment instruments are provided. Even clinicians that primarily do not treat medical patients will benefit from studying this book."

Dr Judith S. Beck, Director, The Beck Institute for Cognitive Therapy and Research, Philadelphia, USA, and Clinical Associate Professor of Psychology in Psychiatry, University of Pennsylvania, USA.

"There is growing recognition of the contribution of clinical health psychologists in the management of chronic medical conditions. Craig White applies Beck's cognitive model to a range of medical problems, including cancer, chronic pain, and cardiac disease. This is a readable, clinically focussed and practical guide, which uses relevant extracts from clinical sessions covering assessment, case level formulations and interventions. It will be of interest to all involved in clinical health psychology applications."

Paul Kennedy, Academic Director, Oxford Doctoral Course in Clinical Psychology, Warneford Hospital, Oxford, UK

"Craig White's Cognitive Behavioral Therapy for Chronic Medical Problems is required reading for any clinician who works with patients who have difficulties related to cancer, pain, diabetes, dermatology, surgery or cardiac problems. Given the increased risk of these problems in our population, this important volume provides much needed information as to how to assess and treat the psychological adjustment that follows from chronic health issues. This book is well-organized, practical, clinically sensitive and extremely valuable in helping the clinician work with these complex issues."

Robert L. Leahy, PhD, Editor, *Journal of Cognitive Psychotherapy: An International Quarterly*, President-Elect, International Association for Cognitive Psychotherapy, Clinical Associate Professor, Department of Psychiatry, Cornell University, USA, and Director, American Institute for Cognitive Therapy

"This timely book by Craig White presents a detailed account of CBT for a range of chronic medical problems: cancer, chronic pain, diabetes, dermatitis, and surgical and cardiac problems. In his approach Dr White shows how problem level and case level formulation can be applied to assessment and treatment of distress and psychosocial problems, and can be used to improve self-management in medical conditions. He provides a wealth of valuable information on interviewing, self-report measures and treatment strategies. This book will be an indispensable resource for health professionals working in this area."

Adrian Wells, PhD, Reader in Clinical Psychology, University of Manchester, UK

COGNITIVE BEHAVIOUR THERAPY FOR CHRONIC MEDICAL PROBLEMS

The Wiley Series in

CLINICAL PSYCHOLOGY

Craig A. White	Cognitive Behaviour Therapy for Chronic Medical Problems: A Guide to Assessment and Treatment in Practice
Steven Taylor	Understanding and Treating Panic Disorder: Cognitive-Behavioural Approaches
Alan Carr	Family Therapy: Concepts, Process and Practice
Max Birchwood, David Fowler and Chris Jackson (Editors)	Early Intervention in Psychosis: A Guide to Concepts, Evidence and Interventions
Dominic H. Lam, Steven H. Jones, Peter Hayward and Jenifer A. Bright	Cognitive Therapy for Bipolar Disorder: A Therapist's Guide to Concepts, Methods and Practice

Titles published under the series editorship of:

J. Mark G. Williams   *School of Psychology, University of Wales, Bangor, UK*

Peter Salmon	Psychology of Medicine and Surgery: A Guide for Psychologists, Counsellors, Nurses and Doctors
William Yule (Editor)	Post-Traumatic Stress Disorders: Concepts and Therapy
Nicholas Tarrier, Adrian Wells and Gillian Haddock (Editors)	Treating Complex Cases: The Cognitive Behavioural Therapy Approach
Michael Bruch and Frank W. Bond (Editors)	Beyond Diagnosis: Case Formulation Approaches in CBT

A list of earlier titles in the series follows the index.

COGNITIVE BEHAVIOUR THERAPY FOR CHRONIC MEDICAL PROBLEMS

A Guide to Assessment and Treatment in Practice

Craig A. White

Department of Psychological Medicine, University of Glasgow, Scotland, UK

JOHN WILEY & SONS, LTD

Chichester · New York · Weinheim · Brisbane · Singapore · Toronto

Copyright © 2001 by John Wiley & Sons Ltd,
Baffins Lane, Chichester,
West Sussex PO19 1UD, England

National   01243 779777
International (+44) 1243 779777
e-mail (for orders and customer service enquiries):
cs-books@wiley.co.uk
Visit our Home Page on http://www.wiley.co.uk
or http://www.wiley.com

Other Wiley Editorial Offices

John Wiley & Sons, Inc., 605 Third Avenue,
New York, NY 10158-0012, USA

WILEY-VCH GmbH, Pappelallee 3,
D-69469 Weinheim, Germany

Jacaranda Wiley Ltd, 33 Park Road, Milton,
Queensland 4064, Australia

John Wiley & Sons (Asia) Pte Ltd, 2 Clementi Loop #02-0
Jin Xing Distripark, Singapore 129809

John Wiley & Sons (Canada) Ltd, 22 Worcester Road,
Rexdale, Ontario M9W 1L1, Canada

Library of Congress Cataloging-in-Publication Data

White, Craig A.
    Cognitive behavioural therapy for chronic medical problems : a guide to
assessment and treatment in practice / Craig A. White.
        p. cm. — (The Wiley series in clinical psychology)
    Includes bibliographical references and index.
    ISBN 0-471-49480-1 (cloth : alk. paper)
    ISBN 0-471-49482-8 (paper : alk. paper)
    1. Cognitive therapy.   2. Chronic diseases—Treatment.   I. Title.   II. Series.

RC489.C63 W52 2000
616.89'142—dc21

                                                        00–047748

British Library Cataloguing in Publication Data

A catalogue record for this book is available from the British Library

ISBN 0-471-49480-1 (cased)
ISBN 0-471-49482-8 (paper)

Typeset in 10/12pt Palatino by Dorwyn Ltd, Rowlands Castle, Hants.
Printed and bound by Antony Rowe Ltd, Eastbourne

For my wife, Gwen and my son, Adam Craig

CONTENTS

LIST OF FIGURES

LIST OF TABLES

ABOUT THE AUTHOR

Craig A. White is currently Cancer Research Campaign Clinical Research Fellow in Psychosocial Oncology at the Department of Psychological Medicine, University of Glasgow. He is the first clinical psychologist to be awarded this prestigious Fellowship. He is a Chartered Clinical and Health Psychologist and has Honorary clinical positions with Ayrshire and Arran Primary Care NHS Trust and North Glasgow Hospitals University NHS Trust. He completed his clinical training at the University of Manchester and worked from 1995 to 1998 as an NHS clinical psychologist in adult mental and physical health. He undertook specialist training in cognitive therapy from 1996 to 1997 at the Newcastle Cognitive Therapy Centre under the supervision of Professor Ivy Blackburn. He is a Fellow of the Royal Society of Medicine. His research interests are in the application of cognitive models to the assessment, conceptualisation and treatment of the psychological consequences of medical and surgical problems.

PREFACE

This book has been written with the intention of providing cognitive behavioural therapists with guidance on how to practice cognitive behavioural therapy (CBT) with chronic medical problems. It is not intended to act as a guide to the practice of CBT with the common psychological problems associated with the medical problems which are covered in this book, nor has it been written as a comprehensive review of the literature on cognitive behavioural aspects of chronic medical problems. There are a number of reasons for this. First, there is insufficient literature on this topic from a clinical practice perspective to be of use to the practising clinician. Second, the aim of this book is to provide readers with a rich source of ideas about how to tailor their work to the problems associated with the medical conditions which are addressed in the book. Parts of the book are, of course, based on cognitive behavioural theory and, when relevant, reference will be made to the supporting literature. Extracts from therapy sessions are provided throughout to illustrate some of the suggestions which are made on assessment and intervention using CBT. These extracts are based on actual sessions with patients treated by the author. Details that may lead to the identification of these patients have been changed.

I have tried to write a book which I would have found useful when I started to work with patients experiencing psychological problems associated with chronic medical problems. I developed an interest in the psychological consequences of medical problems during my training as a clinical psychologist. My training was significantly influenced by cognitive behavioural therapy and this is an interest which developed further during my first years of clinical practice. I often found myself having to adapt findings from health psychology to the practice of CBT—incorporating these into my assessments and trying to adapt CBT protocols for anxiety and depressive disorders to work with patients experiencing cancer, chronic pain and psychological problems associated with surgery.

I hope this book will enable readers to feel competent and confident in the way in which they assess and treat the common problems which present in the physical health settings that this text covers. The book is divided into three parts.

Part I covers the main components of CBT. Chapter 1 outlines current issues within CBT and provides an overview of the themes and issues which are addressed within the book. Chapter 2 outlines a framework for assessment. Formulation is of paramount importance in CBT, and this is reflected in the devotion of Chapter 3 to this topic (an emphasis which is also reflected in the inclusion of formulation sections in each of the chapters in Part II). Chapter 4 summarises cognitive behavioural intervention strategies and the important guiding principles of CBT.

Part II outlines the application of CBT to common chronic medical problems. Chapters 5 and 6 are devoted to two problems for which most has been written on CBT—cancer and chronic pain. Chapter 7 outlines the way in which CBT is tailored to the needs and concerns of patients with diabetes. Chapter 8 illustrates how CBT can be applied to understanding and treating psychological problems associated with skin conditions. Chapter 9 outlines how cognitive behavioural principles can help with the process of surgery, and Chapter 10 addresses the problems which present in cardiac care settings.

Part III consists of two chapters on the professional and service issues which need to be considered by cognitive behavioural therapists working in this area. CBT in this area is in its infancy, and therapists need to ensure that they can participate in service planning and keep up to date with developments in CBT not only in general but also as applied to chronic medical problems. Psychological care of people with chronic medical problems can be marginalised by those who are responsible for commissioning and planning health care services.

My hope in writing this book is that, first, it provides clinicians with some ideas about how to work using CBT with their patients with chronic medical problems. Second, that it may stimulate some people to carry out much needed research into CBT in this area and on cognitive behavioural processes associated with psychology of chronic disease and its management. It is only when there is a greater body of research evidence that therapists can argue for service developments which will ensure that all patients with chronic medical problems can have equal chance of accessing CBT services.

ACKNOWLEDGEMENTS

I am grateful to a number of people who have influenced me during the early stages of my career. I am particularly grateful to the staff and supervisors associated with the University Department of Clinical Psychology, University of Manchester for providing an excellent training in clinical psychology and stimulating my interests in cognitive behavioural psychotherapy. I am especially grateful to Gillian Mayes for introducing me to the discipline of clinical psychology while I was an undergraduate and to Jennifer Unwin who encouraged my interest in clinical health psychology and provided many helpful insights on the practice of clinical psychology while I was training. Zena Wight (Consulting and Clinical Psychology Services) has been a respected colleague and friend from whom I have learned much about the provision of high-quality psychological services. Colin Espie (Department of Psychological Medicine, University of Glasgow) has supported my work. I also extend my thanks to the following people involved with the process of preparing this book: Michael Coombs, Mike Shardlow, Fran Scott-Turner and Lesley Valerio (John Wiley & Sons); Marian Kenny and Alison Carnegie (Department of Psychological Medicine, University of Glasgow); Margaret Wagner (Consulting and Clinical Psychology Services); Lindsay MacLeod (Department of Medical Illustration, Western Infirmary, Glasgow); Louise O'Neill and Brian Callaghan who assisted with literature searches; and Alex Whyte for copy-editing.

I am grateful to the Cancer Research Campaign. By awarding me a Fellowship in Psychosocial Oncology they have afforded me the opportunity in my current position to explore how some of the issues covered in this book applied to understanding psychosocial adjustment to cancer and its treatment. The interest and support of family and friends helped me to complete this book. Special thanks to Andrew and Ann McPhail. I thank the many people I have assessed and treated in my career so far. Their experiences and insights have helped me to write this book. I am indebted to my parents, Gordon and Linda White, for their love and for making so much possible. I could not have completed this book without the support, love and understanding of my wife Gwen, and I have dedicated it to her and to Adam, our son.

Part I

GENERAL COMPONENTS OF CBT FOR CHRONIC MEDICAL PROBLEMS

Chapter 1

INTRODUCTION

CHRONIC MEDICAL PROBLEMS: THE CONTEXT

Chronic medical problems have become increasingly prevalent in recent years. People are living longer and medical problems which might previously have carried considerable mortality risk can now be managed more effectively. Turner and Kelly (2000) have suggested that these improvements in the way chronic diseases are medically managed may sometimes be at the expense of patient quality of life. Scandlyn (2000) has suggested that chronic illness challenges views of life as orderly and having continuity, a challenge which can have significant psychological consequences. Increasing technological advances in medical science and practice form one of the factors responsible for changes in the epidemiology of disease, and have also resulted in a need for greater information and support. This is particularly true for patients who have to endure debilitating and demanding treatments. The publicity which is afforded medical advances often results in patients and their families having increased expectations that all medical problems can be cured. This in turn can make it difficult for patients to accept the personal consequences of a chronic medical problem and to embrace a 'coping' model when it comes to managing their illness.

A multidisciplinary emphasis means that patients are coming into contact with a greater number of health professionals. This involves a need to interact with more people and, for some, increased demands on already limited psychological resources. The move towards care in the community and day care means that patients may spend a longer time in non-hospital settings. This can result in some patients feeling unsupported psychologically and may be one of the factors that mediate psychological problems. Many chronic medical problems require a self-management approach to regulate the course and impact of patient symptoms and problems. Collaborative relationships must be established with health care staff and patients are often expected to adopt a more active role in managing their problems than might be expected with an acute medical problem. Holman and Lorig (2000) have highlighted some further differences between acute and chronic illnesses. These are outlined in Table 1.1. This comparison highlights the factors which can contribute to psychological problems associated with chronic medical problems. Indefinite outcomes and the associated pervasive levels of uncertainty surrounding diagnosis and prognosis are often central to the psychological problems associated with chronic medical problems and their treatment.

Table 1.1   Differences between acute and chronic diseases

	Acute disease	Chronic illness
Onset	Abrupt	Usually gradual
Duration	Limited	Lengthy, indefinite
Cause	Usually single	Usually multiple and changes over time
Diagnosis and prognosis	Usually accurate	Often uncertain
Technological intervention	Usually effective	Often indecisive, adverse effects common
Outcome	Cure	No cure
Uncertainty	Minimal	Pervasive
Knowledge	Professionals knowledgeable; patients inexperienced	Professional and patients have complementary knowledge

From Holman and Lorig (2000), Data Supplement—Box, electronic, *British Medical Journal* (reprinted by kind permission of authors and British Medical Journal).

THE PSYCHOLOGICAL IMPACT

Psychological dimensions of chronic disease are often overlooked (Turner & Kelly, 2000) as most patients adjust well to the psychosocial aspects of their chronic medical problem. Adjustment can become more difficult, however, when patients experience a decline in physical health status (Cassileth et al., 1984). It is generally accepted that around 20–25% of patients with chronic medical problems experience clinically significant psychological symptoms. The diagnosis of a chronic disease can stigmatise patients, by virtue of limited independence and/or the negative impact on daily routine (Scandlyn, 2000). Chronic medical problems often necessitate changes in behaviour by virtue of the increased self-care demands, and these, too, can result in stigmatisation. Holman and Lorig (2000: 526) have summarised the way in which the lives of patients with chronic medical problems are changed:

> With chronic disease, the patient's life is irreversibly changed. Neither the disease nor its consequences are static. They interact to create illness patterns requiring continuous and complex management. Furthermore, variations in patterns of illness and treatments with uncertain outcomes create uncertainty about prognosis. The key to effective management is understanding the different trends in the illness patterns and their pace. The goal is not cure but maintenance of pleasurable and independent living.

Patients with chronic medical problems often find themselves undertaking a delicate balancing act where they must balance the need to be in control of their lives with the fact that there will be times when it will be more functional for them to surrender control to significant others. Patients may have coexisting psychological problems. These can often complicate the management of medical problems and make it difficult for therapists to tailor cognitive behavioural assessments, formulations and treatment plans in a way that takes account of biological, psychological and physical variables. Some patients with histories of psychological problems have increased vulnerabilities to develop psychological problems as a result of the diagnosis of a chronic medical problem. This may occur at the time of diagnosis and/or during the course of the illness in response to elements of treatment or events which occur during the course of the disease. There are a further group of patients for whom the chronic medical problem itself confers a psychological vulnerability to experience problems triggered by other life events. It is also being increasingly acknowledged that psychological problems can result in physical morbidity in their own right. Prat et al. (1996) reported that, when medical factors are controlled for, the risk of myocardial infarction increases four- to five-fold as a result of the presence of depressive symptoms.

Friedman et al. (1995) have suggested that there are a number of pathways by which psychological variables influence patient interface with health care services. They also propose that these pathways are influenced by psychological interventions and that, as such, it is possible for such interventions to have a positive impact on both the quality of clinical care and the financial costs of health care delivery. These pathways are outlined in Table 1.2.

The information and decisional support pathway relates to patient–health service contact, which is mediated by the need for information and assistance relating to the need to distinguish symptoms or acquire information

Table 1.2   Pathways relating to patient–health service interface (Friedman et al., 1995)

Information and decisional support	Social support
Psychophysiological	Undiagnosed psychological disorder
Behaviour change	Somatisation

about medical problems. The psychophysiological pathway typically relates to patients experiencing deleterious effects as a result of the negative impact of stress on conditions such as arthritis. Pathways related to behavioural changes relate to the impact of behaviours such as diet, smoking or exercise in relation to medical problems such as cancer, diabetes or heart disease. Chronic medical problems can result in isolation and Freidman et al.'s social support pathway outlines how some patients' interactions with the health care system are mediated by the need for social support. A further group of patients present with physical symptoms which are the result of an undiagnosed psychological problem or disorder. This may relate to somatisation, where emotional distress is expressed in physical terms. Many of the psychosocial correlates and mediators of adjustment to chronic medical problems can be understood with regard to these pathways. Indeed, cognitive behavioural therapy (CBT) often targets one or more of these. Friedman and his colleagues present evidence that addressing patient health service use as a result of these pathways can result in significant cost offset.

UNDERSTANDING VARIATIONS IN PSYCHOSOCIAL ADJUSTMENT

It is accepted that the physical and psychosocial functions of patients with the same medical conditions vary widely. There is a huge variation in the subjective impact of medical conditions of the same objective severity. Two patients may have the same degree of physical disease or damage but yet have markedly different psychological responses to that physical illness. The variation in the ways in which patients make sense of and respond to illness has been examined according to the self-regulation model of Leventhal (Leventhal, Diefenbach & Leventhal, 1992). This emphasises the importance of the illness representation held by the patient (Weinman et al., 1996). These are often disease specific in nature and, as such, components of illness representations may relate differently to adjustment and quality of life depending upon the nature of the disease process (Heijmans and de Ridder, 1998). It has been shown that the illness representation held by the patient can account for variations in emotional reactions to symptoms (Prohaska et al. 1987) and self-care behaviours (Petrie et al., 1996). Patients with more negative views of their illness are more likely to be depressed (Murphy et al., 1999). Patients who view their illnesses as more serious, chronic and uncontrollable tend to be more passive, report more disability, have poorer social functioning and more mental health problems (Heijmans, 1999). Patient perceptions of control over their symptoms and/or the course of their disease often relate to mood states such as depression (Devins et al., 1981; Thompson et al., 1993; Affleck et al., 1987; Helgeson, 1992). Perceived control has been shown to predict recovery from disability (Johnston et al., 1999). Cognitive components such as core beliefs, intermediate beliefs and thoughts often account for the differences in psychological responses to illness. Lacroix et al. (1991) have illustrated how the symptom schema held by patients influences what they believe is wrong with them. They demonstrated how a patient with a range of physical symptoms tended to make different attributions about their cause than his physicians. The symptoms and the explanation of both patient and physician are out-lined in Table 1.3, which is an excellent illustration of how cognitions are central to the appreciation of patients' experiences of their symptoms.

There has been an increasing emphasis on the importance of the role of meaning in understanding psychopathology (Brewin & Power, 1999). Barton (2000) has suggested that greater emphasis should be afforded

Table 1.3 Importance of symptom schemata (Lacroix, et al., 1991)

Patient complained of choking sensation, runny nose, headache, sore throat, shortness of breath, back pain, muscle pain and soreness, dizziness, skin rash and fatigue.

Grouped by patient into six clusters:

(1) shortness of breath, fatigue, choking sensation and runny nose   *Attribution to cold*
(2) shortness of breath   *Attribution to chest muscles getting tired*
(3) headache   *Attribution 'unknown'*
(4) back pain and sore muscles   *Attribution to improper positioning in wheelchair*
(5) skin rash   *Attribution to dry skin*
(6) dizziness   *Attribution to moving too quickly*

Medical staff opinion on his presentation:

(1) sore throat, choking sensation and runny nose   *Due to tracheotomy*
(2) shortness of breath   *Due to respiratory failure*
(3) back pain, sore muscles and muscle pain   *Due to spinal injury*
(4) skin rash   *Due to medication side effects*
(5) headache and fatigue   *Due to depression*
(6) dizziness   *Due to brain injury*

within cognitive therapy of depression to the meanings attached to precipitating events. Psychological disorders are often associated with the presence of unwanted or painful meanings. Beck (1991), in considering his early work on the development of cognitive therapy, stated how he was 'struck by how ascertaining the idiosyncratic or special meanings people attached to events helped to explain what otherwise might have represented quite inexplicable affective and behavioural responses' (p. 369). The idea that meaning is central to adjusting to physical illness is beginning to appear in the health psychology and nursing literature (O'Connor, Wicker & Germino, 1990). Patients need a framework for ascribing meaning to illness (Holland et al., 1998). Indeed, Fife (1995) has suggested that patients seek meaning to understand experience and situation within life schemas. The ability to find meaning or purpose amidst misfortune may influence psychosocial adjustment.

It has been suggested that therapists need to understand the cognitive interpretative framework from which patients derive meaning for their experiences, and that psychological interventions which do not take account of this may adopt a hit and miss approach (Buick, 1997). Buick (1997) has further argued that the cognitive representations held by patients are central to understanding the types of meanings ascribed by patients to their illness experiences. Cassel (1982), in his article on the nature of suffering and the goals of medicine, stated that: 'Another aspect essential to an understanding of the suffering of the sick person is the relation of meaning to the way illness is experienced.'

The way in which meanings are processed can be as important as the meaning content. The recent emphasis on meta-cognitive processes within CBT is a reflection of the acknowledgement that the processing can be as important as the content of the meanings and interpretations associated with psychological adjustment. Understanding the meanings attached to the diagnosis and management of chronic medical problems is crucial when applying CBT to the problems and issues faced by people with these physical health problems. The cognitive behavioural model is particularly well suited to embrace this approach to the psychology of illness as it places the meaning-making capacity of patients at the heart of the therapeutic endeavour. The consequences on an individual of having a serious illness diagnosed are often understood in terms of patient's pre-existing self-beliefs and assumptions about the world in which he or she lives. Clinicians talk of assumptions being 'shattered' (Fawzy et al., 1990) or 'challenged' (Lepore & Helgeson, 1998), and the need for reformulation of these assumptions and/or for their amendment has also been reflected on the writings of academics in this area (Taylor, 1983; Fife, 1994, 1995). The central role within CBT on meanings and interpretation is one of the reasons why this form of treatment is particularly suited for application to the psychological components of chronic medical problems. The remaining factors which make it particularly so will be outlined in the following section.

WHY CBT?

Enright (1997) has suggested that 'it is logical to assert that there is no psychological or physical problem that cannot potentially be assisted by a cognitive behavioural approach' (p. 1812). CBT can be applied to the assessment and treatment of almost every chronic medical problem, and there are a number of factors which make CBT particularly suited to addressing the problems associated with long-term medical problems. First, chronic medical problems are often associated with the sorts of psychological problems for which CBT has proven efficacy, is the treatment of choice and/or has an established role in their management (see DeRubeis and Crits-Cristoph, 1998); it may even be cheaper than medication when maintenance therapy and related costs are taken into account (Antonucci, Thomas & Danton, 1997). Cognitive behaviourally based interventions form the majority of the American Psychological Association's Division of Clinical Psychology Task Force on Psychological Interventions 'empirically validated therapies' (Chambless, 1998). The importance of adopting a self-management approach, the need for patients to establish collaborative relationships with health care staff, and the active role patients are encouraged to adopt in the management of their illness, each lend themselves to the philosophy and central tenets of CBT. The collaborative nature of the relationship between patient and therapist and the emphasis on building a repertoire of skills for the management of psychological problems are particularly relevant for CBT as well as medical self-management. The current UK health service emphasis on patients having access to evidence-based and cost-effective treatments should make it more likely that patients will be able to access CBT. Although there is a significant amount of evidence on the efficacy of CBT as an intervention for anxiety and depressive disorders, many of these studies have been conducted with patients with no significant medical problems. There is no reason to expect CBT to be any less effective in treating psychological morbidity when it co-exists with a medical problem. However, it is only in the area of cancer and chronic pain that research has specifically established CBT's role (see Chapters 5 and 6). Guthrie (1996) has highlighted some of the difficulties with psychological therapy for chronic medical illness. Research in this area is difficult and challenging; it presents researchers with the challenge of many confounding variables and problems associated with recruiting patients with longstanding medical problems.

CBT: AN OVERVIEW

This book is written from the perspective of the approach to CBT advocated by Aaron T. Beck (Beck, 1976, Beck et al., 1979). However, CBT has increasingly become a range of therapeutic approaches. There has also been a tendency to dilute CBT by dispensing with crucial elements and/ or to amalgamate CBT with other therapeutic approaches (as in the case of so-called cognitive behavioural counselling). CBT is not counselling, and referring to it as such immediately changes the central emphasis. Counselling is generally regarded as an unstructured and non-directive form of psychological support or intervention. CBT is a structured form of therapy and naming it cognitive behavioural counselling is unhelpful. It is becoming accepted that the structure of CBT is important. Shaw et al. (1999) have reported that a therapist's ability to structure therapy relates favourably to treatment outcome. Many practitioners profess to be using CBT when they are in fact using cognitive or behavioural strategies or treatment techniques which are applied in isolation and without sufficient reference to a formulation or as an amalgamat with other therapies. Some practitioners decide to dispense with agenda-setting or homework, and prefer to incorporate cognitive or behavioural strategies as part of an eclectic approach to psychological therapy. The evidence base for the efficacy and effectiveness of CBT is significant, whereas the evidence base for counselling is not—and the two should not be confused.

The cognitive model emphasises three 'levels' of cognition: schema (or core beliefs), assumptions (or intermediate beliefs) and automatic thought or images. The importance of information-processing variables such as biases and memory are also acknowledged. Core beliefs are global and absolutistic, such as 'I am helpless', 'Others pity me' or 'Cancer is always fatal'. Intermediate beliefs (or assumptions), which are more cross-situational in their emphasis and can be thought of as 'rules for living', can be outlined in conditional or unconditional format. An example of a conditional belief would be: 'If I do as the doctor tells me then I will have no symptoms.' Unconditional intermediate beliefs are of the format: 'I must always do as the doctor tells me.' Automatic thoughts are situation specific and easier to identify than core beliefs or intermediate beliefs. Each 'layer' of cognition relates meaningfully to the next. Core beliefs, assumptions and automatic thoughts ('They all look so ill—I will crack up if I end up like that') are thematically linked. Beckian CBT emphasises the importance of understanding the influence of a patient's experiences on his or her belief system. Beliefs and schema are formed as a result of experiences and exposure to events, people and situations. This approach emphasises the importance of critical incidents which, when congruent content of existing beliefs, can serve to trigger them. These in ult in information being processed by patients in a particular manner.

The model emphasises the importance of understanding stable mental representations and their impact in determining how information is processed. Gelder (1997) has outlined how CBT approaches to psychological problems take account of attention and memory. Anxiety and mood disorders are associated with greater levels of self-focused attention (Ingram & Smith, 1984; Wells, 1985). Contact with medical services often results in patients having to pay greater attention to themselves than they might do otherwise, and this can exacerbate pre-existing problems and/ or may precipitate problems with an attentional bias which results in an exaggerated self-focus. It is accepted that emotions are associated with the way in which information is retrieved from memory. Metacognitive factors are being incorporated into the conceptualisations of psychological disorders (Nelson et al., 1999; Papageorgiou & Wells, 1999). Assessment measures, such as the Metacognitions Questionnaire (see Wells, 1997) and the Thought Control Questionnaire (Wells & Davies, 1994; Reynolds & Wells, 1999), have also been developed to enable therapists to assess these elements of patient experience. There has also been an increased interest in understanding the nature and function of imagery in psychological disorders and as a component to target for change in treatment.

An example of the application of this model to understanding a psychological problem would be a patient who, by virtue of exposure to adversity or loss in early life, developed negative beliefs regarding loss, failure and achievement. Blackburn (1998) has stated that the typical themes of core schemata are personal worth, moral worth, abnormality and personal ability. These beliefs will be activated by events which are thematically congruent with the beliefs. A patient with a core belief about worthlessness is more likely to experience activation of this belief following rejection than someone who has a similar experience but does not have this core belief. The activation of this belief leads to the tendency to process information according to the dominant cognitive structures which have been activated. This results in the patient experiencing thoughts and images which are associated with predictable emotional, behavioural and, in some cases, physical reactions.

There are an ever-increasing number of psychological disorders for which cognitive behavioural models and therapy protocols have been developed, many of which have been shown to be effective in research trials. These include CBT for depressive disorders (Beck et al., 1979; Dobson, 1989), panic disorder (Clark et al., 1994), generalised anxiety disorder

(Butler et al., 1991); obsessive compulsive disorder (Salkovskis, 1999), post-traumatic stress disorder (Dunmore, Clark & Ehlers, 1999); hypochondriasis (Warwick et al., 1996; Clark, Cook & Snow, 1998); bulimia nervosa (Ledanowski et al., 1997; Hay & Bacaltchuk, 1999), schizophrenia (Haddock et al., 1998; Jones et al., 1999, Tarrier et al., 1999) personality disorders (Davidson & Tyrer, 1996; Davidson, 2000) and bipolar disorders (Scott, 1996). Rachman (1998) has suggested that the application of psychological approaches to other branches of medicine has been slower than desirable and expected when compared with the developments in psychological models and therapies within psychiatry. In saying this, CBT has also been applied successfully to the management of irritable bowel syndrome (Greene & Blanchard, 1994), chronic fatigue syndrome (Price & Cooper, 1999) chronic pain (Morley, Eccleston & Williams, 1999) and cancer (Greer et al., 1992). It is true that advances in cognitive behavioural approaches to psychological disorder have not been matched by the application of the model to understanding psychosocial aspects of adjustment to physical illness. This is beginning to happen (e.g. Salkovskis & Rimes, 1997) as therapists begin to combine clinical observations with scientific findings (Gelder, 1997).

Readers requiring a comprehensive review of the scientific foundations of CBT are advised to consult Clark and Fairburn (1997). Readers interested in CBT generally are advised to consult excellent introductory texts on cognitive therapy such as those by Beck (1995), Leahy (1996) or Blackburn and Twaddle (1996), which provides both an introduction and an excellent illustration of cognitive therapy in practice.

The importance of empirical process within CBT and the acceptance of the need for rigorous evaluation mean that CBT is in a strong position to take advantage of the emphasis on clinical governance and clinically effective therapies. CBT is becoming increasingly accessible to patients, and both the public and media are becoming more interested in how CBT can be applied to psychological disorders (BABCP News, 2000). Clinical psychology has roots in behavioural theories and therapies; it is the discipline most commonly associated with CBT and has become increasingly cognitive in its emphasis in recent years (Rachman, 1998). Most clinical psychologists who have studied in the UK will have had some training in the use of cognitive and behavioural treatment strategies. There is also a small number of psychiatrists in the UK with specialist training in CBT as psychiatrists are required to treat a small number of cases under supervision using cognitive and/or behavioural therapy as part of their training for Membership of the Royal College of Psychiatrists. Clinicians from disciplines such as occupational therapy and social work are also beginning to be trained in CBT, and the expansion of training opportunities has been mirrored by the need to ensure accreditation of suitably trained therapists. Evidence is beginning to emerge that current CBT training courses are effective in promoting skill development among trainees (Milne et al., 1999).

SUMMARY AND CONCLUSIONS

There are fundamental differences in the impact of acute diseases and chronic illnesses. Psychosocial response to illness rarely correlates highly with disease severity. Psychological variables are particularly important in understanding the way in which patients respond to the challenges which are associated with a chronic medical problem. The literature in this area emphasises the importance of meaning and it is this which makes CBT an ideal approach to helping patients to minimise the negative psychological impact of their illness. The sound evidence base for the application of CBT to the common psychological problems of the physically ill is particularly relevant to modern health care provision and its emphasis on evidence-based therapies. Despite these obvious links between CBT and the context of caring for those with chronic medical problems, therapists are not always clear on how they might tailor their assessments, formulations and treatments to take account of the idiosyncratic elements of working with someone who has a chronic medical problem. This requires an approach which addresses idiosyncratic elements of chronic illness experience while preserving the essential components of CBT theory and practice.

Chapter 2

ASSESSMENT

INTRODUCTION

This chapter will outline the importance of assessment in CBT when working with people who are experiencing chronic physical health problems. Assessment process will be distinguished from assessment content for the purpose of this chapter. In many respects, assessment of the presenting problems of people who have chronic medical problems is no different from the assessment of the common psychological problems which are often treated using CBT. However, there can be particular issues which need to be addressed when complex presentations are being assessed. The assessment of someone with a chronic medical problem, related psychological problems and a history of a pre-existing psychological problem would be an example of such a complex assessment situation. This chapter will make some general recommendations regarding the structure and content of cognitive behavioural assessment. Other chapters in this book will expand on the general guidance given here and provide further detail on the important process and content issues as they relate to particular situations and disorders.

ASSESSMENT PROCESS

Cognitive behavioural assessment is a central component in cognitive behavioural therapies. The primary purpose of assessment is to elicit information for later synthesis within the case formulation (or conceptualisation). It is also important in terms of identifying information to assist with the evaluation of the outcome of interventions. If an assessment is carried out correctly and has an appropriately broad coverage, then it will be easier to formulate the ways in which a patient might be able to meet the treatment goals. There are several methods that can be used during the process of assessment: for example, observation, self-report questionnaires, semi-structured interviews, clinical interviews and the completion of diaries. These methods of gathering information as part of an assessment will be outlined and examples will be provided of their application to psychological aspects of chronic medical problems. Although some of the process and content of a cognitive behavioural assessment will be similar to that of a standard psychiatric interview, there are important differences which will be highlighted.

Patients, particularly those with complex psychosocial and medical needs, will often report their experiences across many different dimensions in a way which overwhelms the therapist. It is important to develop the ability to tolerate the sort of uncertainty that this can produce. Uncertainty of this nature should act as a cue to the therapist that he or she has yet to discover the key cognitive and behavioural factors at the heart of the patient's problems. CBT novices are often advised to concentrate on summarising what they have heard if they are confused or overwhelmed during an assessment session. This is something which all therapists should do regularly, particularly during assessment, as this helps to communicate to the patient that you have heard what you were meant to hear (assuming that you have) and serves to refocus periodically the assessment for patient and therapist.

Some of the key elements of the cognitive behavioural therapy process, such as structure, collaboration and a present-oriented focus (see Chapter 4), are important components of the assessment process. Indeed, it is these process elements that differentiate cognitive behavioural assessments from other psychological approaches to assessment. Assessment validity is enhanced when a number of information-gathering strategies are used throughout the process. The main strategies that therapists might use will now be outlined.

Self-report Questionnaires

There are a vast number of self-report questionnaires available for the assessment of the cognitive and behavioural dimensions of psychological factors in chronic medical problems. Specific questionnaires which can be used for assessment will be highlighted throughout this book as they relate to the disorders being considered. As there is enormous variability in the design and quality of these questionnaires, there are consequently a number of factors that need to be taken into account when choosing which one to integrate as part of the assessment process (see Table 2.1). There are also some 'general' questionnaires that have been produced to measure psychological constructs applicable to a wide range of physical health problems such as illness representation and locus of control. Some of these can be used as part of a core assessment battery.

Table 2.1   Factors to consider in choosing a self-report measure

Has this measure adequate reliability and validity?
Has this measure been developed for the psychological dimensions I want to assess?
Has this measure been applied to people experiencing the problems that my patient has?
Are there aspects of this patient's physical health problems which would make the use of this measure unreliable?
Is this the only way I can get this information from this patient?
How long will it take to administer this test?
Will this patient be able to complete this measure? Will medical problems interfere with this?
Is there normative data for people with this particular medical problem?

Illness Perception Questionnaire

This questionnaire (Weinman et al., 1996) is a self-report measure for assessing the cognitive representation of illness. It comprises five scales which assess *identity*—the symptoms the patient associates with the illness; *cause*—personal ideas about the cause of illness; *time-line*—the perceived duration of the illness; *consequences*—expected outcome; and *cure/ control*—how one controls or recovers from the illness. Patients are required to indicate the degree to which they agree or disagree with statements using a five-point Likert scale (Strongly disagree, Disagree, Neither agree nor disagree, Agree, Strongly agree). The measure can be customised for particular illnesses by replacing the word 'illness' with the specific medical problem experienced by the patient being assessed (i.e. 'illness' replaced with 'cancer' or 'diabetes').

Table 2.2   Sample items from Illness Perception Questionnaire (Weinman et al., 1996)

A germ or virus caused my illness
Diet played a major role in causing my illness
My illness will last a short time
My illness is a series condition
My illness has not had much effect on my life
My illness has strongly affected the way I see myself as a person
Recovery from my illness is largely dependent on chance or fate

Multidimensional Health Locus of Control Scales

These are 18-item scales (Wallston, Wallston & De Vellis, 1978) which measure perceived control over health-related events. Each item is a statement concerning perceived control over health. Respondents are required to outline their level of agreement or disagreement on a six-point scale from 'Strongly disagree' to 'Strongly agree'. There are three versions of this questionnaire. Forms A and B are a general health locus of control scales. They consist of three 6-item subscales: internality; powerful others externality; and chance externality. Form C is designed to be used with specific conditions (users can substitute the word 'condition' with the name of the illness experienced by the patient being assessed (Wallston, Stein & Smith, 1994). Copies of these measures appear at:

http://www.vanderbilt.edu/nursing/kwallston/mhlcscales.htm

Other measures

Readers are advised to consult the helpful guide to *Measures in Health Psychology* produced by Weinman, Wright and Johnston (1995) for a range of other measures which will be suitable for a wide range of conditions.

It may also be possible for therapists to use some cognitive behavioural questionnaires which have been developed for use with mental health problems. However, physical illnesses often produce symptoms which can mimic symptoms that could also be due to the presence of psychological problems such as anxiety and depression. This can increase the risk that self-report measures developed for use in mental health will give rise to artificially high scores when completed by someone with a physical health problem. An example of this would be the administration of the Beck Depression Inventory to measure severity of depressive symptoms in someone with a chronic medical problem (see Beck et al., 1997). The score on the BDI would be artificially high if their medical problem caused appetite disturbance and diminished energy. The Hospital Anxiety and Depression Scale (Zigmond & Snaith, 1983) was developed to overcome this problem and is widely used in physical health settings to measure anxiety and depressive symptoms. For clinical purposes it may be possible to use these mainstream measures and ensure that patients rate the items which are confounded by physical health variables in a way that takes account of the non-physical aspects of their problems.

Observation

Observation can be a particularly helpful component of cognitive behavioural assessments. An individual's behaviour provides a number of clues to cognitive and emotional dimensions of experience, and can inform other elements of the assessment process. There are many variables which could be observed during a cognitive behavioural assessment. Some will be especially relevant for certain disorders (e.g. posture for a chronic pain problem) and dimensions of psychological experience (e.g. loudness of voice is often helpful as an index of anger intensity).

Table 2.3   Observational variables

Eye contact
Facial expression
Posture
Volume and tone of voice
Frequency with which questions are answered and/or avoided
Illness behaviour (e.g. groaning when walking)
Breathing rate
Relationship of non-verbal behaviour and topic of assessment

Examples of variables that might form the focus of observation during a cognitive behavioural assessment are outlined in Table 2.3.

An example of the way in which observation can be used as part of the assessment process is illustrated with the following extract from an assessment session. The factors that were relevant to observational methods of assessment are highlighted in italics:

T: What are the main things which you have been finding difficult since you came into hospital?

P: (*Patient's shoulders slump*) Everything is just so difficult—I don't know where to begin really. (*Eyes fill up with tears*)

T: Would you feel able to tell me what is the biggest problem at the moment?

P: Yes. . . . Well, I feel I will never get over this operation. (*Voice lowers towards the end of the sentence*)

T: How are you feeling at the moment?

P: (*Patient moves eyes away and lowers head*) I am so fed up . . . so tired.

The significance of observations made early on in the assessment process may not become apparent until much later in the process of formulation.

Observation is particularly important regarding the way in which people talk about their problems. It is useful during assessment to make note of verbatim statements made by patients, perhaps emphasising the words which the patient emphasised. Examples of this might be:

- 'I just **had** to take another pill before I went out'—this statement was later shown to be related to the patient's intermediate beliefs that if she did not take her medication she would forget when outside and need immediate hospital admission.

- 'Well the doctor told me it would not be easy. . . . **What is**?'—the therapist and patient later noted that this patient had a belief that 'Living is too difficult for me' which often determined her reactions to practical advice about the management of her medical problem.
- 'It is just **another** example of what I said before'—this provided a clue to the therapist that the patient had beliefs about the personal significance of a sequence of negative events (in this case it was that she was being punished for a previous mistake in life).

Such statements often act as a stimulus to further enquiry to the disclosure of significant emotions and/or information on underlying cognitive or behavioural dimensions. Noting these can provide rich material for later analysis and synthesis as part of the case conceptualisation. It is not always advisable for therapists to highlight to patients what they have observed. In some instances, the patients may feel criticised and/or deny that they have been doing what you have observed. The results of observations made as part of an assessment can usually be shared at the time of discussion of the case formulation. Discussion of the potential significance of an observed behaviour should always be presented in a tentative manner and, as such, be open to further testing or enquiry. It is important to delay discussion of assessment material until the patients are suitably socialised into the generic cognitive behavioural model and any specific models of their medical problems and/or psychological aspects. It is also easier for patients to accept ideas about linking observations with problem origins and maintenance when a collaborative relationship has been established.

Diaries

There are many diary formats which can be used to gather information on patient problems. Some of these are produced according to an established format and are readily available from most experienced cognitive behavioural therapists and/or in cognitive therapy textbooks (e.g. Beck, 1995; Padesky & Greenberger, 1996). Examples of these include Daily Records of Dysfunctional Thoughts, Weekly Activity Schedules, Pain Rating Diaries and Frequency Counts. Most cognitive therapists will have devised their own versions of symptom diaries to accommodate the unique constellation of symptoms for particular individuals and/or their individual way of working within CBT.

Indeed, diaries can often be individually constructed for patients based on their symptoms and individual problem profiles. The use of assessment diaries not only provides information on symptoms, but begins to help patients to appreciate the collaborative nature of CBT and the importance of beginning to work on their problems outside treatment sessions. The use of diaries may also help patients to make discoveries about how their symptoms change over time and/or in relation to other symptoms. Much of the success of CBT depends on a patient's ability to integrate out-of-session tasks with normal living. The introduction of out-of-session monitoring during the assessment phase can enable therapists to address potential obstacles to the later implementation of therapy homework. The completion of this sort of monitoring provides patients with an idea of what a course of CBT involves. When problems with adherence to diary-keeping occur, it can often be a helpful way of introducing a discussion about the patient's thoughts, feelings and behaviour related to adherence to medical care regimes in general.

A Weekly Activity Schedule (WAS) is sufficiently general for it to be applied to a range of physical and psychological problems. It is often used to monitor the relationship between patient activity levels and various other physical and psychological symptoms. There are various questions which can be answered if a patient completes a WAS as part of the assessment process (e.g. At what times of day are the problems worst? What things happen to make the problem better/worse?). These enable people to appreciate links and develop a 'mind set' which promotes self-discovery and analysis of their experiences. Completion of diaries can also act as a direct test of an important cognition (Table 2.4)

In some circumstances patients will find that they make therapeutically beneficial discoveries about their symptoms during a monitoring exercise conducted as assessment homework. Indeed, as therapists become more

Table 2.4   Diary-keeping initiates the process of guided discovery

Mr R was a 54-year-old man referred for cognitive behavioural assessment of symptoms of major depressive disorder which had only partially responded to antidepressant medication. His Beck Depression Inventory score was 30 and Beck Anxiety Inventory score was 29. At the intake assessment interview Mr R reported that 'I am in pain all of the time'. He was observed to start crying at this point in the interview. Mr R and the therapist decided that it was very important that they understood in more detail the relationship between activity and pain levels. This was an important assessment component in its own right. However, it also provided him with the opportunity to evaluate this belief in more detail (the therapist had hypothesised it to be an example of overgeneralisation due to the information processing consequences of depression). Mr R was astonished to discover that his monitoring revealed that all of his pain severity ratings were less than 5 (on a 0 to 10 scale) and that 85% of his ratings were 0 or 1. Mr R experienced a significant reduction in depression and anxiety which was associated with the completion of his diary for homework.

competent and confident at integrating assessment, formulation and intervention, they may be able to set up diary monitoring in a way which furthers the process of assessment, begins socialisation to the cognitive behavioural model and can begin the process of therapeutic change. Patients feel more confident to complete monitoring outside a session if this is started in the session.

Structured Interviews

It is well known that clinicians are as affected by biases in reasoning and decision-making as any other human being. This is one of the reasons that structured interviews can be a useful component of cognitive behavioural assessments. Many of these have been constructed by cognitive therapists for use in their own units and, as such, have not been published. Structured interview schedules such as the Structured Clinical Interview for the Diagnostic and Statistical Manual of Mental Disorders (American Psychiatric Association, 1994) can be a helpful tool in ensuring that a reliable assessment of psychological signs and symptoms of mental disorder is carried out. Much of the cognitive therapy literature for psychological problems is organised around diagnostic groupings. Having information on psychiatric diagnosis can assist with the identification of assessment measures and literature. It may also be relevant to include disorder-specific structured interviews in certain assessments. Examples of this might be the Anxiety Disorders Interview Schedule for DSM-IV or the Clinician Assisted Interview for PTSD.

Hospital Records

Hospital records (medical, psychological or psychiatric) often contain helpful information relating to previous life experiences, medical history and personal history. The information contained in correspondence and discharge summaries is often particularly helpful in enabling therapists to understand the nature and extent of investigations, medical opinion and treatment plans. These events are often trigger events and relate to the establishment of beliefs which will mediate or moderate patient problems. When medical problems have lasted for many years, a detailed review of the medical notes is essential. This can sometimes be done in the presence of the patient and can trigger memories which are important in understanding current problems. Therapists should be familiar with the policies governing disclosure of health-related information where they work. Prior to disclosure, they may need to obtain consent from those colleagues who have made a contribution to the medical record. In some cases it can be useful to check the extent to which 'unexplained' or partially explained physical and psychological symptoms have been investigated. Patient statements about medical investigation may be influenced more by their illness representations and related cognitions and, as such, differ from what has been documented in the case notes.

Review of clinical psychology case notes and psychiatric case records may also assist therapist assessment as these will usually contain information on psychological aspects of their life experiences. In addition to information on past problems, diagnoses and treatment plans, patient case records also contain information on patterns of attendance, dates and times of admission to hospital, the opinions of colleagues on problems, and many useful observations of patient behaviour which may be helpful in the later stages of conceptualisation and treatment.

Clinical Interview

It may seem obvious, but another crucial element of the assessment process (and the most commonly used element) is the clinical interview. Indeed, clinicians usually obtain most of their assessment information by questioning the patient. The art of questioning is a crucial component of cognitive therapy. However, there can be a danger that therapists will rely on this source of information alone without seeking evidence and information on problems using the other assessment methods outlined. Trainees and clinicians who are new to working with people who have chronic medical problems often ask 'How will I know what to ask?'. The content of a general cognitive behavioural assessment will be outlined in the next section of this chapter. Each chapter in Part II of this book has suggestions about which content areas to include in the assessment of particular clinical problems.

ASSESSMENT CONTENT

There are a number of areas which are standard components of any cognitive behavioural assessment and some which are routinely included in any assessment of the psychological aspects of a chronic medical problem. The main headings that can be used to structure the content of the assessment will be outlined. This is not to say that the assessment should always aim to cover these areas in the precise order required. The methods used within each assessment content area will differ between patients and between therapists. There are some situations where following a strict protocol will be the preferred interviewing strategy, and others where it will be possible to map this structure onto information which is obtained after it has been provided. The assessment process should be informed by cognitive behavioural principles. Many of the suggestions regarding assessment content are presented here as if they were questions that are always asked at every assessment that is carried out. In an ideal world, assessments should proceed logically and always seek to cover the main areas outlined in this chapter. However, most clinicians who work in this area quickly realise that there are many situations that require a clinical judgement as to what components will be sufficient for inclusion in their assessments.

Referral Process

There are a number of issues that can act as significant obstacles to engagement in the assessment process, and they need to be addressed at the start of an assessment appointment. If they are neglected, it may negatively influence the nature and quality of any information provided. There is often a huge variablity in the quality of the information provided to patients about their referral to a cognitive behavioural therapist. Furthermore, patients have very different ideas about what therapists do and how this might relate to their referral for assessment. Regarding the validity of their symptoms, their sanity or their relationship with medical and nursing staff, some patients will have interpreted the suggestion of referral as an expression of doubt on the part of the referrer. The following initial questions provide a helpful starting point for establishing a person's understanding of the referral process:

What have you been told about Dr X's reasons for referring you to me? This question will either give rise to the disclosure of the fact that the patients have been told nothing (this may, of course, also mean that they have not retained what they were told) or they will offer information on what they have been told. If the patients say that they have been told nothing, then the therapist should tell them all that is known about the referring doctor's reasons for referral, and what he or she knows about the patients' situation, which not only means that checks can be made that the information is correct, but also that patients start the appointment with an understanding of what the therapist already knows. This is often a useful way of beginning the process of collaboration and information sharing (which many patients will not be used to). This initial component of the introduction to assessment makes sure that the patients and therapist are starting off with a similar understanding of what the referrer thinks. In some circumstances, patients may say that they have been referred because their doctor thinks they are 'mad'. When this occurs, these issues can be placed on the assessment agenda for discussion and/or provide useful material to note for later analysis and synthesis into the formulation.

What did you think would happen during today's appointment? This question may reveal that the patients have no idea about what is going to happen. In this case they should be given information about the proposed duration of their appointment and the therapist's suggestions for the assessment agenda. This is the patients' first experience of agenda-setting and therefore provides an excellent opportunity to introduce this feature of CBT. They should also be given the chance to comment on this suggestion and add anything they wish to the assessment agenda. This will enable them to experience the collaborative nature of CBT.

P: I did not know what would happen—I was a bit concerned really.

T: Was there something in particular that concerned you about what might happen?

P: No, just not knowing I suppose.

T: Would it make any difference if I made some suggestions about what I would like to happen during our appointment today?

P: OK.

T: I wanted to spend about 50 minutes with you today. During this time I hope that I can find out some more information about the sorts of problems that you have been having recently. I will ask you some questions about these and some routine questions which I ask every new patient I meet. How does that sound?

P: I'm not sure . . . I will just have to see.

T: After we have been talking for about 10 minutes, I could check with you again to see if you still have any concerns. Would that be OK?

P: Yes.

T: If you have any concerns or problems with what I am asking then please do tell me so that we can sort them. . . .

Problem List

Patients with a chronic medical problem will often experience problems in other areas of their lives. Some will be a consequence of their physical ill health and others may be (or seem to be) unrelated. A comprehensive cognitive behavioural assessment should take all presenting problems into account. This is important when it comes to planning treatment and formulating the main contributors to patient problems. Given the central role of the problem list in assessment, it is helpful to explain the process of constructing a problem list to a patient (Table 2.5).

Table 2.5   Explaining the problem list

Part of the purpose of our meeting today is for me to get a good idea of the problems which you have been having. This will help me to understand how things have been for you and to work out what sorts of things we might be able to work on together to help you with them. I am going to write down the heading 'Problem List'. It would help if you could begin to tell me in your own words the sorts of things that have been a problem for you over the past month. For each one I will ask you about your thoughts, feelings and behaviours as they relate to the problem.

Some patients will often comment that there will not be enough time to list all their problems, state that they do not know where to begin, that everything is a problem for them or, on some rare occasions, that they have no problems. When someone is concerned that there will not be enough time to list all their problems it can be helpful to reassure them that you will ensure that you will have enough time to discuss all their problems, even if this means arranging another appointment for them. In my experience, very few patients need more than one appointment to report their problem list, which can be used to illustrate the differences between thoughts and reality. Every statement can provide potential clues to patient thoughts, beliefs and images. Patients who predict problems about the assessment process often discover that it is the same thinking processes which relate to their reasons for referral. When people say they have no problems they can be asked to elaborate on why they think they have been referred (and why they came to the appointment).

It is important that the problem list is comprehensive. This can be promoted by offering frequent summaries of what patients have said, followed by probing for further items. Therapists need to understand what is problematic about each item on the problem list. It can be very easy to accept a patient's statement as a problem without fully understanding why it is worthy of inclusion on the problem list. Seeking further clarification on what makes something a problem will often enable the patient to elaborate and provide information on cognitive, behavioural and emotional elements of the problem. This is illustrated in the following extract from an assessment session:

P: Well, I just can't seem to get used to life since the surgery.
T: In what way has getting used to life since the surgery been a problem for you?
P: I just can't do the things that I used to do any more. (*Elaborates on behavioural element*)
T: Are there other aspects of getting used to surgery you find difficult?

P: No . . . just that really.

T: How do you feel about not having to do the things that you used to be able to do? (*Checks for emotional element*)

P: Disappointed and down, quite down really.

T: You have been feeling quite down and low.

P: I have really.

T: What sort of things do you find that you think about when you feel this way? (*Checks for cognitive element*)

P: I wonder if it will ever be better, if I will ever have a life again.

Here the use of a further question to clarify the precise difficulties has provided a more specific response which illustrates how the adjustment process has caused a problem for this person. The effect of clarifying in this case has provided information on a behavioural dimension of this problem. This could then be used to form the focus of further exploration of the problem area. A sample item from a completed problem list is outlined in Table 2.6.

Table 2.6   Sample item from problem list

1. Difficult to get used to life after operation as cannot do things that used to do. Feels tired and exhausted, especially when needs to do housework and when thinking 'I will never get over this'; 'Things will never get better' and 'It all seems so pointless'. Feeling sad and down and mainly sits around doing nothing.

There are times when patients will report problems separately which seem to be differing elements of the same problem. This is particularly common when someone is feeling overwhelmed by their physical symptoms and feelings. If it seems that a patient is reporting different elements of the same problem as discrete problems, then the therapist can use this opportunity to check whether this might be the case. This process of clarifying the discrete nature of problems can be therapeutic in itself for some people as it promotes the process of reattribution. They move from viewing themselves as having many unrelated problems to having some which are related and therefore less in number overall. Patients may begin to notice that problems on their 'problem list' are related. This helps them to begin to make links and can help them to feel less overwhelmed by what was a seemingly unrelated set of problems.

The problem list is a very useful way of structuring the assessment session and assessment process. People often report that it is helpful to specify the problems in some detail and that the idea of numbering them for closer inspection or intervention gives some structure to what previously seemed a 'mess'. It also permits the therapist to retain a structure within the assessment.

Patients will occasionally begin a session by focusing on reporting incidents and experiences from the past. Unless there are specific aspects of their problem list which are past-oriented (e.g. recurrent memories of when they were given their diagnosis), it is not usually helpful to begin the process of determining a problem list by focusing on past events. If, after explanation of the need to initially retain a present focus with the problem list, the patient prefers to discuss past events, then this can be negotiated and the agenda for the assessment session modified accordingly.

In practice, determination of a problem list and the exploration of cognitive and behavioural dimensions are often done at the same time. Experienced therapists can also integrate a review of historical elements. However, some therapists prefer to determine the specific problem list and then explore dimensions and history. Indeed, novice therapists will probably find this an easier approach to assessment initially. The act of exploring cognitive and behavioural dimensions of a problems is illustrated below (based on the earlier example):

T: So you have found that you cannot do the things that you used to do any more—this is one of the ways in which it has been difficult to get used to life after the operation. (*Summary statement*)

P: Yes, it is really dreadful.

T: How have you been feeling when you cannot do the things you used to? (Elicit emotions)

P: Oh, very tired . . . exhausted. (*Patient gives physical sensations which can be noted, but not emotions*)

T: So, physically you have been tired and exhausted . . . is that all the time or just when it is difficult to do things?

P: Just when I need to do certain things about the house.

T: How does it make you feel emotionally, in your mood when you can't do the things that you used to do?

P: Oh fed up, down . . . really sad.

T: And when you are feeling this way—down and sad . . . what sorts of things do you think about—what passes through your mind? (*Elicit thoughts*)

P: Mm . . . (*sighs*) . . . that I will never get over this, things will never get better.

T: When you think this way . . . what do you do, what is your reaction?

P: I just sit and do nothing . . . it all seems so pointless. (*Gets behaviour and a further thought*)

This illustrates that when a problem is elicited it provides a focus for specific cognitive and behavioural dimensions to be explored. The problem description can then be entered onto the completed list to reflect dimensions which have been assessed. Patients will not usually have knowledge about what differentiates cognitive, behavioural, emotional and physical dimensions, and may need help with this before a problem list can be determined. If patients do not mention physical or psychological aspects of their problems then it is important to screen for these.

Some further elements of the cognitive behavioural assessment process (i.e. not just clinical interviewing) can be applied to the assessment of aspects of the problem list. This might involve the use of a self-report measure, observation or a diary. This could be complementing clinical interview with the administration of a questionnaire to assess depressive symptoms or with a Weekly Activity Schedule focused upon activity, energy and depression. There may also be helpful information from nursing observations of patient behaviour, statements made to staff and possibly from hospital records which the clinician could obtain.

Functional Analysis

Each problem on the list will need to be assessed in detail to provide the patient and the therapist with further information on what might have triggered the problem and the factors which reinforce it. The problem list provides some helpful information to determine the problem components that might be related in this way. Some of the questions that might be asked in reaching a functional analysis of a problem are outlined in Table 2.7

Table 2.7   Questions to assist functional analysis

What makes it better/worse?
Are there particular situations/times of day/people present when this problem occurs?
Can you take me through a recent example in great detail?
What situations does this problem occur/not occur in?
What happens right before you feel/think/do this?
How do other people react when you feel/think/do this?
What happens after you feel/think/do this?
What do you do then?
What do others do when you feel/think/do this?
What feelings do you get before this thought/before you do this?
Do you get a warning that this is about to happen? What do you feel/think/do at this time?

For the purposes of cognitive behavioural assessment it is helpful to keep the basic model in mind during questioning. If, for example, someone provides information on their feelings it is then useful to ask information about their thoughts and then their behaviour and so on in a cyclical manner (feelings, thoughts, behaviour, feelings, thoughts, behaviour) until the problem has been adequately assessed. Functional analyses seek to specify the antecedents and consequences of emotions and behaviours in order that a sequence of events can be described. Functional assessment is facilitated by asking patients to focus on discrete examples. It is important to clarify if the example which has been the focus of detailed discussion is typical of further problem occurrences.

History of Problem Development

Assessments should aim to allow people time to provide information on how the problems have developed since their onset. It is important to enable people to stay focused on the historical course of the problem being discussed. It is very easy for people to become distracted by information that comes to mind when reviewing the past. If this sort of wandering is not addressed the assessment process can very quickly lose structure and focus. Therapists can also become confused as information from different dimensions are disclosed, each from a different time perspective.

Patients can be asked to talk through the main problem developments across their life span. Patients often find it helpful to think in terms of the 'main headlines' or to have prompts about the main time points which may have been significant in the problem development. This can be done in terms of chronological development over months or years or, alternatively, in terms of events such as diagnosis, after diagnosis, during treatment and after treatment. Providing anchor points of this nature, and frequent summaries that are structured around the anchor points, can promote focus and facilitate recall.

Information on problem development can be documented using a time-line format. This strategy enables therapists to keep track of what is being said and identify gaps in the history. It is rare for therapists to be able to recall information in exact chronological order, and in this way therapists can enter the information chronologically on a time-line contained within the therapy notes as this is disclosed by patients (see Table 2.8)

This format can be varied according to the particular patient and their own situation and in some circumstances can be used to collect information over longer time periods, such as an individual's childhood experiences. This can also be completed as a homework assignment. Making an assessment of the history of problem development will also

Table 2.8   Chronological account of symptom and problem development

Date	Symptoms/problems
May 1999	Husband commented that looked pale Marie left home to start University
June 1999	Noticed a swelling over eye Visited GP
July 1999	GP invited me back 'looked very worried'
August 1999	My father died (in nursing home) CT scan confirms tumour Off work—very anxious during day Could not sleep 'worried sick'
September 1999	Surgeon removed tumour Panic attacks started

usually lead to the disclosure of information on personal history, medical history and family history.

Personal History

In addition to the sort of information which people might provide about the development of their problems, there may be aspects of their life experiences which will be relevant in understanding their problems. Some practitioners will routinely ask about this and carry out an in-depth analysis of personal history. This is not always necessary for a cognitive behavioural interview, as it could be argued that important historical information will emerge as therapy progresses. However, enquiry about childhood illnesses, parental health and parental responses to illness is often helpful with those who are physically ill as it provides information on early influences on current representations of illness and medical treatments.

Medical History

Medical history is very important to those who have been struggling with medical problems, and including this as part of the assessment is a very helpful way of gaining information. This information usually relates to significant events, thoughts and feelings about medical and nursing staff, satisfaction with treatments, communication skills of staff, facts about their medical conditions and current medical management.

Family History

The behaviour, thinking and emotions of family members are influenced by having someone in the family with a longstanding medical problem.

The behaviour, thinking and emotions of family members will also influence a patient's psychological responses. There are usually some members of the family who have more frequent contact with the person being assessed, who demonstrate greater empathy and understanding, who offer more practical support and in whom the patient will find it easier to confide. These are all important elements of the family history which need to be assessed and which will help with the formulation and treatment plan. Basic information on family composition is also usually gathered and can be done prior to determining which of the patient's family members would be the most appropriate to interview. Interviewing a family member can be a helpful way of gathering information on changes in patient behaviour and is also an alternative source of information. Family 'myths' are also important as these often mirror beliefs shared by the patient.

Psychological Symptoms

The significant problems relating to psychological morbidity associated with living with a chronic medical problem should be screened for. Patients will usually mention various psychological signs and symptoms as part of an assessment interview. These will obviously be noted when mentioned but it is often useful to screen for symptoms which patients may not have talked about. Patients are often not sure whether it is relevant to mention certain symptoms they have been experiencing, and may filter out psychological symptoms in favour of physical ones. Psychological symptoms which are not mentioned are often crucial in assessing cognition, behaviour and emotion. Screening can also access information which the patient may be actively avoiding. Useful information is usually obtained when such screening is carried out and therapists discover signs and symptoms which people may not otherwise have mentioned. The presence of these symptoms can then be assessed from a cognitive behavioural perspective.

Suicide Risk

Chronic medical problems are often associated with hopelessness and suicidal thoughts. Indeed, chronic physical illness is often cited as a factor which contributes to the risk of suicide. Clinicians implementing cognitive behaviour therapy with those experiencing chronic medical problems should be comfortable with and competent at making an assessment of suicide risk. Patients who are experiencing significant problems with suicidal thoughts and hopelessness need to be identified. There is the obvious need to ensure that they do not pose a significant risk to themselves but also the possibility that suicidality will act as an obstacle to assessment and treatment of their medical problems and the psychological consequence. Patients with chronic medical problems will also probably be taking medication which when taken in overdose has a high lethality.

Suicide risk assessment should be included in a cognitive behavioural assessment of someone with chronic medical problems. This should begin by asking about times when the patient has felt that life was not worth living and, if necessary, proceed with graded questions depending on whether patients give affirmative responses to initial questioning (i.e. Do you feel that life is not worth living?; Do you think that you would be better off dead?; Have you been having any thoughts of killing yourself?; What specific things have you thought about to kill yourself?) to the point where specific details on suicide planning are assessed, if this is relevant. If it seems that hopelessness and suicidality are to be the focus of further assessment, then assessment of cognitive (e.g. advantages of living/dying) and behavioural (attempts at suicide) dimensions can be carried out. If the patient provides information on a specific method (e.g. overdose) then proceed with questions to elicit information on the degree of planning and preparation for implementation and the protective factors available. The assessment process may need to be temporarily suspended until any suicide risk is addressed. If there is no immediate risk of suicide then it may be possible to assess how suicidal thoughts and hopelessness related to cognitive and behavioural dimensions of chronic medical problems.

Cognitive Mediators

The main cognitive moderators and mediators of psychological responses to illness should be assessed in some detail. Clinicians should aim to assess illness representation, with particular reference to patient beliefs about illness identity, controllability, time course and consequences. This can be done with the Illness Perception Questionnaire referred to earlier. It is also possible to do this using clinical interviewing and questioning. Assessment of cognitive constructs such as self-efficacy (confidence in ability to attain certain outcomes) and self-worth need to be included. Specific details on how these can be assessed will be covered in the assessment section of specific chapters.

Suitability for CBT

The assessment should aim to determine the degree of patient suitability for a trial of cognitive behavioural treatment. The framework for assessing suitability for short-term cognitive therapy (Safran & Segal, 1996) is useful in this regard, and the factors outlined in Table 2.9 are particularly relevant for those with physical health problems. There are some signs which are definite contraindications to a good response to cognitive therapy (Blenkiron, 1999). People who are not willing to consider any potential relationship between psychological variables and their medical problems (even at the level of coping) are likely to find engagement in CBT difficult. People who make statements about getting a new tablet or wishing the therapist to 'make everything better' will usually find initial collaboration difficult. These factors are not always definitive contraindications to therapy, and therapists may wish to offer a number of time-limited sessions to such patients with the objective of enhancing the patient's suitability for treatment.

Table 2.9 Dimensions relating to suitability for CBT

Ease with which patient can identify and differentiate emotion, feeling and
    behaviour
Degree to which patient accepts some responsibility for changes in problems
How readily patient accepts the cognitive theory as applied to his or her
    problems and situation
History of interactions and relationships with medical and nursing staff
Number of previous attempts to deal with problems being referred and duration
    of problems
Degree to which patient's self-schema is allied to illness representation

Treatment Goals

Assessments should always aim to include some information about the goals on which the patient would like to work. This can be determined by asking the patient 'What would you like to change about the problems you have told me about?' or 'If there were things that we might work together to improve, what would they be?'. Goals should usually be expressed in terms of specific, measurable outcomes (e.g. to increase the frequency of blood sugar checks per day) and not global outcome which would be more difficult to evaluate (e.g. to improve my self-care).

PROBLEMS ACCEPTING ASSESSMENT RELEVANCE

It is particularly common when working with those struggling with physical health problems to encounter people who find it very difficult (or in some cases even impossible) to appreciate that their physical symptoms, emotions, behaviours and thoughts are all interrelated. There are others who will acknowledge that this is possible 'theoretically', but certainly does not apply to their particular life situation. It often turns out that the beliefs which are mediating their reluctance to engage in a psychologically oriented assessment are also the same beliefs which mediate their problems. If patients will not engage in assessment then it is obviously difficult to enable them to modify the problematic beliefs which are themselves blocking access to assessment. It can sometimes be possible to negotiate with patients to leave this intact and emphasise that the reason for their referral is to help them to cope and adjust to their illness. It is best to acknowledge their refusal or scepticism rather than convince them that psychosocial variables influence their physical sensations and symptoms. It is often helpful to suggest to patients that they are right to be sceptical and that they should not 'give up' this scepticism until they have evidence to the contrary. People will have evidence to support their views on the role of psychological factors and it is often possible to engage them in assessment by focusing on what they believe. ('Tell me what sort of things make you think that every feeling about your illness is chemically based?')

Patients often become more engaged in the assessment process if the focus is on their problems in accepting that psychological aspects are important. It can be helpful to assist them to focus on previous experiences which have supported their belief. There are some useful strategies which can be used to address problems in this area (see Table 2.10). The work of Salkovskis and others on engagement of people with problems of health anxiety and hypochondriasis is relevant here (Salkovskis, 1989). Patients can be provided with examples of how psychological variables influence physical health—these can often be illustrated 'in vivo'. Therapists need to ensure that the desire for information about psychological aspects does not compromise the collaborative working relationship.

Table 2.10   Strategies to deal with problems accepting relevance of psychological variables

Acknowledge and summarise patient's viewpoint about psychological variables
Acknowledge that the patient may be correct in the view that this is irrelevant for the patient
Increase the frequency of questions about physical symptoms to promote engagement
Try to find some common ground
Provide the patient with an example of link and use the patient's reaction to assess the problems accepting

T: How did you feel when the doctor told you that it was something which would not go away?

P: What is it with all these questions about how I feel? (*Patient screws up face*) It is pain. Pain is pain and I am at my wits end.

T: Mm . . . the pain has really been getting to you . . . you are feeling at your wits end.

P: Yes.

T: Is there something about the questions I am asking you which is upsetting for you?

P: Well, I don't see what all this about feelings has to do with my pain. . . . I want someone to help me with my pain.

T: I see, you are wondering how emotions and feelings can have anything to do with your pain. Sometimes emotions and feelings have very little to do with pain. However, sometimes there are links between these which can be helpful in helping people to cope so that they are less likely to get to their wits end. . . . It may be that this does not apply in your case—but in order to find out I need to ask you some questions about feelings and pain.

It is also helpful to try to clarify the nature of their difficulty in accepting the links between psychological and physical variables. This may reveal information about a problem or concern that is easily resolved by the provision of information or an agreement to spend time during a later session sorting out this problem.

SUMMARY AND CONCLUSIONS

In many respects the assessment component of CBT is the most crucial element of this approach to the problems of those with chronic medical problems. It provides many opportunities to socialise patients into a new way of understanding their experiences. If it is carried out using various methods and with reference to the content areas outlined in this chapter, then it will provide ample information for patients and clinicians to synthesise into a model to explain the origins and maintenance of their difficulties. This is reflected in the problem and case formulations—the crucial link between assessment and intervention and is the focus of the next chapter.

Chapter 3

FORMULATION

INTRODUCTION

When sufficient information has been collected from the patient about his or her presenting problems, links can be made between this information and psychological theory. This is then linked with plans for treatment. The process by which these links between assessment and treatment are made is known as the formulation (or case conceptualisation)—an essential part of the process of delivering any psychological intervention. A formulation outlines how a particular problem/concern or symptom has emerged, the way in which it has manifest itself and how it is being maintained. The formulation process embodies the way in which theory to practice links are made—it seeks to impose an explanatory system (Butler, 1998) upon the patient's physical, psychological and social problems. It is by the process of formulation that clinicians are able to synthesise the findings from assessments and integrate these into an explanation of the mediators and moderators of an individual patient's problems. Mediators are the variables responsible for the occurrence of problems (e.g. types of interpretations, relationships between behaviours) and moderators are the variables which account for the severity with which an element is expressed and the way in which the links between mediating variables are manifest. An example of this might be panic which is mediated by catastrophic misinterpretations of physical sensations and moderated by the concerns about being noticed by others. In other words, the patient experiences panic when she misinterprets her breathlessness as a sign of impending collapse (the mediating link). The degree of panic is worse when others are present because she believes that they are all looking at her (the moderating link) (see Figure 3.1).

Formulation seeks to offer a framework within which the multiple problems, contexts and historical aspects of a patient's life can be understood. This book will differentiate between two levels of formulation: case-level

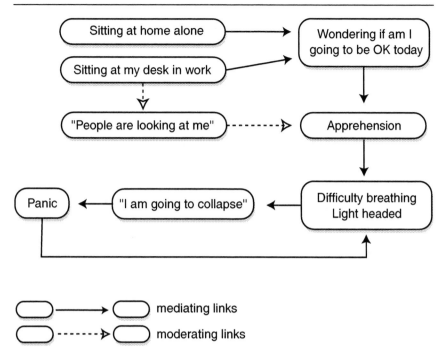

mediating links

moderating links

Figure 3.1.   Mediating and moderating links

formulation and problem-level formulation. Problem level formulation involves the application of cognitive behavioural theory and principles to account for the main factors contributing to the occurrence, severity and nature of problems on the problem list. If a patient presented with problems relating to avoidance of social situations, then the *problem-level* formulation would outline the cognitive, behavioural and emotional components of the situation-specific elements of this problem. It would not outline the origins of the problem or key events in the course of the problem—these would be outlined in a *case-level* formulation. A patient presenting with chronic pain in his lower limbs would have a problem-level formulation outlining the ways in which his thoughts, behaviours and emotions contributed to discrete episodes of pain. It would remain focused on situation-specific aspects of pain occurrence and intensity and less on contextual or historical variables. The case-level formulation might include information on previous experience of illness, beliefs about self and illness, the presence of other medical problems and how these relate to the patient's experience of pain. Case-level formulation becomes an individualised account of each problem on the problem list, integrated with elements of the patient's life history and current life context.

PROBLEM-LEVEL OR CASE-LEVEL FORMULATION: SOME ANALOGIES

Imagine a theatre stage where some actors are standing among some scenery and props. Problem-level formulation can be thought of as what might be seen when focusing the spotlight on a particular area of the stage. Two of the actors, the stage and some scenery can be seen. The remainder of the actors and stage are not illuminated by the beam of the spotlight. The case-level formulation can be thought of as the overall picture—broadening the area covered by the spotlight to take account of surrounding problems, historical events and life circumstances. Problem-level formulations do not seek to be as encompassing in their scope as their case-level counterparts, preferring to focus upon specific clinical problems which make up the larger picture. Both types of formulation are used to understand and plan interventions related to the psychological aspects of most chronic medical problems.

This distinction between case and problem level can also be thought of in terms of a road map. Imagine that you are looking at a map of your local area. Locate the two nearest major cities to where you live (e.g. Glasgow and Edinburgh). This can be viewed as analogous to the process of looking at a list of patient problems and locating two of the biggest problems (e.g. social anxiety and depressed mood). When you have identified the two nearest cities on this map, you could choose to look at each city in detail—outlining the minor roads, landmarks, suburb names or even getting an 'A to Z' to study how the streets link together. This process is analogous to examining discrete patient problems in detail. (When does the social anxiety occur?; What thoughts are experienced at these times?) Problem-level formulation confines itself to discrete occurrences of the problem. Within this analogy, the cities on the map constitute patient problems and the detail within each city constitute components of the problem-level formulation.

Consider now the distance between each city on the map. What towns and cities are between them? Which is the best/quickest/safest route from one city to the next? Are there surrounding landmarks, towns or villages closely situated near the city? In order to address these questions, the complete map would need to be examined. This process of considering first a small section and then all of the map is analogous to the process of moving from the problem level to the case level of formulation. Therapists move their focus from considering discrete problems to examining how they might link and looking for other background detail that might help to understand their size and nature. Therapist and patient examine the ways in which problem-level formulations can be linked together to ensure that they have an explanation of how these component parts make up the larger picture—the case formulation.

Problem formulation examples are outlined in Figures 3.2 and 3.3. Figure 3.4 outlines an example of a case formulation.

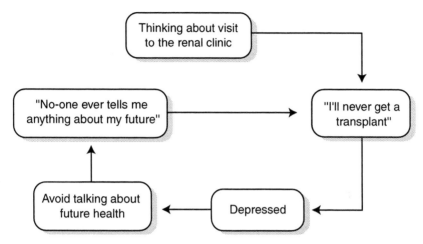

Figure 3.2. Problem-level formulation

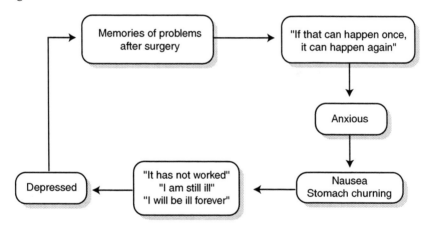

Figure 3.3. Problem-level formulation

USING FORMULATIONS TO PLAN TREATMENT

Distinguishing problem-level formulation and case-level formulation in this manner enables therapists to begin to deliver formulation-driven interventions for presenting problems, while still gathering information to form the more comprehensive case-level formulation. While treatment based on a problem-level formulation is being implemented, therapists can use information they obtain about links with related problem areas

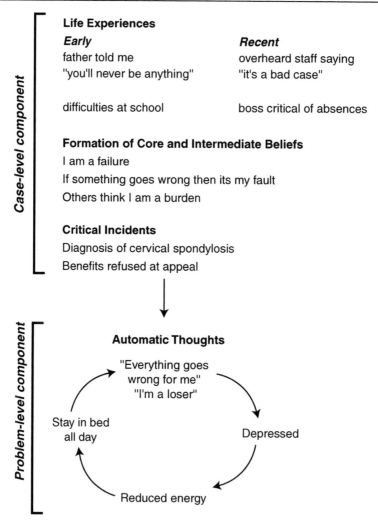

Figure 3.4. Case-level formulation

and/or information from patient history. Patient responses to interventions derived from problem-level formulations will also be important for inclusion in the case-level formulation. An example of this might be when a patient with panic disorder and diabetes demonstrates a partial response to verbal reattribution of catastrophic misinterpretations. It emerged during the early stages of treatment that the patient had been drinking heavily when her partner was home from working abroad (information which had not previously been disclosed). This contextual information belongs within the case-level formulation. The drinking problem became the focus of a further individual problem-level formulation, which complemented the existing problem about the role of interpretations on panic experiences.

Clinicians who are familiar with and competent in cognitive behavioural case and problem formulation usually find that most aspects of this skill are applicable to the emotional, behavioural and cognitive aspects of longstanding physical health problems. However, it can be more difficult to formulate psychological components of a chronic medical problem as this requires the need to integrate knowledge of both psychological problems and medical problems. Cognitive behavioural formulation draws upon the cognitive behavioural literature to offer hypotheses which explain the phenomena outlined during assessment. Therapists formulate hypotheses to account for patient experience of problems and how factors such as prior life experience might interact to produce the problems for which the patient is seeking help.

The hypotheses that are used to plan assessment and treatment strategies can also be thought of in terms of problem-level and case-level components. Problem-level hypotheses are links which are embodied within problem-level formulations. Problem-level formulations will often suggest case-level hypotheses by virtue of the fact that discrete problems are often associated with particular life experiences, beliefs or coping strategies (e.g. teasing as a child is often associated with the occurrence of social anxiety). In this way, therapists can tentatively begin to list case-level hypotheses when they have a robust problem-level formulation. These hypotheses will in turn become the guiding principles to further assessment and evaluation throughout the course of therapy. The following extract from a session illustrates how therapists can use statements related to problem-level hypotheses and emerging case-level hypotheses to structure their work within sessions. Some further examples of problem- and case-level hypotheses are outlined in Table 3.1.

T: You noticed that you had started to feel more depressed on your way home from the clinic?

P: Yes, that always happens.

T: What were you thinking about as you travelled home?

P: It was just the same old journey home. (*Problem-level hypothesis*: some depressive symptoms are mediated by thoughts about the unrewarding and repetitive nature of life experiences)

T: Tell me about it if you can.

P: I waited for about 40 minutes to be seen—to be told 'That's you—fine, see you in 6 months'.

T: . . . And that's the same as what usually happens when you attend that clinic?

P: Yes, same old story.

T: What else passed through your mind at that time?

P: I kept thinking about the last time—what a waste of time it was. Nothing ever changes with them—same old see you in 6 months. Keep smiling—I've heard it all before.

T: Is this something that you feel about any other situations in your life? (*Case-level hypothesis*: patient may have intermediate beliefs relating to the monotony of repeated exposure to situations and/or experiences which lead him or her to expect that all clinic attendances will be pointless)

P: What are any situations when I feel depressed? It is quite a lot now— always when I feel that I should be doing more. (*New case-level hypothesis*: may relate to intermediate belief that should always be a success, being applied to illness)

Table 3.1   Examples of problem-level and case-level hypotheses

---

Case-level hypotheses

Patient has been exposed to negative experience of others with the same illness

Partner is critical and this is maintaining low self-esteem

The news that this patient's arthritis is now affecting more joints was the trigger for her depression

The neglect that this patient endured as a child has resulted in his belief that all caregivers are selfish

Problem-level hypotheses

The anxiety following appointments is mediated by doubts about what the doctor said

Visits to the GP serve to reduce the anxiety which unexplained symptoms causes

The intrusive memories that this patient experiences of her sister's funeral are the primary mediators of her low mood

---

A formulation enables a clinician and patient to understand why problems have occurred, how they were initiated, how they are being maintained, possible strategies for their amelioration (or solution) and the ways in which it might be possible to prevent their future occurrence. A formulation assists therapists in making predictions and should enable clinicians not only to know which components to target in their treatments but also which outcomes should be monitored in evaluating the impact of a cognitive behavioural intervention. Figure 3.5 outlines how outcomes to be monitored can be determined from the problem-level and case-level variables in individual cases. Formulations can also help with predictions of how other events, problems or situations will influence the person whose problems have been formulated (e.g. what might happen if they were to experience a particular complication associated with a chronic medical problem).

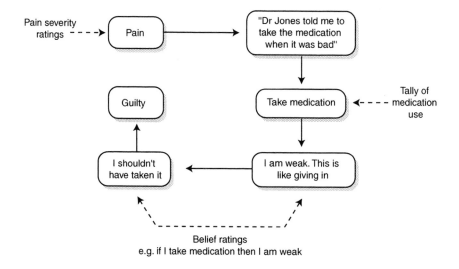

Figure 3.5. Using formulation to determine outcome variables for monitoring

When patient and therapist have constructed a preliminary formulation (problem or case level) this should contain enough information to answer the sorts of questions outlined in Table 3.2. These can be used to determine whether there are missing elements within the formulation and whether there is sufficient information to use the formulation for whichever therapy tasks need to be addressed. When review of these questions indicates missing information it is often necessary to carry out further assessment.

The cognitive behavioural formulation of psychological components of chronic medical problems is a difficult skill to master. However, the competency and confidence with which this is tackled are very much dependent on the therapist's knowledge of cognitive behavioural models of mental disorders and the literature linking cognitive and behavioural psychology to the experience of physical ill health. A huge amount of information is obtained during a cognitive behavioural assessment. It can be difficult to know how best to organise this when formulating the main mechanisms for a particular case. The construction of a case formulation is made easier if a number of problem-level formulations have already been devised. This enables thematic links to be made between problem-level formulations and it is easier to link historical and contextual information in a way that is relevant to understanding the origins and the maintaining factors for a particular individual. The way in which

Table 3.2   Questions which a formulation seeks to answer

Problem level

What cognitive/behavioural/situational factors make this problem better/ worse?

What is the main factor behind changes in symptom severity?

What would need to change in order for this cognitive/behavioural/emotional element to cause less of a problem?

What makes this a problem for this patient?

Case level

Why should this set of problems have occurred for this person at this time in her life?

Which problem components are linked?

Which life events are most important in understanding why this is a problem now?

Are there times that this has not been a problem for this patient? Why was this?

Were there particular cognitive, behavioural and/or emotional factors which explained this?

What have been the most important incidents in influencing this person's beliefs about her illness?

What are this person's beliefs about herself, her illness, medical staff and how are these relevant in understanding her adjustment to her medical problems?

How does this patient's past psychological history relate to her current experience of chronic medical problems?

Has this person developed a strategy/set of strategies to cope with her problems? If so, how does this relate to her beliefs and the course of her problems?

---

problem-level formulation and case-level formulation might be linked is outlined in Figure 3.6.

MECHANICS OF FORMULATION

Problem-level Formulation

During the early stages of assessment, patients will provide information about various different times when their problems have caused them difficulty. These difficulties can usually be understood in terms of the patterns of thoughts, feelings and/or behaviour. The problem formulation can be thought of as the framework that is applied to understanding why these situations are problematic—it explains what aspects of thoughts, emotions and behaviour are responsible for mediating and moderating the problem on the patient's problem list. Like all formulations in psychological therapy, the cognitive behavioural problem formulation can be expressed diagrammatically or in writing. Expert therapists become proficient at constructing formulations 'in vivo' as

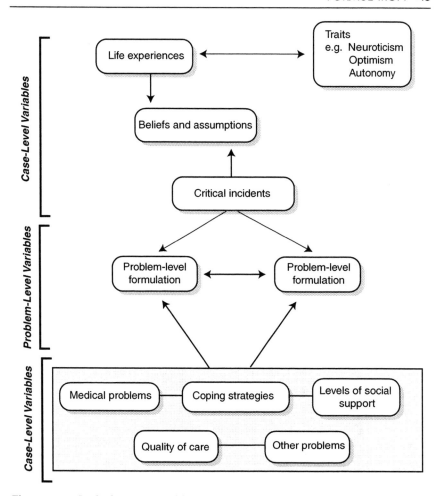

Figure 3.6.   Links between problem-level and case-level formulation

patients provide information during assessment. Less experienced therapists often find that they, too, are able to do this if they use principles
from one of the many cognitive frameworks that exist to aid understanding of these problems. Therapists with less experience in formulating
problems should first construct a list of information using the various
sources of information gleaned during their assessment. Particular effort
should be made to avoid imposing an explanatory structure at this early
stage. Therapists may conclude at this stage that they have insufficient
information within which to formulate presenting problems, and it is
often easier to identify gaps which require further assessment from such
lists of information. When sufficient information has been collected, it is
possible to begin to make links between items and construct an idio-

syncratic explanation that outlines the key elements, mediators and moderators of the particular problem being formulated. This is a highly recursive process, involving, as it does, the repeated analysis of why particular elements merit inclusion in the formulation. Formulations should offer some explanation of why certain elements have been linked, and this collection of information can then be linked in a formulation summary and/or diagram.

Therapists should assess more than one discrete example of problem episodes as they construct a problem-level formulation. Detailed assessment of recent problem examples is often the most productive way of generating such information and should always aim to cover situation and environment, emotions, behaviour, thoughts/images/memories and physical sensations. The main decision-making criterion for inclusion in a formulation is the amount of explanatory power that is achieved by inclusion. ('Does adding this to the problem-level formulation add understanding to why or how this problem occurs?') Problem-level formulations should aim to account for problem absence and occurrence, frequency and severity. It should be possible to make links between every subcomponent of a problem-level formulation and each link should be supported by assessment data. Formulating at this level almost always results in the discovery that there are elements which require further assessment, either to provide missing data or to refute or confirm potential links. Problem-level formulations in cognitive behavioural therapy seek to explain links between these domains of experience in a manner that make sense to the individual experiencing the problems and takes account of cognitive behavioural theory. One of the most helpful principles to keep in mind in constructing a problem-level cognitive behavioural formulation is cognitive content specificity. It is well recognised that specific themes in thought content are accompanied by corresponding emotional states: *anxiety*— thoughts associated with danger or threat; *anger*—thoughts associated with the violation of what is seen as a personal right; and *depression*— thoughts associated with the negatives of a situation and an inability to do anything about it. Some cognitive behavioural problem-level formulations make the mistake of simply *describing* an individual patient's experiences in each of the domains. This is undoubtedly important, but the essence of a formulation is captured in the extent to which it *explains* the nature and strength of the links between domains of patients' experiences. The contrast between description and formulation is outlined in Table 3.3.

The initial statement in Table 3.3 certainly represents the beginnings of a problem-level formulation but falls short of providing the degree of explanation that should be aimed for.

Table 3.3 Problem-level formulation—more than a description

Description of problems
Mrs X experiences episodes of guilt which are associated with thoughts that her parenting skills are substandard because of the demands of her chronic illness.

Problem-level formulation
Mrs X is particularly concerned by episodes of guilt of moderate intensity which always occur when at home alone (usually at night) associated with thoughts of being a bad mother which, at these times, she believes completely. The guilt increases gradually in intensity as more and more intrusive memories of perceived failures in mothering are recalled. The guilt is such that the patient is unable to look at her children because this seems to intensify the frequency and intrusiveness of the memories. This difficulty further reinforces her belief of substandard parenting which, in turn, perpetuates the problems with guilt. Mrs Smith's husband is dismissive of her concerns and finds discussion of the topic too distressing. Unfortunately, his wife often interprets the lack of information on his part to be evidence that he agrees with her views on her parenting.

Case-level Formulation

A case-level formulation aims to synthesise the information contained in multiple problem-level formulations and seeks to integrate this with historical information on the problems, details on core cognitive structures, the patient's life history and current living situation. Case-level factors, such as coping style and personality traits, should be included when these are relevant to understanding how the formation of particular beliefs and/or exposure to life experiences might have occurred. Links between historical events and core cognitive structures are featured in the case-level formulation (e.g. the development of the belief 'I am useless' following repeated criticism at school or 'Doctors cannot be trusted' following exposure to an earlier mistake by a GP). This is another area where knowledge of cognitive behavioural theory is helpful. There are a number of core cognitive themes which are predictably affected in certain clinical problems. In the case of depression, these usually surround themes of failure and self-worth. With anxiety problems, these are often thematically related to vulnerability to harm or illness and/or a pervasive inability to cope. This level of formulation should also endeavour to outline compensatory strategies which individuals may have developed in an attempt to minimise the negative impact of their beliefs and assumptions on their well-being. These strategies are similar to avoidance behaviours mentioned earlier but are usually more cross-situational in their focus. Formulation construction at this level can be tricky, is often confusing and may provoke uncertainty in the therapist. Confusion and uncertainty are usually signs that further information on a formulation element would be helpful and/or that the therapist is feeling pressurised to formulate and/or intervene prematurely. In such cases, further assessment should definitely be conducted. Sharing the preliminary case formulation with the patient is often a productive step in that it usually provides confirmation for some of the elements and ideas for refinement.

T: This is the eighth time that you have visited the clinic. You might remember last week that I suggested we spend some time on my understanding on how some of your problems might fit together.

P: I remember that you said that, yes.

T: Over the past few appointments we have been discussing in some detail the situations, feelings, thoughts and behaviours which have been causing you some difficulty. We have worked out together that there are some common thoughts, feelings and behaviours which always go together. For example, we have discovered that when you have any unexpected physical sensation you tend to think your illness is getting worse, you feel anxious and usually bring forward your hospital appointment.

P: My urge to do that is getting less.

T: We have also discovered that when your doctor suggests an increase in your medication, you usually start to become very depressed because of predictions that this will result in a downward spiral followed by certain death.

P: That happened again last week.

T: We know from our work with other people in similar situations that these examples are small pieces of a larger jigsaw, that it is possible to work out how you think about yourself and the world and what beliefs underlie your concerns that you are destined to become very ill soon.

P: If you tell someone something often enough then they'll believe, won't they?

T: I guess they might do, yes. How does that relate to your view of things and the concerns about illness?

P: Everything my mother did gave me the idea that I couldn't cope. In fact she always referred to me as the weak one. I tend to see myself as a wee soul, too weak to withstand the stresses and strains of life.

Detail on life experiences, critical incidents and the current life circumstances of patients are all incorporated into the case-level formulation. The type of information which may need to be included for these areas is outlined in the remainder of this section. It is not possible to provide a universally applicable list of all of the early life experiences which may be potentially relevant to constructing a case-level formulation. However, there are certainly some common themes among the idiosyncratic experiences reported by patients which can help therapists to identify core cognitions commonly seen among patients with difficulty adjusting to their chronic medical problem. Some medical problems are associated with prior exposure to traumatic events. These are often pivotal in establishing dysfunctional beliefs about self or illness. The presence of important life events can be elicited by reviewing personal history in detail or by asking socratic questions which enable patients to make links between present and past events ('Does how you felt in the clinic remind you of any other times in your life when you felt that way?'). In some cases patients will spontaneously report a memory of an earlier experience which proves to be significant in understanding how they developed particular beliefs about themselves or their problems. Questionnaires such as the MultiModal Life History Questionnaire (Lazarus & Lazarus, 1991) can be helpful in providing clues to the sort of significant information that might be included in a case-level formulation. Some patients prefer to provide historical information in this format. There are others for whom direct questioning ('Did you ever experience bullying at school?') is preferable and still others who prefer to be given the chance to offer a chronological account of their earlier experiences (see Chapter 2). It is not always early life experiences that result in the formation of unhelpful schema or intermediate beliefs—a single recent event can be enough to lead to the formation of a dysfunctional belief. The most common early life experiences that are relevant in formulating illness-related aspects of patient problems are often parental statements and behaviour in relation to physical well-being and/or family or prior personal experience of illness (see Table 3.4).

Critical incidents are essential components of a case-level formulation and provide a rich source of information regarding the ways in which hypothesised cognitive mechanisms can manifest particular psychosocial problems as a result of the interface between belief and life event. They are usually easy to identify in that they are associated with the onset, exacerbation or recurrence of physical and/or psychosocial problems. Critical incidents are usually affect laden and, as such, patients will

Table 3.4 Examples of early experiences from case-level formulations

Physical, sexual or emotional abuse
Neglect
Witnessed negative consequences of relatives chronic medical problem
Parental anxiety about ill health
Overprotective parental responses to illness
Critical parents or significant adult (e.g. teacher)
Traumatic hospital experiences as a child

usually find them easy to recall. Some common examples of critical incidents are outlined in Table 3.5. An assessment will provide important information on dates and times which may be relevant trigger-points for problem development or exacerbation. These should be noted as critical incidents in the case-level formulation and may be helpful in planning treatment. An example of this might be the anniversary of the diagnosis of a chronic medical problem and/or key events in the course of a problem (dates of surgery, worsening of symptoms, when the patient stopped work).

Table 3.5   Examples of critical incidents from case-level formulations

When diagnosis of chronic medical problem confirmed
Reactions of other people to news of problems
Having to give up work because of difficulties
Actions or memorable statements by medical/nursing staff
Acute exacerbations in symptoms
Hospital admissions
Media coverage relating to own medical problems
Deterioration in physical health status
Development of a new physical health problem
Change in arrangements for the provision of medical and/or nursing care (e.g.
    new member of staff)

FORMULATION FRAMEWORKS

There are a number of cognitive behavioural theories and models which therapists can choose from to assist with the conceptualisation and formulation of the psychological problems associated with chronic medical problems. The remainder of this chapter will outline some frameworks which can be used to guide the formulation of psychological aspects of chronic medical problems. Details are provided of the sorts of questions therapists should seek to answer in their formulations. Having a framework enables therapists to generate hypotheses which can be tailored specifically to individual presenting problems as the formulation begins to take shape.

General CBT Framework

The framework proposed by Padesky and Greenberger (1996) is particularly helpful for the construction of problem-level formulations in cognitive behavioural therapy. Its appeal is that it can be applied to almost any situation experienced by patients with chronic medical problems. The inclusion of a component consisting of physical variables makes it particularly useful in that it acknowledges the importance of taking physical symptoms into account. This is particularly helpful when socialising patients to a cognitive behavioural model of their psychosocial adjustment. Patients usually respond well to the idea of paying equal attention to physical factors (especially those who may have been concerned about referral to a psychologically oriented therapist). It is also a framework that is well suited to the formulation of problems for which there are no established cognitive behavioural models or they are not immediately apparent to the therapist. The framework is outlined in Figure 3.7.

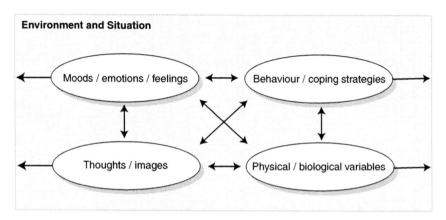

Figure 3.7. Generic cognitive-behavioural framework. (This framework is based on that outlined by Greenberger and Padesky (1996); reproduced here with permission)

Panic and Anxiety Problems

People who are troubled by anxious feelings will often report thoughts concerning themes of threat, danger and an inability to cope with threatening or dangerous situations. Much of their thinking can be conceptualised as 'What if' thinking, and is usually future oriented and focused on negative outcomes over which they have limited control. Episodes of anxious mood are also often accompanied by cognitive and behavioural efforts to minimise anxiety. These avoidance tactics often have paradoxical effects in that instead of minimising anxiety they maintain it. This occurs as a result of processes which prevent confrontation with feared stimuli and deny access to disconfirmatory information. Indeed, patients who are troubled by anxiety disorders or symptoms will often report that it is their avoidance which is protecting them from the outcomes they fear. Anxious patients most often display an attentional bias towards threatening information and are often unaware that their avoidance behaviour is making their problems worse. The cognitive model of panic outlines how patients tend to catastrophically misinterpret benign physical sensations as evidence of an impending catastrophic mental or physical event. These cognitions serve to mediate anxiety which subsequently increases the severity of physical and mental symptoms. Patients then perceive this as further evidence of their worst fears. Clark (1999) outlined how six main processes maintain distorted beliefs about the dangerousness of events or stimuli. These are: safety-seeking behaviours, attentional deployment, imagery, emotional reasoning, memory processes and the way in which threat is represented. These processes should be outlined in formulations of anxiety and panic problems when relevant.

Patients with generalised anxiety often experience what Wells (1997) refers to as type I and type II worries. Type I worries among the chronically physically ill are often about the nature and impact of medical problems, and type II typically relate to concerns about the potential which worry has to exacerbate medical and/or psychosocial correlates of medical problems (e.g. 'This worrying will cause another heart attack' or 'If I worry about the cancer then it will make it come back'). Type I worries are the worries themselves (e.g. worry about outcome of treatment, worry about childcare) and type II worries are worries about worry. Table 3.6 outlines some of the questions which therapists will find helpful in applying a framework to their formulations of physically ill patients with anxiety disorders.

Recent conceptualisations of anxiety disorders have emphasised the role of safety behaviours as key maintaining factors. These behaviours are often subtle and are usually best identified by working with a patient to

Table 3.6   Formulating anxiety problems among the chronically physically ill

Does this patient's medical condition cause physical sensations which he catastrophically misinterprets?

Has this patient been privy to any information recently about people with the same condition experiencing catastrophic or tragic outcomes?

Are any of the patient's coping strategies designed to prevent perceived physical catastrophe?

Has the perceived catastrophe occurred in the past? If so, what are the predominant memories of this?

Do any of the patient's medications produce physical sensations which could be misinterpreted?

Has this patient received instruction in how to cope with the consequences of his medical problem?

determine the function of behavioural changes that have developed to manage their symptoms ('What things do you do to manage your symptoms that you did not do before?'). Safety behaviours are sometimes difficult to detect. The implication that these can only be behavioural strategies should not divert therapists from identification of cognitive responses which are designed to protect patients from harm, danger or serve to reduce a perceived threat. The concept can be presented to patients as 'safety strategies'. Safety strategies (cognitive or behavioural) serve to inflate patient perceptions of actual risk. After all, if it were not really dangerous then patients would not believe they had to implement strategies designed to keep themselves safe. Patients deny themselves the opportunity to discover that the safety strategy serves only to exacerbate their problems. It also denies them the opportunity to elicit evidence that things are not as dangerous as they think they are. The role of safety strategies can be especially problematic when behaviour serves to increase symptoms as a result of psychophysiological pathways. Checking behaviours which are designed to identify physical symptoms often result in increased anxiety as patients develop hypervigilance for a range of physical sensations.

Social Anxiety

The cognitive model of social anxiety disorder (or social phobia) emphasises the important role of unhelpful processing strategies for information about the self in relation to others in social situations. People with social phobic and/or anxiety symptoms tend to perceive themselves from the perspective of other people and to experience thoughts about being the centre of attention and/or being humiliated. They too develop safety behaviours which have a paradoxical effect. Although they are designed to reduce social visibility, they increase the likelihood of patients being noticed by others and serve to magnify their level of self-focused attention. Cognitive conceptualisations of social anxiety and social phobia are particularly relevant when working with people who have been disfigured and/or who have medical conditions that require them to rely on aids and adaptations to maximise their functional abilities. Some patients have medical care regimes which require that they pay close attention to physical symptom changes. These patients have a well-developed ability to tune their attention towards themselves at the expense of other stimuli—a process which is functional when it comes to their self-management. This process can become dysfunctional when patients begin to have an exaggerated degree of self-focused attention.

Table 3.7 Formulating social anxiety problems among the chronically physically ill

Does this person's symptoms worsen when he is in a social situation?

How does he think that other people perceive his medical problem?

Are there elements of this person's behaviour and appearance which make it apparent to others that they he has a problem? If so, might he be exaggerating the extent to which this is the case?

Does his medical management involve his having to pay attention to his physiological functioning? If so, would this have generalised to such an extent that this has generalised?

Was he teased or bullied at school because of a medical problem?

Has he heard or witnessed others with similar experiences being embarrassed or humiliated in social situations as a result of their medical problems?

Does his medical problem actually result in drawing greater attention to himself than would otherwise be the case?

Post-traumatic Stress

Cognitive conceptualisations of PTSD and related symptoms emphasise the importance of the way in which people assimilate information about trauma within their existing belief structures. It is also important to understand the ways in which patients think about the normal psychological phenomena which occur after exposure to a traumatic event (Dunmore, Clark & Ehlers, 1999). It is believed that some of the common signs and symptoms of post-traumatic stress reactions are the result of an inability to assimilate such new information about the self or the world. Stimuli that are traumatic for one individual can act as a minor inconvenience for another. There are clearly a set of events which are likely to be universally traumatic for anyone who has the misfortune to experience them (e.g. near death, rape, etc.). However, even these events will result in a wide range of effects on pre-existing beliefs and psychological responses. It is often helpful to assess and examine the extent to which people adhere to what has become known as the 'just world' view. To work effectively with this model in formulating cases, the therapist must first understand the sort of beliefs and assumptions which the experience of chronic physical illness has shattered. In some cases, it is possible to determine those beliefs that have been shattered by directly questioning ('When you found out that the liver disease could not be cured, do you find that some of the things you always thought were instantly shattered?'). More commonly, details of the beliefs and assumptions which have been shattered by experiences of physical illness emerge from themes within problem formulations.

An example of this might be a patient who experiences problems with intrusive thoughts relating to events which he may not be alive to witness. Many chronic medical problems and their treatments can be associated

Table 3.8 Formulating post-traumatic reactions among the chronically physically ill

Does the content of the person's re-experiencing symptoms relate to aspects of his chronic medical problem? If so, are these themes reflected in the person's thoughts about other presenting problems and/or do they contribute to other problems on the problem list?

Does this person have concerns about the significance of his re-experiencing symptoms on the course of his medical problem?

What elements of this person's premorbid lifestyle has he given up since the diagnosis/treatment and to what extent is this contributing to him being frozen in time?

Which aspects of the course of his chronic medical problem have been most shocking? Which beliefs might have been shattered to produce this degree of shock?

with repeated exposure to personally threatening information. This can have the cumulative effect of overwhelming previous belief systems and resulting in post-traumatic symptoms. Indeed, some people may live with the constant threat that their life expectancy is compromised and it is this which mediates traumatic psychological reactions. Patients may suddenly be given news or information which they cannot assimilate into pre-existing belief systems and this, too, may be the factor which results in the emergence of the symptoms of PTSD or related phenomena.

Depression

The most common cognitive contributors to depression are negative thoughts and images related to self, world and future. Patients may attribute negative events to be the result of global, internal and stable factors. Behavioural manifestations of depression also include avoidance of activity but this is most often related to predictions that activities will be unfulfilling. Depressogenic thinking is characterised by biases towards the negatives in any situation, the view that things will not improve and that the patient has a significantly compromised ability to affect the outcome.

Table 3.9 Formulating depression among the chronically physically ill

What losses has this patient experienced with regard to her medical problem?

How much time does this person spend thinking about the negatives of her situation compared with the positives in her life?

Has this patient been told that her condition will deteriorate?

Has this patient had experience of witnessing (directly or indirectly) the negative consequences of this or similar illnesses?

Is this patient perceiving events to be more permanent and uncontrollable than might be the case?

Stages of Change Framework

Prochaska and diClemente (1986) have outlined five discrete stages which are helpful in understanding the views people may take when changes in their behaviour are being considered. These stages can be applied to a wide range of behaviours and, as such, are useful concepts for inclusion within case-level formulations and treatment plans. The model has been used to understand a patient's readiness to adopt a self-management approach for pain (see Chapter 6). It can be applied to a wide range of aspects of individual adjustment to life with chronic medical problems such as a patient's level of acceptance of a diagnosis and/or the need to undergo investigation or treatment.

Patients who have no intention to change their behaviour are said to be at the *precontemplation* stage. Indeed, patients at this stage may be unaware of problems. People who have an awareness that a problem exists, and are thinking about tackling it, are said to have reached the *contemplation* stage. To be classified at this stage of change, patients must not have made any decisions to make behavioural changes. *Preparation* is the stage at which patients intend to engage in activity designed to make changes. When this intention is followed by attempts to modify the factors responsible for the occurrence of problems, patients are said to have reached the *action* stage. This is followed by *maintenance*—the stage within which patients work to consolidate gains and, in so doing, prevent the recurrence of problems or relapse to a prior problem status. The sorts of behaviour to which the stages of change model can be applied in working with people with chronic medical problems are outlined in Table 3.10.

Therapists will find that the formulation of patient problems is much easier when reference is made to the cognitive frameworks outlined in this chapter. There are many more which may be helpful and therapists need to keep up to date with emerging cognitive models of psychological adjustment and disorders. The principles from these frameworks can be integrated with findings from theoretical frameworks addressing illness

Table 3.10   Behaviours which can be understood within the stages of change model

Completion of CBT homework tasks
Self-examination (e.g. testicular self-examination)
Smoking
Alcohol use
Attending regular hospital appointments
Exercise
Diet
Self-monitoring of health status (e.g. peak flow in asthma)

representation, self-efficacy or locus of control. Indeed, most theoretical findings from within clinical health psychology can be incorporated into a cognitive behavioural conceptualisation of presenting problems. It has already been suggested that formulation is an iterative process. In this sense therapists are constantly engaged in a process of formulation and reformulation of hypotheses. There are times when there is a need for a more significant review of the way in which theory is being applied to the particular case being worked on. This need for a reformulation is addressed in the final section of this chapter.

REFORMULATION

The process of formulation continues throughout the course of therapist contact with patients. Reformulation is required when new psychological symptoms emerge or problems cannot be explained by existing elements of the formulation. Patients may experience deterioration in their physical health which require that therapists reformulate the nature of hypotheses to explain problems and symptom occurrence and patterns. This could be in the form of a new problem-level formulation which takes account of a new problem as it occurs. Patients may develop a new set of problems, which means that the case formulation requires radical alteration and/or suggests that there were major elements of the prior formulation that were 'incorrect'. Patients may disclose new information, which means that revisions are necessary in the details of early experiences or cognitive structures.

The use of general principles from mainstream CBT can help therapists to formulate hypotheses and ensure that formulations, although tailored to the needs relating to medical problems, do not neglect the core components of many of the established cognitive behavioural models of anxiety and depression.

SUMMARY AND CONCLUSIONS

CBT is always driven by a formulation. Assessments are conducted with the aim of gathering sufficient information to formulate hypotheses and then link these in a way that enables therapists to plan intervention. Problem-level formulations outline the factors which contribute to discrete problems. The way in which these interact with the presence of other problems and factors such as life history, support and beliefs, make up the case-level formulation. In some instances formulations of psychosocial aspects of chronic medical problems will be very similar to those for patients without medical comorbidity. However, in most cases, formulation requires therapists to tailor cognitive behavioural formulation frameworks to the patient's medical problems and in some cases to integrate these with concepts from health psychology research and practice. This enables therapists to plan intervention strategies and evaluate the outcome of therapy. The main principles of intervention and therapeutic strategies will now be outlined in order that Part II can begin to outline how assessment, formulation and intervention can be applied to particular medical problems.

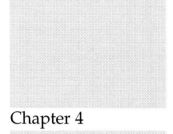

Chapter 4

TREATMENT STRATEGIES

INTRODUCTION

When a formulation has been constructed, therapists must then consider which treatment strategies are most appropriate to target the mechanisms that have initiated, accelerated or maintained problems. Treatment strategies need to be chosen with treatment goals in mind. Many books have been written to provide therapists with an outline of the main components of cognitive behavioural treatment strategies and their application to the ever-increasing range of problems where there is evidence of CBT efficacy and effectiveness. This chapter has been included to provide an outline of some of the main cognitive and behavioural strategies which can be implemented when working with the chronically physically ill.

Treatment strategies should not be implemented in isolation using what is sometimes referred to as a 'cook book' approach. CBT treatment strategies are based on the formulation and should be implemented with regard to the guiding principles of CBT. These principles will be outlined in this chapter, with discussion about how they can be particularly tailored to the treatment of psychological aspects of chronic medical problems. Treatment strategies are presented here in isolation and as discrete categories, but in reality, treatment strategies are integrated with an overall approach to intervention which uses a range of strategies, each based on the cognitive behavioural formulation. Indications for when therapists might choose one treatment strategy in preference to another will be mentioned when this is relevant. Variations in implementation or emphasis to take account of the chronicity of medical problems will be highlighted when this is relevant. Although socialisation will often have taken place before treatment strategies are implemented, therapists should not miss the many opportunities for re-socialisation which exist during treatment. Indeed, socialisation throughout the active treatment phases may make it easier for patients to appreciate how therapy links with the cognitive behavioural model and their formulations.

DISTINGUISHING CBT FROM OTHER PSYCHOLOGICAL THERAPIES

Several key themes are unique to the practice of CBT and distinguish it from other psychological therapies. These can be thought of as the guiding principles for implementing CBT. It is essential that they are not 'lost' or 'diluted' when CBT is applied to the problems associated with people with longstanding medical problems. It can become easy to apply cognitive or behavioural techniques without the structure, collaboration or integration of homework which are the hallmarks of CBT. This is more likely to happen when therapists are treating patients with multiple chronic physical health problems which present in the context of multiple psychological problems and a complex historical and environmental context. Paradoxically, it is with these more 'complex' cases that preservation of the central CBT principles will be of most help to therapists. In such clinical scenarios, it may seem to therapists that there are too many obstacles to achieving the degree of structure or collaboration that CBT demands. Novice therapists often offer rationalisations to account for their departure from structured CBT (e.g. 'It was all so tragic, it seemed cruel to talk about agendas and that sort of thing'). Insurmountable medical problems may be presented by patients as evidence in support of a nihilistic view of the possibility of psychological change, and this too can persuade therapists to adopt a more eclectic and generically supportive therapy.

T: We agreed that it would be helpful for you to keep a note of the times when you were feeling at your most weak.

P: I couldn't do that—I had a check up, they have told me that I need to restart the steroids. I have too many side effects. Our next door neighbour was ill too and I said I would help her.

T: I am sorry to hear about the side effects. That can make diary monitoring difficult—not to mention the fact that you had the additional demands of helping your neighbour.

P: It was a hectic week.

T: How would you feel about discussing the ways in which you might be able to fit some of the therapy tasks into weeks like the one that you had to complete?

P: Fine—I filled in the form that you gave me.

T: Thank you—that's very helpful. I will score it up and tell you next time how this information might link in with the goals that we are working on.

P: See if I pass?

T: It won't be a matter of pass or a fail—it will give a score which will tell us the sorts of coping strategies that you have been using. That might be a good place to start . . . despite the busy week and the new medical problems, you managed to fill in the form. When did you do that?

P: This morning. I knew I could get it all done, you see.

T: Was knowing that you could get it all done important to you?

P: Yes.

T: The sorts of problems that you have with your health will mean that there is always the risk that something will happen which gets in the way of other things that you might have planned. I wonder if we might be able to help you feel that you could try things like filling in the diary when you get a chance, accepting that initially there may be blank spaces and that you might not get all of it done?

P: OK.

Therapists who plan their work with reference to the core components of CBT will find it easier to tailor therapy to patients' problems than therapists who implement CBT in an 'ad hoc' manner without consistency and attention to the important principles already mentioned. CBT involves the patient and therapist working together as a 'scientific team'. This can be seen in the way in which therapist and patient keep an open mind about the potential contribution of cognitions and behaviours to the presenting problems—evaluating and reviewing the evidence as they proceed. Therapy sessions are structured by an agenda. Limited time is used effectively, specific problems are highlighted and complex problems (which may seem overwhelming to the patient and the therapist) can be enumerated and stated in specific terms. There are some 'standing' agenda items which appear on every therapy session agenda. These include a summary of, and reaction to, the last session; a brief update on mood and significant events; a review of homework; and, towards the end of the session, an opportunity for a session summary, setting of new homework and a feedback on the session. In adapting CBT for work with patients who have longstanding medical problems, it can be helpful to add a further specific standing item which relates to a review of the patient's physical health status, the course of that person's medical problems and/or related treatments. This is often the point within therapy sessions where patient and therapist have the opportunity to discuss the role of the medical problem in relation to the other agenda items. This approach serves to orient therapist and patient toward the role of the medical problems in the initiation and maintenance of their psychological problems.

T: How did you feel about the last session?

P: It was very interesting. I don't think I have ever had the chance to tell a doctor what I really feel and think about my problems—and that's after 10 years of coming to this hospital!

T: I am pleased . . . I certainly learned a lot about how you see your situation. Was there anything that you wanted to add or anything you wished would have been different?

P: No, I don't think so.

T: How has your anxiety been this past week?

P: OK until yesterday, I went to pieces in the GP's.

T: Is that something you filled in on the diary?

P: Yes, it's here.

T: We'll review that in a second. What about your arthritis, how has that been?

P: It has been bad in the mornings . . . it takes me an age to get out of bed.

T: Was that why you were at the GP?

P: Yes, I need something for the stiffness.

T: Is that something else we could put on the agenda—dealing with the stiffness in the morning?

P: I thought that would be more of a medical thing.

T: There might be ways of responding to it—things that you could do differently or new coping strategies which would help. Let's add it to the list and we can explore it later. OK—we'll review your monitoring, spending some time on the panic attack at the surgery and then look at ways in which you could deal with that stiffness when you get up.

P: Sounds good to me.

The collaborative nature of CBT is reflected in the fact that the 'non-standing' agenda items are negotiated by therapist and patient. Agenda-setting reduces the likelihood of the therapist imposing his own agenda and/or excluding items which are important for the patient. Non-standing agenda items vary according to the nature of the patient's problems and the stage of therapy.

Therapists should aim to elicit feedback from their patients in a bid to enhance the spirit of collaboration which is central to CBT. Information can be obtained on patient understanding and interpretation of significant events within and between sessions. Specific feedback forms can be incorporated into treatment to ensure a more structured approach to the provision of feedback. Patients with no prior experience of psychological therapy and/or prior exposure to traditionally oriented medical care often find this element of collaboration a novel idea and one to which it takes them time to adjust. It may be necessary for therapists to address this with patients, as illustrated in the following session extract:

T: As part of this type of therapy, I will often ask you about how you feel things are going or what you think we need to do differently to help you reach your goals.

P: Whatever you think best Dr White, I will be guided by you.

T: I will certainly make recommendations on what I think might be best. However, I need to help you to feel able to test things out for yourself—to not always accept my word for things.

P: Oh.

T: That is part of the 'mind set' that you will develop during this therapy—testing things out, saying what you think about things—you need to feel able to give me honest feedback on what we are working on.

P: I agree that honesty is essential.

T: Have other people in the clinics given you a chance to give your thoughts on treatment or feedback on their opinions?

P: I got a little survey to fill in while I was waiting last week—that sort of thing?

T: Did you discuss it with the doctors or nurses?

P: No.

T: The difference with the sort of feedback that I will encourage you to give is that I want to hear it and I want to act on it to make sure that we make best use of the time we have in these sessions and that I do all that I can to help you reach your goal of being able to go out without feeling anxious about collapse.

Patients treated with CBT are almost always assigned homework tasks between sessions. This active involvement is crucial. It provides vital information for the ongoing development of problem and case formulations as well as enabling patients to make changes in dysfunctional behavioural and cognitive processes. It has been suggested that CBT is a process which 'needs to be constantly lived' (Freeman, 1987). The regular completion of therapy homework is an example of this and one which has been shown to relate favourably to treatment outcome. Improvements in symptoms and a faster rate of progression towards the attainment of treatment goals occur when patients complete out-of-session tasks. This is something that can be explained to patients and which may help with motivation to implement homework tasks. Mainstream cognitive therapy literature offers a number of helpful pointers to maximise the likelihood that homework tasks will be completed (e.g. completion within session, negotiation of manageable tasks).

However, there are a number of further issues which need to be taken into account when considering homework adherence with the physically ill. Certain homework tasks may be genuinely more difficult because of the competing demands of attendance at other medical appointments: the demands of medical self-care; the debilitating effects of medical problems; and unexpected deterioration in physical health state. Weishaar (1993) has suggested that empirical hypothesis testing is the primary vehicle for change in CBT. Therapists must therefore ensure that a significant number of homework tasks relate to testing the central problems or case-level hypotheses. All of this should be done in a manner that is sensitive to the nature and importance of the medical problems in each particular patient's presentation. Table 4.1 outlines some example of homework assignments from the author's clinical work with people with chronic medical problems. Patients should be encouraged to write important discoveries from within sessions in a notebook or on coping cards to read regularly at home.

Therapists should routinely endeavour to pre-empt patient difficulties with the completion of homework tasks. Therapists should ask patients how likely it is that they will complete the homework assignment between sessions. A response of less than 90% usually indicates the need for more time addressing difficulties (Beck, personal communication). These difficulties commonly relate to misunderstanding, hopelessness about the possibility of change, cognitive avoidance and/or an inability to regulate time for the completion of homework. The format outlined in Table 4.2 is useful to consider as a means of maximising the chances of patients being able to complete CBT homework.

Therapists should endeavour to provide capsule summaries as a way of reinforcing the main issues in treatment, mechanisms within the formulation and to educate patients in the main principles of cognitive therapy. CBT aims to foster skill development after discharge and the use of summarising is one of the most helpful ways of promoting this. Process-oriented summaries include statements about what has been achieved

Table 4.1   CBT homework tasks

Monitoring thoughts when experiencing nausea
Write down predictions about what the surgeon will say if you ask him to
    explain the problem again
Count the number of times that your wife tells you to 'be careful'
Test out the belief: 'If I take the medication Dr Jones gave me, I will be drowsy
    all day'
Write down in the present tense a description of everything that happens in 'My
    nightmares of the operation'
Every time you feel sad or angry, fill in the first three columns of the Thought
    Record

Table 4.2 Questions to structure CBT homework

Before
What homework have you agreed to do?
What is the purpose of the assignment?
How often will you carry out this homework assignment?
Where will you carry out this homework assignment?
When will you carry out this homework assignment?
What are the possible obstacles to carrying out this assignment?
How can you overcome these obstacles?

After
What did you actually do as homework?
What happened to prevent you from being able to complete the homework?
What have you learned from completing this homework?

within a session and can provide a bridge to what will be focused on next within treatment. These summaries can serve to demystify the nature of the therapeutic encounter for the patient.

T: Can you think of what your husband might say to you if he knew that you were thinking of giving up on the treatment?

P: No.

T: If he were here right now and you said Frank, there's no point, it won't work—what would he say to you? Would he agree? disagree?—what would he say?

P: He would probably tell me not to be so silly.

T: Do you think that he would have a reason for telling you not to be silly?

P: He would probably think that I would be giving up any chance I had of feeling better—that it would be certain that it would not work if I did this, I'd be making it a certainty. (*Patient and therapist have further discussion about different view of husband*)

T: It is important to summarise what we have been doing. What we did might be helpful when you have other thoughts which make you feel depressed. We identified the thought by focusing on what you thought when you felt low. I asked you to keep thinking about what your husband might say if he knew you thought that—this helped you come up with other ways of thinking about your situation. This might help if you have any more depressing thoughts which you find difficult to challenge.

Content summaries are helpful in reorienting the therapist and patient to the agenda or when at a 'stuck' point within a session. These summaries should reflect the gist of patient statements, except when a subtle 'twist' in the summary is required to illustrate a point or move the patient's perspective as a precursor to a cognitive intervention.

It has been suggested that questions are the 'principle therapeutic tools' of the cognitive behavioural therapist. Questioning is a key strategy for identifying cognitions and behavioural dimensions of patient experiences and for enabling patients to make therapeutically significant discoveries (Overholser, 1983; Padesky, 1993). It enables the patient to discover information which helps them to think about their problems from an alternative perspective. Therapists should choose their questions to test out hypotheses as a formulation emerges and help people to collect evidence for and against problematic interpretations. McDaniel and Schlager (1990) have suggested that people who discover relationships by themselves learn more than when they are explained to them. Information obtained from questioning should be subjected to a process of inductive reasoning. Questioning can be used to help to synthesise information into new ways of thinking or responding ('How might this be linked with what you discovered during the homework?').

BEHAVIOURAL TREATMENT METHODS

The range of behavioural responses to and components of psychological problems in chronic medical problems is vast. The huge range of behavioural components within any one person's experiences of a medical problem makes it difficult to determine the component to target using a behavioural strategy. This range of behavioural responses, and the many possibilities which exist for behavioural change, becomes even larger when one considers that the behaviour of others in the patient's life will also influence the patient's psychological adjustment and the self-management of his or her medical problem (e.g. the behavioural responses of a family member or a junior doctor's comments in a clinic).

Behavioural treatment strategies are based on the premise that behavioural components of presenting problems are the result of past and present learning processes and exposure to particular environments. These strategies are usually applied when therapists wish to change the frequency of behaviours which do not occur frequently (Leahy, 1996). Behavioural treatment methods within cognitive behavioural therapy are not implemented in isolation from cognitive factors. The academic debates on the reasons for the effectiveness of behavioural treatment methods (are they changes in contingencies, cognitive changes, or both?) are important but are not considered here as they are beyond the scope of this book and are rarely issues that concern patients. Assessments often result in the identification of behaviours which are pivotal in compromising functioning in discrete quality

Table 4.3 Problem behaviours and related treatment goals

Missing doses of medication	Increase the number of times I take my medication
Avoiding contact with family members	Decrease avoidance; increase ability to respond to criticisms about illness
Seeking inappropriate reassurance from nurse specialist	Increase belief conviction that no deterioration in health state

of life domains; access to medical care; or as an integral part of a psychological disorder. When treatment strategies are targeted at behavioural elements of patient problems, both the problem behaviour and the desired behaviour should be specified in observable and measurable terms. Indeed, many treatment goals will often be stated in behavioural terms, and Table 4.3 outlines some examples of problem behaviours and goals of treatment.

The way in which behavioural treatment strategies are presented to patients is crucial. In many ways the simplicity of some of behavioural principles is a strength. However, it can also result in the view that they are too simplistic to be useful or relevant for complex and multifaceted elements of a patient's problems and experiences.

Exposure-based Treatment Strategies

Exposure-based treatments are based on the principles of conditioning. Two stimuli become linked so that one stimulus takes on the ability of being able to elicit responses previously elicited by an original stimulus (as a result of links between this stimulus pairing). Patients may have been exposed to stimuli during episodes of physical ill health which later become the focus of problematic conditioned reactions. An example of this might be clothing worn during kidney dialysis, which subsequently elicited the fear previously only associated with the kidney dialysis machine. It is possible to implement exposure-based therapeutic strategies in these situations. These treatment strategies often involve patients modifying the links between a stimulus which has become conditioned with fear. This can be done in progressively more difficult steps as in graded exposure or by arranging prolonged exposure to the feared stimulus. Systematic desensitisation is a variation on graded exposure in that it incorporates the use of relaxation or some other response which is inhibitory to the fear produced by exposure to the conditioned stimulus. In common with many behavioural treatment strategies, desensitisation emerged as a treatment strategy for anxiety-related problems. Patients with phobias were first taught relaxation strategies and were then encouraged to develop hierarchies to reflect scenarios that give increasing levels of distress. With the support of their therapist they then began to confront elements of the hierarchy while engaging in relaxation (or some other response which was inhibitory to anxiety). The rationale for this was that the physical effects of relaxation would inhibit the arousal which was consequent upon exposure to the distressing element of the hierarchy. Although these treatment techniques were developed in the context of treating anxiety, they can be adapted for other clinical problems where the concept of a graded approach regarding exposure to a stimulus might be helpful. They can also be applied where the conditioned response is something other than fear and the inhibitory factor could be something other than relaxation. The principles of exposure and response prevention can also be transferred to situations where exposure to a stimulus results in an unhelpful response by the patient. An example of this might be exposing a patient to intrusive thoughts about his illness and enabling him to inhibit responses designed to seek reassurance.

Using Reinforcement

The principles of *reinforcement* are based on the observation that behaviours which are followed by positive consequences are likely to increase in frequency, whereas behaviours which are followed by negative consequences are likely to decrease in frequency. Reinforcement is the term given to actions which result in increases in the frequency of a behaviour. Positive reinforcement is characterised by the provision of a reward following a behaviour, and negative reinforcement is characterised by the termination of exposure to an unpleasant experience. Therapists can integrate treatment strategies based on reinforcement with good effect across a wide range of behaviours. The application of the principles of positive reinforcement can be extended to the process of CBT itself—providing praise when patients complete homework or attending to patient statements which are consistent with the principles of a CBT approach. Extinction is designed to reduce the frequency of a target stimulus by terminating reinforcement of the stimulus and can be used when patients exhibit unhelpful or dysfunctional responses as part of their psychological reactions to chronic medical problems. It can often be applied to clinical problems believed to be reinforced by the attention of relatives or healthcare staff. Implementation of this treatment strategy should be accompanied by monitoring of the number of times that unreinforced presentations of the conditioned stimulus occur. The following extract from a supervision session with a ward-based nurse outlines how this technique might be applied:

T: So from what you are saying, you have noticed that every time you go near Mr Jones he is rude.

S: Yes, when any of the nurses pass him he mutters comments about us.

T: What sorts of comments?

S: All sorts of things.

T: What is a recent thing that he has said?

S: He called me a useless cow yesterday when I was seeing to another patient's dialysis machine.

T What do you usually do when he makes these comments?

S: Well I look over at him to let him know that I have heard what he said, finish what I am doing and then, if I can, I go over and tell him that there is no need to be rude, that I am only doing my job.

T: Is that what you did yesterday?

S: I think so.

T: Have you noticed any change in how often he is doing this?

S: The girls think that he is doing it more now, to get a reaction.

T: The monitoring that you have all being doing would support this—it seems to happen around four times a visit, whereas a weeks ago it was one a visit. This is probably because the attention he gets is reinforcing the problem.

S: So we should ignore him?

T: If that is what is keeping it going then ignoring him for long enough should stop it. It will probably worsen first though.

Modelling and Role Play

Behavioural treatment strategies are not always concerned with engineering changes in the links between existing stimuli. There are some situations where learning can occur or new behaviours can be acquired through observation (without the need for tedious practice). These techniques can result in patient acquisition of new patterns of behaviour, inhibition or disinhibition of unhelpful responses and in some cases can facilitate the expression of already established responses. New responses can vary from adopting a different posture when experiencing a particular symptom to developing a series of responses to use when medical staff are minimising or avoiding important psychosocial problems. Therapists using modelling should ensure that: a patient's attention is directed towards the most significant aspects of the model; conditions are optimal for retention in memory of what has been observed; the patient is physically capable of reproducing the behaviour or behaviours being modelled; and the patient is suitably motivated to want to apply what has been learned. Attempts should be made to ensure that the implementation of modelling is relevant to the patient's clinical condition and life situation. These elements are illustrated in the following extract from a treatment session with a patient who found it difficult to cope with intrusive questions about her physical health.

T: You have really been struggling with how to deal with the questions that you keep getting from other people.

P: It is really getting to me.

T: One of the ways that we can deal with this is to help you practise how to respond when this happens

P: I need to do something about it, that's for sure.

T: We can do this by doing a role play—you can pretend to be one of the people who have been asking you these questions and I will show you some of the ways in which you can try to respond. This way you can copy me and we can practise this until you are ready to try it out for real. How does that sound?

P: OK.

T: First I need to know some more about what sorts of things they ask you.

P: Are you going to be cured? is a favourite question. They also want to probe more and more into the detail, 'What sort of kidney problem is it?', 'Will you need a transplant?'.

T: What do you say when they ask you these sort of things?

P: I tend to clam up. I say that it is amazing what can be done and that there are people worse off than me.

T: What happens then?

P: They are never satisfied—some are, but most people want to know about me. I am a private person and I want to keep it to myself—I don't want people knowing my business.

T: Perhaps we could role play this, you be the people who pry and with each response I give try not to be satisfied with it—always keep prying more and more about my health.

P: Your health?

T: Yes, remember I will be role playing you.

P: Sorry (*laughs*), yes, I see.

T: When we have done this you can see if any of the things that I say might be worth trying out—we can role play it again with you as yourself . . .

Activity Scheduling

Chronic medical problems are often associated with significant changes in the activity levels of patients, reports that patients are overwhelmed by the resumption of activity, a loss of structure to their daily routine and changes in the extent to which activities are associated with pleasure or achievement. For each of these difficulties, planning of daily activities and levels of activity can help. This might involve planning the amount or the type of activity. Patients can be encouraged to plan a series of smaller tasks as part of a graded resumption of previously avoided activities and/or activities which are difficult to engage in because of medical problems. This intervention strategy is most useful for patients with depressive symptoms and is particularly helpful for patients whose medical problems result in changes in their functional abilities. It can be combined with the use of Weekly Activity Schedules and incorporated into other treatment strategies such as the evaluation of thoughts or exploring alternative beliefs during a behavioural experiment.

Behavioural Experiments

In some cases it is clear that patients' behavioural responses to physical symptoms are the product of dysfunctional or, in some cases, factually inaccurate beliefs about their disease and its management. In some instances educationally based strategies will change these beliefs. However, some patients are reluctant to accept new information until they experience it for themselves. Examples of such behavioural responses include patients who take non-prescription medicines because they believe that these alleviate their symptoms (when in fact they exacerbate or cause the symptoms) or patients who avoid physical activity in response to physical sensations as they believe that this avoidance will relieve or prevent symptoms. In these cases, therapist and patients need to work together to enable them to appreciate that the behaviour being discussed is the product of a belief. This can then be linked with the suggestion that their evidence base may be questionable and/or that it is possible that an alternative belief will be better supported by new evidence and experiences.

Behavioural responses to physical symptoms, behavioural elements of interactions with healthcare staff, and behaviours which are designed to avoid physical sensations often become the targets of behavioural experiments (Table 4.4). Behaviours which are more appropriate for the management of acute episodes of illness can become transferred to patient responses to chronic illness. Therapists may need to help patients to test

Table 4.4   Behavioural experiments

If I think about my future health then I will be overwhelmed with fear and have
   a panic attack

Experiments	What do you predict will happen?	Outcome

On the basis of these experiments:

What are the main conclusions?
How do they relate to the thought that you were testing?
Are the results of this experiment of relevance to any other beliefs/thoughts that
   you have?
Are there any other beliefs you have on which you could do experiments like
   this?

out more appropriate responses. These elements of a formulation can be
targeted using behavioural experimentation where the experiment is designed to enable patients to appraise the evidence base for 'acute' illness
behaviours and 'chronic' illness behaviours. Therapists must be able to
fully understand and be able to empathise with the evidence base which
seems to mediate the behavioural response being treated by behavioural
experimentation. This can be difficult to do with behaviours which, on the
surface, seem illogical. When this has been achieved it will be easier for
patients and therapists to collaborate on alternative beliefs and behaviours to put to the test.

COGNITIVE TREATMENT METHODS

Identifying, Evaluating and Modifying Automatic Thoughts

In order for cognitive treatment strategies to have an effect, patients need
to have developed strategies for identifying the cognitions that will later
form the focus of therapy. Automatic thoughts and images are probably
the most easily identifiable types of cognition as they are situation specific. They are often easily accessed by discussing problem examples
within sessions and/or reviewing thought records that have been com-

pleted outside of sessions. Patients need to know what thoughts they are to pay attention to, otherwise they may report thoughts which have limited scope for further analysis or do so in a way which makes further evaluation or modification difficult to implement. Patients with chronic medical problems often have many realistic negative automatic thoughts. This does not always mean that these thoughts are the ones which should be the focus of attempts at further evaluation and/or modification. Beck (1995) outlines a number of examples of how patients often provide automatic thoughts which are difficult to work with. The automatic thoughts which are the most useful targets of therapy are those which relate to patient's interpretations about events and their experiences. It is helpful if this can be explained to patients during the early phases of therapy. Therapists should ensure that they distinguish patients whose problems are mediated by intrusive thoughts, worry or meta-cognitions as these will require different socialisation and monitoring strategies to automatic thoughts.

The most common strategy for evaluating automatic thoughts is the use of a *Thought Record*. There are different versions of these available for use by therapists. Many therapists decide to modify these or develop their own for use with their patients. The core components of Thought Records are the provision of a structure for the identification and evaluation of the thoughts that are experienced. Most Thought Records involve the monitoring of situation, mood and thoughts; some require patients to rate the intensity of emotion using a 0 to 100 scale and/or the degree to which they actually believe the thoughts that have been identified (also using a 0 to 100 scale). Some include space for recording the presence of physical sensations. Most vary in the extent to which they provide prompts or explanations on the recording form itself. The use of Thought Records for the identification of negative automatic thoughts among the physically ill often requires monitoring forms to be tailored to the specific needs of patients (see Figure 4.1).

Therapists often rely upon the use of Socratic questions to help patients to identify their negative automatic thoughts. Therapists should not always ask the same set of questions as this can jeopardise the process of guided discovery. CBT will work best with people with chronic medical problems when therapists integrate patient experiences of the physical health problem with their questioning style. This maximises the chances of patients and therapists discovering the thoughts and images which are most related to their experiences of being physically ill. The examples in Table 4.5 illustrate the differences between generic questions and those which are specific to the cognitive and behavioural aspects of being physically ill.

Situation	Physical symptoms 1 What symptoms 2 How bad? 0 - 100	Mood 1 What mood? 2 0 – 100	Thoughts and images List the thoughts and images accompanying your symptom and mood	Working on alternative ways of thinking
				⌐ What supports this way of thinking?
		Memories		What does not support your way of thinking? What is unhelpful?
				Putting it all together: └
		Which thought makes you feel worst of all? ┘		

Note: Patients who used this had lists of notes on how to complete sections (based on components from previous sessions).

Figure 4.1.   Individually tailored thought record

Attentional Control

Attention control training (or attention training) has been shown to be an effective intervention for patients experiencing health anxiety (Papageorgiou & Wells, 1998). This intervention enables patients to develop the ability to lessen self-focus and gain metacognitive control of their attention. This is achieved by regular practice of attentional manipulation, which involves practise of selective attention, divided attention and attention switching. Full details of this intervention are outlined in Wells (2000). Attention control training is particularly useful for patients experiencing high levels of preoccupation with their chronic physical symptoms.

Distraction (a different intervention strategy from attention training) is most likely to be effective when patients have a good understanding of the role of thoughts in their experiences of emotions, behaviour and thinking. Distraction can be thought of as a first-aid technique to be used when patients have not yet mastered how to modify their thinking or when this would not be practical (e.g. while undergoing an invasive medical procedure). Distraction should not be recommended when patients seem to be experiencing intrusive thoughts, as the thought suppressant effects of distraction are likely to result in more frequent intrusions.

Table 4.5 Generic and specific questions to identify and evaluate automatic thoughts

Generic

Identifying thoughts
What was passing through my mind just before I felt this way?
What did that situation mean to me? What does it say about me as a person?
What is the worst thing that could happen in this situation?
What have I just been thinking about?

Evaluating thoughts
What experiences have I had which show me that this thought is not completely true all of the time?
If I were trying to help someone I cared about to feel better if they were having this thought, what would I tell them?
What advice might someone I cared about give me if they knew that I was thinking in this way? What would they say? Would they agree with my way of thinking? If not, why not? What aspect would they have a different view on?

Specific

Identifying thoughts
What does this mean to me about my health? my future health? my life expectancy?
What is the worst thing that could happen to my health?
When I felt (*physical symptom*) what went through my mind?

Evaluating thoughts
If someone I loved had (*name of chronic medical problem*) and thought this, what might I point out to them?
When I am feeling better physically, how do I tend to think about this?
Are there any aspects of my experiences of (*name of chronic medical problem*) which contradict this thought?

Identifying Thinking Biases

Once patients have mastered the ability to identify the thoughts mediating their problematic mood states they can begin to be introduced to the concept of biased thinking. These are sometimes referred to by therapists and in some of the cognitive therapy literature as thinking errors or mistakes. They will be referred to in this chapter as thinking biases. Patients often find it easier to appreciate the role of biases in their problems if they can be provided with examples that are specific to their problems and/or are generated from monitoring that they have completed (see Table 4.6). There is a variation in the extent to which patients are able to identify and make use of this phenomenon in addressing their problems.

Table 4.6   Common thinking biases

All or nothing thinking: tendency to think in terms of extremes, e.g. something is a complete success or a complete failure

Overgeneralisation: thought characterised by a generalisation from one event to a number of other events

Mental filter: thinking which filters out positive information so that only negative information is processed

Discounting the positive: thoughts which dismiss the importance of a positive or helpful event

Jumping to conclusions: concluding something on the basis of no or little supportive evidence

Magnification: thinking which exaggerates the degree to which something is important

Emotional reasoning: thoughts which are the result of feelings being taken as primary source of evidence about an event or situation

Personalisation: thoughts which relate events or situations to be related to the self when this is not (or only partly) true

Catastrophising: thinking about events as if they are significantly more negative that they are, i.e. as if they were a catastrophe

Mind reading/Fortune telling: thoughts which are based on estimations of what others are thinking/what will happen in the future

Some thinking biases are often referred to by different names and some texts outline variations on those that are presented here.

Looking for these biases within thoughts can be a useful adjunct during the initial phases of therapy, where patients have mastered the ability to monitor their thoughts but have not yet developed the skills to evaluate them. Patients can be encouraged to think about which modifications would need to occur with each biased thought to remove the bias and change the associated affect.

> T: Did you notice any of the sort of biased thoughts we spent time on last week?
> P: I was so amazed at how many of them I was having.
> T: Really? Can you remember some examples?
> P: I noted them down here at the side of the 3-column form.
> T: That's great.
> P: I am a big style 'fortune teller'.
> T: You noticed that bias in your thinking?
> P: Definitely. That one and also magnifying things . . .
> T: Are there examples of this within your Thought Record?
> P: When I was at work and they took a message from the nurse . . . I was really on edge.
> T: (*Looking at diary*) You were thinking 'That's it—they're going to sack me. They'll think that my health is getting worse'.

P: The worrying thing is—I am convinced that I know this when I think it.

T: That's the thing with automatic thoughts—you think of them as facts when they are interpretations of events and experiences. They may be true, as you think they are. However, the important thing is that they may not be or they may only be partly true. This is something that we will come on to later.

Identifying, Evaluating and Modifying Intermediate Beliefs

Intermediate beliefs, by virtue of their cross-situational nature, are usually more difficult than automatic thoughts to identify. It is rare for patients to be able to identify these on the basis of questioning alone and more usual for patients and therapists to begin to appreciate themes in their thinking which they can then synthesise into intermediate beliefs, usually with the guidance of therapists. The following session extract outlines how therapists can help patients to combine themes, discovered as part of other therapy components, into intermediate beliefs.

T: When you felt anxious at the surgery, did that remind you of any other situations when you felt a similar type of anxiety?

P: What, in the surgery you mean?

T: Not necessarily, could be anywhere—times when you recall having similar anxiety.

P: Mm, I always get it at the surgery.

T: Is there another example that sticks in your mind?

P: The day I was told about my kidneys, he asked me to wait while he called the hospital—I was pacing up and down, it was dreadful.

T: That was the same sort of feeling you had as last week in the surgery? What sorts of things were going through your mind as you were waiting?

P: I was concerned that he'd think that I was a pest, that I was taking up too much time.

T: So, in each situation you felt anxious, you were thinking about what the other people would think about you.

P: I suppose I was. I worry that they will be angry with me.

T: Have there been other times in your life when you felt this sort of anxiety?

P: I got it a lot on the way to and from school as a child.

T: You felt the same anxiety?

> P: Yes. I used to be so nervous about asking a question at school. One day I said that I didn't understand something and the teacher made me stand up in front of the class—I started to cry, it was a dreadful experience.
>
> T: It sounds dreadful. Do you think that this experience might relate in any way to your nervousness when you think other people might be thinking badly of you?
>
> P: I always seem to think that people will have it in for me when I ask something of them.
>
> T: What is the rule that you seem to operate by in these situations?
>
> P: It's as if I assume that if I ask someone to do something then they will be angry with me.

Intermediate beliefs cover a wide range of patient experiences. Many of these will outline the way in which patients link discrete elements of their problems. Examples of some intermediate beliefs of people with chronic medical problems are outlined in Table 4.7. Patients are often fascinated to discover the existence of intermediate beliefs which seem to link many of their problem moods, behaviours and situations. Discovery of them often makes it easier for patients to begin to appreciate where their beliefs have originated from and how problems have developed. This is a crucial element in evaluating them and an essential precursor to any attempts to modify them. The worksheet in Table 4.8 can be used to structure attempts to evaluate and modify intermediate beliefs. This first enables patients to think about their belief in terms of its advantages, disadvantages, and origins and to use this as a framework for considering an alternative. This can then be linked with a behavioural plan which specifies how they might arrange experiences to structure the reinforcement of their more helpful alternative. The details in this example relate to a patient awaiting a transplant. Her intermediate beliefs meant that she often felt obliged to engage in behaviour which she was physically unable to sustain as a result of her severe levels of physical debility and significantly compromised functional abilities. Modification resulted in less anxiety and frustration.

Table 4.7 Examples of intermediate beliefs of patients with chronic medical problems

---

If I feel unwell then it means that my condition is deteriorating
If I take all my medicines as indicated then I should have no health problems
If I stay as healthy as I can then it will stop my disease from worsening
If my doctor tells me something then it must always be correct
Doctors should be able to answer all my questions
If I have a new symptom then it means that my disease has progressed

---

Identifying, Evaluating and Modifying Schemata

The chronicity of the sort of medical problems being outlined in this book often means that the medical condition has itself been responsible for the development of pervasive cognitive structures about self, world and illness. Patients may also have a set of beliefs about themselves and their lives which, although not directly related to their chronic medical problems, are activated by the onset or exacerbations in their chronic medical problems. A schema can be thought of as a mental template which serves to assist with information processing. Socialisation to the concept can be done by providing general examples of the way in which a schema operates, using non-emotionally valenced material and/or using an example which seems relevant to the patient. The decision on which to use will depend on the therapist's assessment of which might be easier for the patient to assimilate. Personal examples may make it difficult for patients to learn the basics due to the affect which is triggered by discussion of schematically relevant topics. The following session extract illustrates how schema can be explained to patients:

T: We have been spending time talking about the ways in which your thoughts have an effect on your feelings and reactions. You might remember some weeks ago that I talked with you about core beliefs or schemas.

P: Yes, things like 'I am worthless'.

T: Was that the example that I gave you when I mentioned what a core belief was?

P: Yes I think so.

T: A core belief can be thought of as an information store—someone with the core belief that they are worthless will have a store labelled worthless. This is where they store all the information that they think makes them worthless.

P: I don't think that's my problem though.

T: No, I would agree with you. I wanted to use 'I am worthless' as an example. We can start to think about what core beliefs you might have later—is that OK ?

P: Yes.

T: If someone criticises someone with this worthless belief what do you think they do with this information?

P: Put it in that information store?

T: Exactly—it goes straight to that information store.

P: Have you any idea what they might do if something neutral happens, something that is not necessarily negative?

T: I don't know—put it in another information store?

P: They may do, but more usually core beliefs make people distort infor-
    mation so that it can go into the worthless store of information. They
    may even do this with positive information. Someone may give them
    some really positive feedback. Instead of putting it here in the positive
    store they might distort it by saying 'they don't know the real me'—
    and so, the worthless store is full while the store for the belief 'I am
    worthwhile' is empty.

This idea of a schema as an information store can be outlined diagrammatically as patient and therapist discuss this concept. This is outlined in Figure 4.2.

There are other ways of socialising patients to the idea of schemata. The
concept of a schema as a prejudice is often easily understood by patients
(Padesky, 1993). Therapists should be collecting information on possible

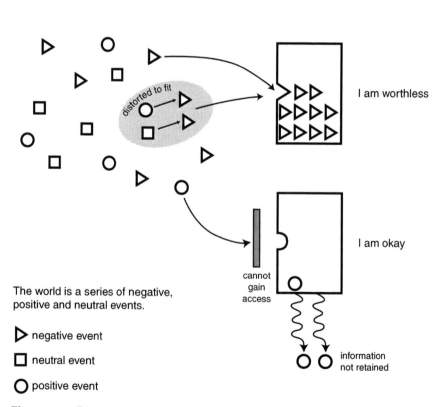

Figure 4.2.   Diagrammatic representation of schema maintenance

themes for possible themes for salient patient schemata while they are working with behavioural treatment strategies and with the other levels of cognition such as thoughts and intermediate beliefs. In some cases sentence completion can result in information about the content of patient schemas, especially if this is preceded by a discussion about recent examples of emotionally challenging situations. It is likely that this acts according to a priming effect where this discussion increases accessibility of the schema.

T: So when you heard that there had been some problems with the way in which you had switched the blood pressure machine on and off, you felt empty and dejected.

P: . . . to the bottom of my stomach.

T: An empty and dejected feeling which you experienced in the pit of your stomach.

P: I felt sick to the core.

T: If you were to keep this reaction in your mind right now and think about how you might complete the following sentence, 'I am . . .'—what would you say?

P: How would I finish that?

T: Yes, keep the empty feeling and the blood pressure machine in your mind and think about how you would complete that sentence 'I am . . .'.

P: Useless. . . . No good to anyone.

If therapists have hypotheses about possible constellations of schemas then they may collate these into a monitoring form for assessment and further refinement of schematic elements of the formulation. When patient and therapist have established the existence of a problem schema, it is possible to begin to discuss the ways in which being physically ill might reinforce it and how cognitive behavioural interventions might be used to modify the schema. As schema change can take many weeks, patients should be provided with an explanation of the process of schema change. This should cover the need to operationalise the schema; to understand where patients place themselves on the schema (using continua); where they would wish to be and how they might begin to achieve this. Schema change emphasises weakening problem schemas and strengthening new schemas. There are various ways in which this can be achieved. Positive data logs and historical tests of core beliefs are helpful, and examples of their application are outlined in Figure 4.3. The following extract illustrates how therapists can begin to enable patients to begin the important therapeutic task of weakening the old schema and strengthening a new and more functional alternative.

T: So it seems that there is a need to weaken this old belief of yours—and to strengthen a new alternative.

P: I hadn't thought of seeing things like that—old and new, weak and strong.

T: What do you think about viewing things in this way?

P: It makes good sense.

T: One of the ways we can start to do this is to help you to look out for things that happen each day that might strengthen your view as competent. We also need to help you hang on to the information—keep it in the store so that it doesn't slip out.

P: Mmmm . . . that's my problem. I am good at looking for things to put in here. (*Points to a diagram of schema*)

T: It can help to think about what you mean when you think about being a competent person. This way you will know what you are looking for.

Identification, Evaluation and Management of Imagery

Therapists must consider images as mechanisms underlying psychological distress and targets for intervention (Hackmann, 1998). Not all patients will experience imagery and those that do will vary in their ability to identify it. The strategies for the identification of imagery are similar to those for the identification of negative automatic thoughts in that patients need to pay close attention to their thought processes at times of significant emotional change. Therapists can re-create situations within sessions by asking patients to focus on a recent emotionally charged situation and begin to elicit the presence of an image by asking questions such as 'Did you get an image?'; 'Was there a picture of something in your mind ?'. This can lead to the identification of imagery which may then become the focus of further detailed assessment. This further assessment can focus upon characteristics of the image itself and/or how it may relate to other presenting problems or cognitive behavioural elements. Images often represent themes which are reflected in thoughts, intermediate beliefs and in core schema. When therapist and patient have identified an image, it is useful to begin to enable the patient to describe the image content in greater detail by asking him or her to elaborate on sensory modalities. This way imagery can be described in a way which acknowledges auditory, olfactory, gustatory, tactile and kinaesthetic modalities. This can be particularly helpful later when patient and therapist might decide to explore the possibility of modifying these aspects of imagery or using them to explore the significance of the image to earlier and/or similar life experiences. Images can be used to help patient and therapist access thoughts, beliefs and schemas.

Positive data log

Old belief: I am a freak

New belief: I am acceptable

1   Moira said she liked my new hairstyle

2   _____

3   _____

4   _____

5   _____

Historical Test of Core Belief

I am a freak

Ages	Evidence	An alternative explanation
0 - 5	My mum said I was always "different"	She might not have meant this in a negative way. Even if she did it is just her opinion
5 - 10		
10 - 15		
15 - 20		
20 - 25		
25 - 30		

Figure 4.3. Frameworks for schema change

T: When you were feeling anxious, did you notice any pictures or images in your mind?

P: I get a picture of myself standing at the edge of a black hole.

T: I'd like to ask you some more about your experiences as they relate to this image. Would that be OK?

P: Yes—but I feel anxious when I think about it.

T: I will need you to tell me if the anxiety gets too much for you so that we can work out a way to lessen it.

P: I should be OK. I am getting it now. It comes on so quickly.
T: What is happening in the image?
P: I am standing at the edge of a big black hole.
T: Go on. Tell me what else you see, if you can.
P: It is huge and gaping right in front of me.
T: Where are you in relation to the hole?
P: I am right at the edge, my toes are right over the edge.
T: Can you look into the hole?
P: Yes.
T: What can you see?

Imagery management strategies will depend upon the degree to which the image relates to an actual event, a symbolic representation of an actual event or one that has a tangential relationship with real life experiences. Images can be modified by enabling patients to change the imaginal representation in the same way that one might use guided discovery to enable patients to discover less affect-laden verbally encoded cognitions. Images can contain similar sorts of biases to those seen in verbal cognitions. There are also some biases which are unique to images—and these are outlined in Table 4.9.

Exposure-based techniques can be used to lessen the distress associated with images which form part of a larger traumatic experience. This involves having patients rank the images in terms of distress and practising repeated exposure to these images until the associated distress lessens. Patients might also rescript their images by changing elements from a written narrative. Patients with nightmares can be encouraged to create alternative endings to their nightmares: these can be rehearsed when awake and used to regulate affect if they experience further nightmares. In some cases, it will not be the image which is the mediator of a behavioural or emotional problem but the metacognitive factors which influence the way in which the content and experience of imagery is processed by the patient ('I can see it so it must be true'). Verbal reattribution of these metacognitions can help. Dysfunctional thought control strategies such as thought suppression may need to be addressed, and imaginal rehearsal can be used when it is not possible to role play model behaviours or responses.

Addressing 'Realistic' Cognitions

Approaches aimed at correcting bias inherent in such thoughts are not appropriate in work with realistically negative thoughts. Socialisation to the cognitive behavioural model, particularly when working with people

Table 4.8 Intermediate Belief Worksheet

I hold the belief that . . .	I must always please people and live up to their expectations or they will think less of me
It is understandable that I hold this belief because . . .	1. My mother said things like 'No wonder you don't have friends if you behave like that' 2. Always having to try to be as good as Jean 'living in her shadow' 3. Because of my health I had to try extra hard to please people 4. Having to overcompensate/be nice to avoid being bullied
However this belief is unreasonable because . . .	1. I can feel anxious when I find out someone expected me to do something and I didn't 2. It is not always reasonable what others expect of me e.g. people's expectations might be based on lack of understanding 3. It means I am always worrying about what others think and this causes me fatigue and stress
Advantages of holding this belief . . .	1. People will approve of me/like me 2. It is good to please and help others
Disadvantages of holding this belief . . .	1. I'll hurt other people (think) if I don't do what pleases them 2. I feel guilty when I do something that doesn't please them 3. It's tiring trying to live up to expectations 4. Can't relax and be myself

The consequences of changing this belief . . .	PROS 1. Less stress and feeling more relaxed 2. It would help Frank and I as I talk a lot to him about it 3. Less need to explain, justify and apologise to others 4. People might be more relaxed in my company and I might feel less tired	CONS 1. Might overlook a situation where my behaviour could have been different

A more helpful belief is . . .	It is good to be able to please people but it is not always possible to do this and people's pleasure isn't always in your control. Even if I don't meet someone's expectations then this doesn't mean they think I'm globally a lesser person

Since I have held this belief a long time it will take time to modify it. My action plan for change is . . .	1. Monitor using a diary when the old belief is activated—situation, mood, thinking
	2. Need to put things in perspective:
	  (a) Complete responsibility pie
	  (b) See if I am applying difficulties—would I view me the way I think he/she/they view me?
	  (c) Look at chapter
	3. Communicating to other people that it is not always possible to meet their expectations
	4. Thinking of having a behavioural test—behave in a way to see what happens
	5. Instead of assuming I am responsible I could ask other people if they are not pleased and this would mean it would get sorted out

with longstanding physical health problems, should emphasise that the cognitive elements of treatment are not always based on the modification of negative thinking. Sometimes the management of negative thoughts is a more realistic alternative. Treatment emphasis in these cases can be on managing the occurrence of these thoughts by distraction or activity scheduling. It may also involve enabling patients to fully engage with the affect associated with the thoughts. This may be blocked by thoughts about the consequences of expressing negative emotion or a general tendency towards avoidant coping. Patients may need help to understand metacognitive aspects of their experience of realistic thoughts. Cognitive therapy strategies may need to be applied to beliefs and assumptions which mediate unhelpful behavioural or emotional responses to realistic thoughts. The need to accept the reality of certain negative appraisals should not be interpreted as equivalent to colluding with a nihilistic and defeatist view of a patient's problems. Realistic automatic thoughts are often accompanied by biased thoughts which can be treated, and patients can also be helped to adopt more active coping strategies, which is particularly helpful for patients who, because of the negative situation they face and the reality of their thoughts, become passively accepting that there is nothing they can do to regulate the emotional impact of their problem situation. Moorey (1996) provides an overview of working with realistic automatic thoughts in CBT.

The following extract from a session with a patient with multiple sclerosis illustrates the need for therapists to strike a delicate balance between accepting the reality of a tragically negative situation while promoting an orientation to the problem which helps them to minimise the emotional impact, addresses unhelpful aspects, and evaluates secondary appraisals in response to realistically negative thinking.

T: You were thinking about not being able to walk.
P: I was so incredibly sad. . . . I felt sick and really thought I would throw up.
T: It sounds as if you had that awful feeling of sadness that you get in the pit of your stomach.
P: That's it . . . so unpleasant.
T: And your thoughts were focused upon not being able to walk any more. Was there anything else that went through your mind?
P: I just see myself out with the kids you know (begins to cry)
T: You see it like it used to be.
P: I can't get it out of my mind.

T: This is different to some of the work that we have worked on in previous sessions. Some of the other things that you have been thinking at times of sadness have been quite biased, haven't they?

P: I see that now.

T: This thought about not being able to walk is a bit different because it is true, not biased. There are different ways of dealing with this. You say you can't get it out of your mind—do you try to do this, to push it away?

P: Yes.

T: Perhaps we could help you to try to gain control over the times you think about it and the times you focus on other things. This way you may have times when it is not in your mind?

P: OK.

Cost–Benefit Analyses

People with longstanding medical problems often have to make decisions such as when and when not to embark upon treatment, which treatment is preferable to none, whether they are able to return to work or who they should tell about their problems. There may be times when making these decisions is difficult and/or impossible to do without help. The use of the principles of cost–benefit analyses can be helpful. Patients can be encouraged to think about the nature of their problem and generate all the possible alternative decisions open to them. They then list the advantages and disadvantages of each option (which can be done from both a short- and a long-term perspective). If necessary therapists can help them to rank these in terms of importance so that patients can calculate the decision that seems to be most favourable.

SITUATIONAL AND ENVIRONMENTAL METHODS

A cognitive behavioural formulation might highlight environmental or situational factors which influence the presentation of psychological problems. In some cases, these need to be addressed before the therapist and the patient begin to address emotional, cognitive or behavioural factors. This might be the case because exposure to a particular environment makes it impossible to treat these mediators—for example, a patient's living situation may be such that he or she is unable to devote the necessary time or energy to psychological therapy because of an abusive partner or child care demands. There can be yet other scenarios where failure to address environmental or situational factors would dilute the effects of treating cognitive and behavioural factors. This might relate to the need to modify exposure to unhelpful members of staff, modifying the reactions of staff or re-engineering the healthcare environment to ensure that the factors responsible for negative emotional, behavioural or cognitive reactions by patients are minimised or completely removed. This often involves making the healthcare environment more psychosocially sensitive. In some cases, therapists may wish to communicate information about the interface between patients' well-being and hospital environment to hospital management. The following session extract outlines how the patient and the therapist decide that elements of their interactions with the hospital environment need to be modified as a further strategy in treating their anxiety disorder.

T: The score certainly shows that your anxiety is much less than it was when you started to come to the clinic last month.

P: Really, it was forty something wasn't it?

T: Forty-five.

P: What is it now?

T: Twenty.

P: Great.

T: I thought we might spend some time today looking at what other factors might be making you anxious—in addition to your tendency to focus on the worst possible outcome. If you keep going the way you have been and you can challenge thoughts about things going wrong, what things will you be left with that make you anxious?

P: I feel a bit bad saying this—it is about the hospital. You never get the information you need.

T: This is a big problem sometimes. I want to know about this sort of problem—so that we can work on it together. Is there something which would have been helpful for me to tell you?

P: No, it's not you. It's the way the blood clinic is set up.

T: I see. If it had been me would you have said?

P: I think I would have—you ask for my feedback any way.

T: What has been the problem with the blood clinic?

P: Well, I like it when I get my test results as I at least feel that that's another chunk of time that I have been healthy, . . . but they take more blood and this means that I then start worrying about what they have found.

T: Oh yes, this is a common problem. You are working on a time lag effect.

P: Yes.

T: Changing this would make you less anxious?

P: It would because if I get thoughts about what is happening, I always doubt it as there is still one test result that I do not have.

In some cases it may be appropriate to use arousal modification methods such as relaxation. However, these are rarely based on a personalised formulation and relaxation is more usually as a broad-based strategy which is implemented in the name of anxiety management. When relaxation is used, therapists should ensure that patients do not use relaxation as a safety behaviour (most patients will use relaxation in this way), that patients are competent and confident in the application of relaxation, and that this is only used when it has not been possible to enable patients to identify ways of promoting relaxation from their own lives (e.g. engagement in relaxing activity). If therapists decide to use relaxation then they should endeavour to link this with an element of the formulation.

CBT PROCESS

Unless patients are referred for cognitive behavioural treatment early in the course of their illnesses, they are likely to have had the experience of problems which have developed over many years. It is unlikely, therefore, that behavioural patterns or thinking processes which may have been in operation for years and years will change within a few weeks. Chronic medical problems are likely to last a lifetime. Therapeutic work with people who have had (and who may continue to have) lives which are significantly influenced by their physical health needs to be planned and implemented with this in mind. Appointment duration and frequency will differ according to the clinical problems presented by patients. However, sessions are usually conducted weekly or fortnightly for 50 minutes each time. Patients should be offered review appointments at intervals following the achievement of therapy goals. This might be arranged following a three-month interval, in which case they should be preceded by sessions which are progressively more widely spaced (2 weeks, 4 weeks apart then 3 months). In some cases, for particular conditions it can be helpful to schedule yearly review appointments or to time these with a schedule of medical reviews.

Some therapists consider offering an open-ended arrangement to patients where they can re-initiate contact again in the future. This can encourage dependency, and a preferable alternative is to explain to patients that as CBT is a problem-oriented intervention and it is more usual to proceed from active therapy to follow-up and then to discharge (unless there is a particular need for ongoing review by a cognitive behavioural therapist).

It is important that patients appreciate how the main cognitive and behavioural treatment strategies have had an impact upon their problems and how they might apply these to their future. Relapse prevention should aim at enabling patients to be mindful of the main mechanisms which seemed to mediate and moderate their problems, the therapy strategies by which they have learned to address these, and how they might apply these strategies to any similar future problems. It may be possible to make predictions about the potential future critical incidents relating to the course of their chronic medical problem, particularly when the course of their illness involved predictable events. Therapists should highlight any vulnerabilities that are obvious to them as some patients may wish to focus on these in relapse prevention sessions (e.g. discussion of patient feelings and thoughts relating to time when mobility problems occur as a result of multiple sclerosis). There are others for whom this is not likely to be helpful and therapists must respect patient wishes not to consider these future possibilities in any detail. This group of patients should also be encouraged to think about the signs and symptoms which might indicate a return of their problems. This is often paired with an action plan for how they can minimise the development of symptoms and/or seek professional help at the time. This does not, of course, mean that formulations which suggest major difficulties in connection with future incidents should not be mentioned.

T: You really have come a long way since March.

P: I have?

T: It certainly seems that way to me. I was looking back at what you were telling me when we first met up on the ward.

P: I do feel a lot better—more like my old self.

T: I think it is important that we spend some time thinking about what has changed and noting why this has happened. We need to work out a way of ensuring that these changes are maintained and how to stop them coming back.

P: You mean they might come back?

T: The fact that you have had these problems once means that there is an increased risk they may come back in the future. However, the fact that you have made changes to the way you think about things means that this is less likely than if you had had drug treatment on its own.

P: That's what the leaflet said.

T: There are three things we need to talk about. First, what has helped you to feel better. Second, how you can keep doing this and, third, what you would do if there were signs that you were developing problems again.

P: The Thought Records have been so helpful—that must have a lot to do with the improvements.

It is often useful to follow up sessions which have focused on relapse prevention with homework designed to reinforce within session content. This can be done using a worksheet which enables patients to record their

Table 4.9 Biases in imagery

Frozen	The image which is experienced is the one which represents the worst moment in an event
	Example: Patient with angina has image of clutching chest when in pain
Distant	Image is experienced as distant
	Example: Patient floating above a scene of her family attending her funeral
Spectator	Image represents a view from the perspective of another person
	Example: Patient with hepatitis has image from perspective of family members looking at a 'bright yellow version of me'
Metaphorical	Image is a thematic representation of an experience, event, thought or belief
	Example: Patient with image of self standing at the edge of black hole as a metaphor for being told that progression of her disease was very likely

experiences of CBT. Table 4.10 outlines the content of a worksheet of a patient (treated by the author) who had a major depressive disorder following the recurrence of breast cancer.

Therapists may need to modify their practice to take account of the nature and context of the life experiences of people with chronic medical problems. This may mean reviewing the location of therapy sessions (i.e. home visits may preserve continuity of sessions when a patient experiences an acute exacerbation of symptoms) or the way in which treatment strategies are presented and/or implemented (e.g. a patient with limited ability to write due to arthritis). Some physical health problems may require therapists to be more flexible about the process of case management. Patient illness episodes may prevent timely cancellation of appointments and/or therapy may have to be suspended when there are medical needs which must take priority.

Table 4.10 Questions for thinking about relapse prevention

What aspects of therapy have helped you to feel better/your problems to improve?
How has this aspect of therapy changed your thoughts/beliefs/behaviour?
What is the most important discovery/change that has happened during CBT?
What would be the first sign to you that your problems were returning?
Of all the things that you have learned in therapy, what would you be able to do to prevent this happening?
What would you be able to do to stop this problem from getting any worse?

Table 4.11   CBT patient summary at discharge

What were the main problems you had when you first saw Dr White?

I felt worthless, isolated in an unreal world. I felt that there was no purpose in life for me. I felt unable to make decisions or concentrate and was confused. I thought that I had lost everything in life and that everything I continued to happen was bad news. I had no faith in anything or anyone.

What things did you learn to help with the problems?

I have learned to plan my daily activities to include things that are enjoyable to me. I am able to change my thoughts most of the time by using a Thought Record. Sometimes now I am able to change my thought mentally without writing it down. I have learned that it is better to get up and do something than lie in bed and think.

What would signal to you that you might be developing problems again?

To be unable to cope with everyday life. Withdrawing from other people and feeling hopeless and negative about everything. Stopping doing pleasurable activities. Feeling sad and unable to look towards the future.

SUMMARY AND CONCLUSIONS

CBT involves the application of a range of behavioural, cognitive and environmental interventions, and this chapter has provided a brief over-view of some of the aspects of CBT practice. (Readers are advised to consult specific CBT texts for more information on some of the strategies outlined.) Patients must first identify the problematic components of their behaviours, thoughts or beliefs as it is only then that therapist and patient can work together on the evaluation and modification of these as a way of minimising psychological problems or enhancing the patient's quality of life. The application of CBT can be complicated in the presence of multiple physical and psychological problems and/or the presence of realistic negative thinking. The challenge for therapists in this area is to implement treatment strategies in a manner which ensures that the integrity of CBT is not compromised and the reality of the problems of living with a chronic medical problem is not denied.

Part II

THE APPLICATION OF CBT TO SPECIFIC CHRONIC MEDICAL PROBLEMS

Chapter 5

CANCER

INTRODUCTION

Increasing medical advances mean that more people are cured of cancer than ever before. People with cancer are now tending to live longer than previously (even when cancer treatment is being given without curative intent). These changing circumstances mean that cancer is increasingly being conceptualised as a chronic illness. Cancer is a range of illnesses and diseases, each with a different aetiology, treatment regime and prognosis. Almost everyone who is told that they have cancer will experience a period of psychological distress. For some this will be a self-limiting experience, one which does not cause any lasting psychological problems and can be understood as part of a normal adjustment reaction. However, there are some people who will experience psychological problems which significantly interfere with their quality of life and ability to function on a day-to-day basis. These clinically significant psychological problems usually occur as part of an adjustment disorder, major depressive disorder or an anxiety disorder. The sorts of problems which are commonly treated using CBT in cancer care settings are outlined in Table 5.1. Cancer treatment is also associated with a number of psychosocial concerns, some of which comprise quality of life and contribute to anxiety or depression. Non-physical treatment side effects such as anger, anxiety or apprehension are often rated by patients as being more severe than physical side effects such as nausea or hair loss (Coates et al., 1983). Indeed, some patients may drop out of chemotherapy because of psychological problems (Gilbar & De-Nour, 1989). Some treatment procedures (e.g. bone marrow transplantation) result in psychological problems because of the demands which they involve, and many patients have to face treatment regimes that are difficult to tolerate, may involve behavioural demands such as frequent hospital visits and levels of motivation which may be difficult to generate or sustain. Advances in drug therapies have resulted in a reduction in the incidence of nausea and vomiting associated with chemotherapy; however, conditioned nausea and vomiting do still occur

Table 5.1   Cancer-related psychological problems commonly treated using CBT

Anxiety associated with clinic attendance and/or treatment sessions
Depression which interferes with demands of treatment
Unable to get out of the house because of fears of meeting people
Avoidance of discussion about cancer and its impact
Anger and irritability with staff and family members
Depression relating to negative thoughts about self-worth and appearance
Depression about prognosis
Problems with maintenance of daily routine because of physical debility
Sexual problems

and aversions to food and other elements of the cancer experience can also develop. Even after the end of treatment, patients' lives may be affected throughout the follow-up period, as they attend appointments to determine whether the cancer has returned.

Research into psychological aspects of cancer has undergone what Montgomery (1999) has referred to as a 'mini-renaissance'. Progress in cancer genetics has resulted in increased awareness of the possibility of negative psychological reactions to increased genetic predisposition for cancer (Hopwood, 1997; Cull et al., 1999). Researchers have examined the way in which patients manage uncertainty about this, make decisions about treatment (e.g. prophylactic mastectomy) and how, in some cases, beliefs about a genetic risk of cancer can precipitate or mediate psychological problems. The psychological sequelae of cancer and its treatment have been the focus of much research activity. There are a vast number of different concerns which can develop as a component of psychological distress, and become the focus of cognitive behaviourally oriented treatments. Psychological models of adjustment and principles for psychological management of the problems associated with cancer are now beginning to emerge. Cognitive behavioural interventions and therapies have been shown to be effective when applied to the psychosocial issues and problems experienced by cancer patients (Fawzy et al., 1990, Meyer & Mark, 1995). Cognitive behaviourally based interventions such as adjuvant psychological therapy have been shown to improve anxiety and depressive symptoms (Greer et al., 1992) and be superior to supportive counselling (Moorey et al., 1998). Researchers have started to explore the thoughts and images associated with cancer experiences (Manson, Manderino & Johnson, 1993) and the psychological aspects of cancer have been the focus of a study into cognitive processes in disorders such as depression (e.g. Brewin et al., 1998a). This chapter will outline how cognitive behavioural models can be used to structure assessments and formulate cognitive and behavioural intervention strategies which address the psychological consequences of cancer and cancer treatment at the various stages of the illness.

PSYCHOLOGICAL MORBIDITY

It is generally accepted that around 20% of patients with cancer experience clinically significant psychological symptoms. Faulkener and Maguire (1994) have suggested that psychosocial adjustment to cancer is associated with six hurdles: managing uncertainty about the future, searching for meaning, dealing with a loss of control, having a need for openness, needs for emotional support, and needs for medical support. They suggest that a failure to deal with these results in psychosocial problems. Psychosocial problems can, of course, occur at any time following the diagnosis of cancer. The occurrence of problems is thought to relate to the number and size of individual hurdles for patients and their unique circumstances. Although this is not a conceptualisation that is empirically validated, it is a useful heuristic for assessing and conceptualising psychosocial aspects of adjustment to cancer.

The nature and extent of patient psychological problems will depend upon an interaction between factors such as prior cancer history, levels of social support and the precise nature of the patient's experiences of cancer. Patients' psychological experiences will differ according to the nature of their cancer experiences and will depend on whether they are waiting for tests results to confirm the diagnosis, are attending for follow-up or are in the middle of a course of chemotherapy. Some psychological problems are more commonly experienced at particular times in what is sometimes referred to as the patient's 'cancer journey' (though I am not always sure that this is an appropriate analogy, as a journey is something that one usually chooses to embark upon). This is most commonly when the illness is diagnosed, during the early months of treatment, when all treatment has ended or when a recurrence or spread of the cancer is discovered. The strength of Faulkener and Maguire's concept of hurdles is that they are relevant to understanding adjustment at all stages of patient experience of cancer. Each hurdle can also be understood in terms of a number of cognitive and behavioural features which may influence psychosocial adjustment (see Table 5.2), and therapists will sometimes find it helpful to structure their assessments and problem-level formulations around this concept of hurdles.

Cancer-related psychological problems are related to a set of commonly occurring themes. In addition to core themes, there are a number of cognitive themes which are seen more often among patients with cancer at particular anatomical sites, and some of the common interpretations and meanings are outlined in Table 5.3. Some patients find that it is only after their treatment ends that they will notice any lasting negative psychological consequences (Arai et al., 1996; Ell et al., 1989), but most, however, will not experience any lasting negative psychological

Table 5.2   Cognitive behavioural elements of common cancer hurdles

Hurdle Cognitive and behavioural factors

Uncertainty about the future
Preoccupation about what may go wrong
Anxiogenic thoughts about recurrence and inability to cope

Search for meaning
Avoidance of reminders of the cancer
Muddled thinking about how cancer experience relates to prior self or world view
Avoidance or withdrawal from previous activities as a result of thoughts about lack of meaning and inability to accept living in world where cancer can happen

Dealing with loss of control
Attentional bias towards compromised control
Thoughts about lack of control resulting in anxiety
Generalisations about lack of control

Need for openness
Thoughts about inability to talk to other people
Avoidance of discussion of upsetting topics with staff

Need for emotional support
Thoughts about being alone
Avoidance of emotional expression (self or others)
Lack of access to confiding or supportive relationships

Need for medical support
Care environment is not responsive to psychosocial needs

consequences. Others develop an increased vulnerability to future problems as a result of the psychological impact of cancer. The psychological effects of cancer and cancer treatments may also result in patients becoming more avoidant in their thinking about illness, having greater illness concerns and diminished capacity to work (Cella & Tross, 1986). Cella and Tross provide a useful framework for understanding the stages which someone with cancer may pass through, and refer to the 're-entry to the premorbid lifestyle' for those people who have experienced cure or remission. These ideas are helpful ways in which to think about the assessment of someone with cancer.

ASSESSMENT

Assessment of psychosocial aspects of problems related to cancer and its treatment needs to take account of the unique aspects of a patient's cancer experiences. It should be sensitive to the issues which relate to the site of the patient's cancer, the person's previous life experiences (particularly

Table 5.3 Common interpretations and meanings experienced by cancer patients

Cancer rules my life
It is not fair that I developed cancer
Cancer interferes with living my life
My faith will see me through my cancer
Cancer is not as bad as it is made out to be
I wonder if my cancer has spread
Cancer is a death sentence
I must have done something negative in my life to have developed cancer
Everything about cancer is bad news
My family will be left without me
Luck will determine what will happen to my cancer
I have lost control of my life because of cancer
Having cancer restricts my life
I cannot escape reminders that I have cancer
My life will never be the same again because of cancer
I am a completely different person because of cancer
I have no control over the course of my cancer

family and personal experience of cancer), treatment regime, experiences following diagnosis and unique hurdles associated with cancer. Therapists should determine the most personally threatening aspects being faced by the patient. Almost all of the suggestions which follow for cognitive behavioural assessments of people with cancer are equally applicable to patients with normal adjustment reactions, adjustment disorders, discrete psychological problems and the symptoms of psychological disorders. Novice therapists may find that comprehensive assessment of the content of the psychosocial experiences of people with cancer can be overwhelming—an experience that is particularly common when therapists struggle with their own beliefs about mortality and such concepts as 'justice' and 'fairness' in the world.

In addition to the idea of cancer hurdles, therapists can use milestones in cancer management to structure their assessments chronologically. Indeed, many patients find that this is the easiest way to provide information as part of an assessment session. Some patients do not talk to their family and friends about their thoughts and feelings, while other patients may not have had the opportunity to talk to staff about their 'cancer story' in its entirety. Some psychologically based therapies and support strategies emphasise this from a therapeutic perspective, and CBT acknowledges the importance of enabling people to talk about their experience in this way. However, the 'cancer story' is much more than just an opportunity for patients to talk about their cancer. It is a way of picking up clues to thoughts, feelings, coping strategies, critical incidents and contextual information for detailed cognitive behavioural analysis. The degree to which people require prompting and/or capsule summaries is variable, and this approach to the structuring of the initial interchange of assessment is illustrated in the following session extract:

T: It would be useful if, to start off with, you could tell me in your own words the events leading up to your visits here to the cancer centre and what has been happening to you more recently.

P: What, from the early diagnosis?

T: Yes, from the beginning if that's OK with you.

P: Right, well, I didn't really feel any sort of real symptoms until sort of summer last year, when I was sailing with a friend who was a vet, and I passed quite a lot of blood and I wasn't too happy about that. With one or two questions that he asked me, we deduced that it wasn't piles, so then he advised me to go and see my doctor as soon as I got back home, which I did. The doctor wasn't happy, because he inspected and said it wasn't piles, and he got me to see the surgeon very quickly, very quickly. So it was a growth, they took a biopsy and it was malignant, so from then on it progressed quite rapidly. It all happened very quickly—within a matter of weeks.

T: What happened?

P: I had the operation probably about two or three weeks after seeing the surgeon for the first time. At the time of the operation the surgeon was able to cut out the tumour from the bowel, which was fine, and resected, although he did say at the time he'd found two small growths on the liver. So from there I came here.

T: You felt no symptoms initially and it was after you passed the blood while sailing with your vet friend that you went to the doctor. The surgeon confirmed that you had cancer, you had the surgery but because of the small tumours on the liver you have been coming to the chemotherapy ward.

P: Yes.

T: Things happened very quickly for you—what would you say has been the main day-to-day impact of that, the cancer, surgery and now the chemotherapy?

P: Probably my outlook—your outlook on life changes somewhat. You think well, today I'm here, we live for today. I tend not to think about the future because you don't know what you've got, so you just live day to day. As such, life becomes a lot easier in that respect.

T: Do you think you were like this before the event?

P: I was pretty easy-going before the event, but now . . . it's so simple, life now. I find it a lot easier to cope with.

T: Because of the mindset of living for today?

> P: That's right, yes. You tend not to consider the future at all.
> T: So one of the main ways it affects you is really your perspective of life and the present versus the future?
> P: Yes, that's right.

The chronological sequence of events leading to the confirmation of the diagnosis will often be significant. It can be important to ask people if there are key phrases which they recall from out-patient consultations around the time of diagnosis. The statements that they recall will be influenced by their mood at the time of a consultation and this often provides clues to the salient issues or cognitive themes predominant at this time. This can also provide clues to the ways in which patients interacted with staff. Did they ask the consultant questions? Did they accept what was being said? It may be possible to use this is an assessment of mood around the time of diagnosis to demonstrate the effects of mood on recall or how pre-existing beliefs about cancer might have influenced their thoughts and feelings when they first attended the oncology clinic (important for socialisation to the cognitive behavioural model). The way in which the news about cancer was given to a patient will be significant and should be assessed. This experience can become very significant in terms of the formation or activation of beliefs about staff sensitivity and support (crucial when it comes to later efforts to access support for patients who experience problems during chemotherapy or radiotherapy). When the chronological events have been fully elicited the therapist should then explore problem areas in detail. Assessment proceeds by eliciting examples of each problem and exploring with the patient the main cognitive, behavioural and emotional components.

> T: So it sounds as if it was all quite a shock—you had thought all along that you had pulled a muscle.
> P: I did—and never did it cross my mind that it was cancer.
> T: How did you feel when he said it was cancer?
> P: I didn't believe him.
> T: How long did that go on for?
> P: In some ways, I still find it difficult to accept—I think that's because it was such a shock.
> T: Were there things that Dr McGhee said that made it more difficult to believe the diagnosis?
> P: Don't get me wrong, he was great. I just felt that it was going too fast for me—I was thinking he would be telling me that I needed to go to the physiotherapy department—not for surgery and then weeks of radiotherapy.

T: So you needed more time to transform your thoughts from a pulled muscle to cancer?

P Absolutely.

T: Were there problems that you experienced after this?

P: I became petrified about the surgery.

T: Petrified?

P: I was convinced that they were going to find that it was even worse than the scan said.

T: Was this what you thought when you felt petrified?

P: Yes.

T: What other sorts of thoughts did you have when you felt petrified?

P: I didn't think I would make it . . . even though I was told that it was routine and I had a good outlook.

There has been an increased interest in viewing cancer as a trigger for post-traumatic stress symptoms (Smith et al., 1999). Models of adjustment to post-traumatic stressors are particularly applicable to understanding cancer adjustment. The occurrence and frequency of intrusive memories and thoughts about cancer experiences should be assessed (Baider & De-Nour, 1997). The Impact of Events Scale—Revised (Weiss & Marmar, 1996) is a useful way to assess the dimensions related to the experience of intrusions. Therapists should determine the degree of intrusiveness and avoidance associated with each memory. Images often have their origins in real-life events such as a relative with cancer, witnessing another patient on a ward with the same cancer and/or re-experiencing actual events such as the recall of statements that have been made by medical or nursing staff.

It is important to assess beliefs about the causes of cancer and predicted consequences of the disease for the patient. Patients will have very different views of cancer and its treatment, which often depend on the extent of their exposure to information about this in their personal history and/or from the media. Patient beliefs about treatment, particularly mechanisms of action, are often linked with predominant emotions, thoughts and behaviours and it is vital to include these in assessments. Patients may have had life experiences when their relatives have had a diagnosis of cancer and find that this significantly influences their beliefs about the nature and course of their illness. The Illness Perception Questionnaire can be a useful framework for assessing these aspects of a patient's internal representations. Therapists should ask what patients think and feel about the reactions of relatives to their cancer, especially to what degree they feel that they have to manage this in addition to their own problems. The nature and level of support has already been mentioned in relation to the hurdles patients must address. This should always be assessed. Criticism by spouses has been shown to moderate the relationship between intrusive thoughts and distress (Manne, 1999). This is one of the reasons why therapists should determine the impact of cancer diagnosis on the behaviour of spouses. Patients who have had cancer before may have positive memories and experiences which will be relevant in the assessment of their current problems. Some memories and experiences will be helpful and enable patients to develop positive beliefs which will moderate or buffer distress. Patients do not always view cancer negatively and therapists should assess whether patients have any positive beliefs which might buffer the impact of negative beliefs about cancer. The following session extracts illustrate how prior experience of cancer can have very different effects. This is often a primary factor in determining responses to cancer-related events.

Positive prior experience

P: Well I have had cancer before, when I was 15 years old.
T: How has that experience had an effect on how you see things this time around?
P: Well it makes it easier because I know what it is like when they tell me about chemotherapy . . . that makes a difference.
T: Is there any other way in which it makes it easier?
P: Well I know that when I found it difficult before, the nurses were there for me to get support and help.

Negative prior experience

P: If I am ever told that I have cancer again or that it has come back—I will kill myself. (*Starts to cry*)
T: What would it be about getting cancer again that would result in you killing yourself?
P: It is horrendous—a living nightmare the last time I got it. I have worked out what I will do—that's the only way I can cope with living, knowing that I will kill myself if it comes back.
T: Are there particular things that you predict would happen to you if it came back?
P: (*Starts shaking*) . . . I can't bear to think about it—killing myself would stop it happening.

Patients may find it difficult to offer examples of the ways in which the cancer has affected their lives. This can be assessed by asking people to provide detail on a typical week before their cancer was diagnosed. This is then followed by questions about specific domains from their prior life routine which elicit information on cognitive, behavioural and emotional correlates of changes.

T: I am interested in discovering more about how your daily life has changed because of cancer.

P: Oh, I would not know where to start.

T: Perhaps you could tell me a bit about the main features of your life before the cancer was diagnosed—your work, what you did in your spare time, feelings about life—that sort of thing?

P: Things were fine really—no major problems. Well, I had the usual worries about paying off the bills and whether I would have a job at the end of the month. I wish I had appreciated what I had—it is just as well that you don't know what's ahead of you.

T: What did a typical weekday involve for you before the cancer was diagnosed?

P: Well, I would wake up about 4 as my husband starts his work at 5— then I would fall over until about 5.30, get up and get dressed and then get my son ready for school—I would drop him off at about twenty to eight on my way to work.

T: Thinking about days like that, how do they differ from a typical day at the moment?

When using this strategy to elicit information, the patient and the therapist continue to talk about life before cancer and the therapist notes down key events and thoughts from the patient's life before and the ways in which there have been changes. The therapist may suspect that the patient is presenting an unusually positive (or in some cases negative) picture of her experiences. It is possible to assess by asking about 'split second' experiences. This is outlined below:

T: As far as I can gather then, you are telling me that you have no particular problems and, although you have been anxious before appointments, this does seem to have been the normal amounts of anxiety for this situation.

P: Yes, quite good really.

T: I wanted to take you back to something that you said earlier.

P: Uh-huh.

T: You were talking about your son . . . I noticed that you had difficulty catching your breath. . . . How did you feel then?

P: Fine . . . it's just . . . no problems. My thoughts are focused on the fact that all will be well.

T: Is there ever a time when, even for a split second, you find you can't focus on all being well.

P: (*Patient begins to sob uncontrollably*) . . . Its . . . it is so painful.

T: Your son?

P (*Patient nods*)

P: He is so young . . . he comes into my bed and asks if mummy is OK today . . . I have the most awful sinking feeling, I feel sick. . . . I might . . . (*difficulty catching breath*) . . . might never see him again.

T: A very painful and overwhelming thought.

P: Mm—uh huh.

T: What happens when he asks you this?

P: I have to hide it from him . . . he is too young to understand. I just tell him that mummy is sick and needs to take strong medicines. That mummy will be better soon and be able to take him to the park again.

There are some patients who survive by developing a global avoidance strategy. This can make assessment difficult (as this involves reversal of avoidance). Avoidance is often a key maintaining factor for problems associated with anxiety and depression. It should be distinguished from denial as the concepts used in formulation and the strategies which are used to manage each are different. Avoidant patients differ from those in denial as they know that they have cancer and choose not to think about it. This can often be determined quite easily by asking patients 'What is your understanding of what disease you have?', or in some cases more directly, 'Do you think you have cancer?'. Some patients will experience psychotic symptoms as a result of disease activity such as cerebral metastasis and/or the effects of medication and/or radiotherapy. Some of the emerging literature on cognitive behavioural management of positive psychotic symptoms (see Chapter 1) can be helpful in assessing cognitive, emotional and behavioural responses to these symptoms ('When you hear the voice of your aunt, how does that make you feel?'; 'What do you think will happen if you do not do what the voice says?'). A small proportion of cancer patients will have had the experience of anxiety and depressive symptoms prior to their diagnosis. Assessment should aim to determine which cancer-related psychological problems are related to premorbid problems and which have been specifically triggered by their experience of cancer ('Of all of these problems we have been talking about, which do you see as being a result of the cancer?'). Katz, Rodin and Devins (1995) stated that 'the integration of the illness into the self-concept without undue loss of self-esteem may protect those with serious medical illnesses from clinical depression'. Information should be obtained on a patient's self-esteem as this can be vitally important in conceptualising psychological reactions to cancer. It can be done by asking screening questions such as 'How do you feel about yourself compared to other people?' or 'Do you ever feel worthless?'.

Self-report Measures

There are many cancer-specific assessment measures which can be incorporated into an assessment to complement the questions that have been asked and the observations that have been made. Two measures are outlined here.

Mental Adjustment to Cancer Scale (MACS)

This 40-item scale (Watson et al., 1988) measures coping styles used by people with cancer. Respondents are asked to rate the degree to which statements apply to them (using a scale which varies from 'Definitely does not apply to me' to 'Definitely applies to me'). The MACS takes approximately 10 minutes to complete and provides scores on five subscales when it is completed. The subscales are 'fighting spirit', 'helpless/hopeless', 'anxious preoccupation', 'fatalistic' and 'avoidance'. The MACS has been used as an outcome measure in evaluations of cognitive behavioural interventions among cancer patients and has acceptable reliability and validity. It does not provide an adequate assessment of avoidance and users should aim to complement MACS use with other strategies to assess avoidance related to cancer. A shorter version of this measure is also available (Watson et al., 1994). Some items from the MACS are outlined in Table 5.4. Osborne et al. (1999) suggested that the

Table 5.4   Sample items from the Mental Adjustment to Cancer Scale (Watson et al., 1988)

Fighting Spirit
I believe that my positive attitude will benefit my health
Since my cancer diagnosis, I now realise how precious life is and I'm making the most of it
I have plans for the future, e.g. holiday, jobs and housing

Fatalistic
I feel that nothing I can do will make a difference
I've left it all to my doctors
I've put myself in the hands of God

Helpless/hopeless
I am not very hopeful about the future
I feel like giving up
I feel completely at a loss about what to do

MACS may be measuring six independent constructs: Positive Orientation to Illness, Minimising the Illness, Fatalism (revised from the original MAC development work), Loss of Control, Angst and Helplessness/ Hopelessness.

Cancer Behavior Inventory

This self-report measure (Merluzzi & Martinez-Sanchez, 1997) is designed to assess self-efficacy for coping with cancer. Various versions of this measure are available—the brief version has 12 items and the longer version has 36 items. Respondents are required to rate the degree to which they feel confident in their ability to accomplish the behaviour being asked about. Factor analysis of the long version suggests that there are seven subscales; these are outlined in Table 5.5. This measure can provide helpful ideas for the ways in which interventions should be structured. A copy of this measure is reproduced by kind permission of Dr Tom Merluzzi in Appendix 2.

Table 5.5   Sample items from the Cancer Behavior Inventory (Merluzzi & Martinez-Sanchez, 1997)

Maintenance of activity and independence
Keeping busy with activities
Maintaining independence

Coping with treatment-related side effects
Managing nausea and vomiting
Coping with hair loss

Accepting cancer/maintaining a positive attitude
Maintaining hope
Accepting that I have cancer

Seeking and understanding medical information
Seeking information about cancer or cancer treatments
Asking doctors questions

Affective regulation
Expressing negative feelings about cancer
Ignoring things that cannot be dealt with

Seeking support
Sharing feelings of concern
Seeking consolation

Stress management
Remaining relaxed throughout treatment
Reducing any nausea associated with treatment

Other Self-report Measures

There are a number of other self-report measures which can be incorporated into cognitive behavioural assessments of patients with tumours at particular anatomical sites and/or when particular constructs seem to predominate the thoughts or feelings of patients. The *Sexual Self-Schema Scale* (Cyranowski & Andersen, 1998; Andersen, Cyranowski & Espindle, 1999) consists of a list of adjectives for which respondents indicate the degree to which the term describes them (on a seven-point scale ranging from 0 (not at all descriptive) to 7 (very much descriptive of me). The items which comprise the sexual self-schema scale are embedded within the larger list of adjectives. Andersen, Woods and Copeland (1997) and Yurek, Farrar and Andersen (in press) have found that the sexual self-schema of their samples of women cancer patients accounted for significant amounts of variation in patient sexual behaviour and responsiveness. Patients should be asked about whether they have any spiritual beliefs which might be relevant in understanding their adjustment to cancer (Holland et al., 1999). The *Systems of Belief Inventory* (Holland et al. 1998) may be useful when more formal assessment of this is required. This 54-item inventory measures patient spiritual and religious beliefs and comprises subscales of 'existential perspective on life and death', 'religious practices/rituals', 'social support from religious and/or spiritual community members' and 'the relationship to a superior being'. The *World Assumptions Scale* (Janoff-Bulman, 1989) may be helpful in accessing patient beliefs about constructs such as the malevolence of the world, justice and luck (see Table 5.6 for sample items).

Table 5.6   Sample items from the World Assumptions Scale (Janoff-Bulman, 1989)

Misfortune is least likely to strike worthy, decent people
Bad events are distributed to people at random
Generally, people deserve all they get in this world
I almost always make an effort to avoid bad things from happening to me
The world is a good place
I am luckier than most people
When bad things happen it is typically because people have not taken the
   necessary actions to protect themselves

FORMULATION

In many clinical situations cognitive behavioural therapists working with cancer patients will only ever construct problem-level formulations for their work with patients. This is usually because therapists are engaged in the delivery of brief interventions designed to address an emerging problem which has not generalised to other life domains or when it is more appropriate to restrict therapeutic focus purely to symptom change (e.g. when patients are transferred to other care settings and continued psychological therapy is not possible). In such cases, therapists may merely acknowledge the role of factors such as life history or complex family problems in their assessments. There are, of course, cases which require the construction of both problem- and case-level formulations. The following sections will outline some of the common themes that should be taken into account in formulating problems and taking account of case-level variables in CBT with cancer patients.

Problem-level Formulation

Most problem-level formulations with cancer patients end up as explanations of the mediating and moderating factors for anxiety, panic, worry and depression. Therapists should consider the themes in Table 5.3 when formulating cancer-related problems. It is has been shown that a helpless response to the diagnosis is predictive of later affective disorder (Parle, Jones & Maguire, 1996) and those patients with symptoms of an affective disorder should certainly have the cognitive, behavioural, environmental and physical elements of helplessness outlined in problem-level formulations. Patients who believe that they are successful in resolving concerns are less likely to experience significant affective disorder and therefore a low level of confidence in their ability to resolve concerns may be the primary maintaining factor to feature in some problem-level formulations. Brewin et al. (1998b) have found that intrusive memories relating to prior personal illness or illness of family member or friends are associated with depressive symptoms. Indeed, the amount of intrusion and avoidance associated with these memories is as significant as that associated with patients experiencing symptoms which meet diagnostic criteria for post-traumatic stress disorder. These memories can be stable over time and those patients who experience the same intrusive memory for a few months are more likely to be experiencing greater depressive symptoms. Patients who engage in greater levels of avoidance of memories experience greater anxiety. This link should be explored and, when relevant, included in problem-level formulations of depressive symptoms and intrusive memories. The occurrence of intrusive memories is often related to the reactivation of traumatic memories which have been incompletely processed and, as such, this element of problem-level formulation needs to be linked to case-level elements which outline the hypothesised problems with the assimilation or accommodation of cancer-related experiences to existing schema about illness, cancer, self, their own mortality, the regulation of emotion or other personally salient schemata.

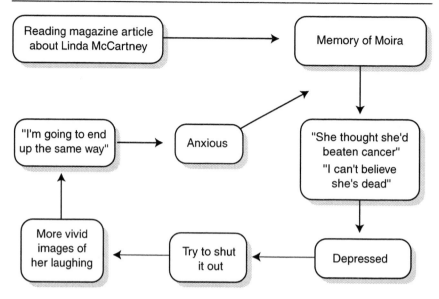

Figure 5.1. Problem-level formulation (cancer)

Patients' perceptions of the severity and course of their illness has a crucial role in determining their psychological responses to all aspects of their attendance at hospital and interactions with staff regarding their cancer. In most cases, patients' perceptions are accurate and reflect what they have been told by their oncologists. However, there are some patients who have unrealistic perceptions (e.g. overoptimistic or inappropriately pessimistic) regarding their illness and its treatment and it is these which mediate problems in other areas. Patients' time perspective seems to be an important element in understanding their psychological reactions to cancer. Some patients are aware of the tendency of their thoughts to become oriented towards the future and are able to stay focused on the present as a way of dealing with day-to-day issues without becoming preoccupied about what may happen at some future point. Time perspective is important in formulating the problems of patients who spend most of their time thinking about future events.

The setting in which people spend most of their time is an important contextual influence on the mechanisms outlined in a psychological formulation. Someone who spends all day sitting in a day room within an oncology unit is exposed to a completely different set of stimuli to someone who spends his or her days sitting in a conservatory at the back of the house. Cognition and behaviour can be modified or influenced by changing context and situation and the influence of these factors on problem occurrence can be used to inform clinical case management. Patients who are ambulatory and have good levels of physical functioning generally

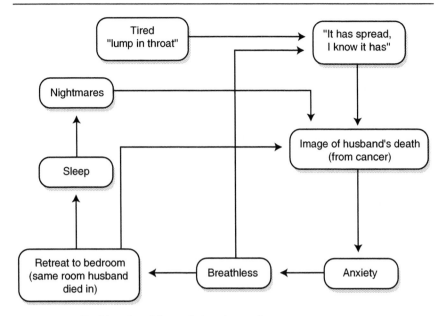

Figure 5.2. Problem-level formulation (cancer)

have lower levels of clinically significant psychological problems. The degree to which a patient engages in ambulatory activity is often included at the level of problem formulation. Activity levels are often targeted in treatment as they commonly mediate other problems, such as preoccupation with negative thinking and/or low mood. Some patients who report lowered levels of functioning are actively avoiding activity for fear of exacerbating physical or psychological symptoms. These mediating factors can appear at the level of discrete problems and also within the case formulation, where avoidance is more likely to be pervasive and determine behavioural responses to a variety of situations.

The way in which the early investigation and diagnosis of symptoms was handled can be a significant determinant of psychosocial adjustment and result in an interactional pattern which is repeated and generalised to all patient–staff interactions. An example of this might be a patient who believed that the consultant oncologist who informed her of her diagnosis did not care about the impact on her. She believed that all staff in the Cancer Centre were uncaring and tended to be rude to them when she was in their company. Discrepancies between the thoughts of patients and their relatives can produce real difficulties and problem-level formulations should outline any discrepancies between patient and other perspectives (actual and perceived). The concept of problematic re-entry to a premorbid lifestyle can be used to conceptualise obstacles for patients who have psychological problems after treatment has ended. Patients may experience clinically significant fears of recurrence (Lee-Jones et al., 1997). Problem-level formulations should also outline which internal and external triggers (e.g. physical sensations, exposure to media) are salient and how processes such as checking, avoidance, reassurance seeking and misinterpretation may mediate such fears.

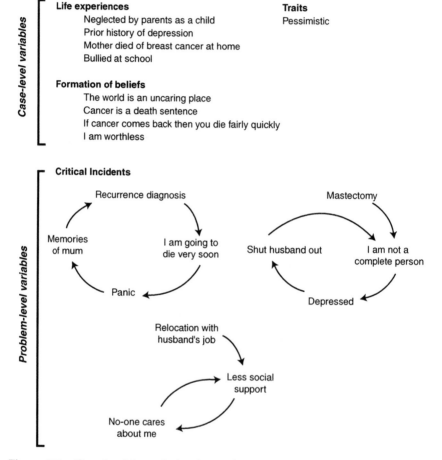

Figure 5.3.   Case-level formulation (cancer)

Case-level Formulation

Case-level formulations should endeavour to outline all relevant aspects of the patients' current and past life experiences in relation to their cancer (e.g. how cancer-related problems link with events such as prior abuse or current problems with social isolation) which might be relevant in conceptualising their current psychological experiences of cancer. These experiences need not be events which they have experienced personally but can be experiences which they have witnessed or read about. In addition to personally relevant historical information, the current life context of a patient can be important in understanding the origins and maintenance of problems at a 'case' level. One such example of a contextual variable is the level of social support. This is relevant as the number and frequency of interactions with others moderates psychological adjustment. Patients with high levels of trait anxiety may experience heightened sensitivity to somatic symptoms. Cameron, Leventhal and Love (1998) have suggested that this phenomenon may be a result of trait anxiety fuelling perception of heightened risk for illness, and that this results in the formation of unhelpful illness representations which, in turn, impacts upon coping and related behaviours. Cancer patients with high levels of trait anxiety should have case-level formulations which outline the ways in which this may link with other aspects of their experiences (e.g. cancer worry, estimations of the likelihood of recurrence). Dispositional optimism should be incorporated into case-level formulations as this can significantly buffer the levels of distress experienced by patients in response to cancer-related events (Epping Jordan et al., 1999). The related, but not identical, construct of hope (Magaletta & Oliver, 1999) can also be incorporated into case-level formulations.

A diagnosis of a life-threatening illness such as cancer challenges patients' core beliefs and assumptions about themselves and the world in which they live. Cella, Mahon and Donovan (1990) have suggested that more 'rigid' assumptions are likely to shatter. Patients who report prior beliefs with marked conviction ('I was sure that I was a healthy person') often suffer most from having their assumptive world shattered. Lepore and Helgeson (1998) suggest that the integration of cancer into pre-existing mental models should promote psychological adjustment, and intrusions are markers of incomplete information processing. Case-level formulations should try to explain the process by which a patient's experience of cancer has been integrated (or not) with pre-existing mental models and make links with any intrusive thoughts or memories that might have been included in problem-level formulations.

When patients have had past psychological problems which resurface or are exacerbated by the cancer diagnosis, cognitive behavioural formulations should seek to determine which cognitive and behavioural mechanisms underlie the previous symptoms and whether it is these same mediators that relate to the present episode. Formulations of cancer-related psychological problems should aim to take account of the chronological course of events with regard to a patient's cancer. An overall case formulation may need to include formulations of different problem-level phenomena that have occurred at different time points following diagnosis.

Research has not identified any consistent or reliable relationship between a person's self-esteem and cancer (Curbow et al., 1990). However, this is not to say that the role of self-esteem will not be important for particular patients. Curbow and Somerfield (1991) highlighted the ways in which cancer can have direct or indirect effects on self-esteem. Case-level formulations of patient problems with self-esteem should discriminate whether cancer is hypothesised to influence self esteem directly (as in the case of a patient who believes cancer to be a further example of her longstanding worthlessness) or indirectly (via diminished social support, disrupted social roles or low perceived control). CBT for self-esteem can be applied in both scenarios, though it is likely that the former will require more intensively tailored therapy for common elements of low self-esteem (Fennell, 1997). Patients with a greater perception of discrepancies between actual experiences and ideal aspects of their self-concept tend to be more depressed (Heidrich, Forsthoff & Ward, 1994).

The predominant coping pattern preferred by the patient should be outlined in the overall case formulation. It may be that there is a restricted pattern of coping where patients rely on one strategy for all problems, as opposed to varying strategies depending upon the demands of the situation. Escape-avoidance coping has been consistently shown to be associated with distress (Dunkel-Schetter et al., 1992; McCaul et al., 1999) and should be featured in the case-level formulation when it appears to be influencing the distress in the range of individual problems faced by patients.

TREATMENT STRATEGIES

Most cognitive behavioural approaches to psychosocial morbidity in cancer are short-term, characterised by time-limited interventions which enable patients to regulate their feelings about cancer and its impact on their lives. They aim to enhance confidence with ability to cope with the hurdles that cancer can present and successfully manage the practical aspects of living with cancer. It may be necessary to devote more therapy time to the coverage of existential themes, particularly when working with those patients who have advanced disease (Kissane et al., 1997). The Cancer Behavior Inventory is a useful tool for assessing the outcome of a range of treatment strategies, and can also be used to plan treatments based on patient scores on subscales (see Table 5.7). Cognitive behavioural therapies can also be delivered in a group format for cancer patients (Bottomley, 1996).

Table 5.7 Using the Cancer Behavior Inventory to plan CBT

Maintenance of activity and independence

Activity scheduling during Week 2 of chemotherapy

Coping with treatment-related side effects

Distraction exercise when travelling on the bus
Pacing when troubled by fatigue

Accepting cancer/maintaining a positive attitude

Identifying and modifying negative thoughts about recurrence
Trying to refocus thoughts on the 'here and now' when thoughts wander

Seeking and understanding medical information

Role play on how to ask Dr McPherson questions about my tumour
Arrange to contact the nurse specialist

Affective regulation

Spend 15 minutes at night talking to James about my main emotions (instead of
  avoiding them)

Seeking support

Make contact with Sarah again—see if she is free to visit me (especially Week 2
  after chemotherapy)

Stress management

Week 3 of chemotherapy—swimming on Friday mornings
Have a relaxing bath before going to bed

Tackling Avoidance

Avoidance is often a significant maintaining factor for many cancer-
related psychological problems. It may involve avoidance of people,
situations or appointments and frequently extends to the avoidance of
sensitive topics within sessions. People usually avoid things when they
find them frightening and/or think they will be unable to deal with them.
Interventions should therefore target both the nature of the fear and
thoughts about coping ability. Avoidance is usually mediated by intermediate beliefs about the predicted consequences of not avoiding ('If I
talk about cancer then I will be overwhelmed'). Patients are often very
reluctant to give up their avoidance behaviour and often need to be
offered an explanation of why avoidance should be addressed. This may
involve exploring advantages and disadvantages of the strategy and testing out the effects of dropping avoidance for a period of time.

T: This is certainly a common experience of many of my patients—they would rather avoid everything to do with cancer than have the unpleasant feelings associated with facing up to whatever it is that they are avoiding.

P: My view is why feel bad if you can avoid it.

T: I would agree with you. Avoidance certainly makes you feel better at the time. Some people find that avoidance does not work in the long run or that it gets more and more difficult to avoid unpleasant feelings.

P: It seems to work for me.

T: It may be that there is no downside to your avoidance, in which case this may have nothing to do with the agitation and unpleasant thoughts you were telling me about. On the other hand, it may be that it is this which is making things more difficult and we may need to work on helping you to reverse the avoidance.

P: I can see that it might be a problem.

T: Do you find that there is any change in how often you have to push the thoughts out of your mind or how often you have to make an effort to avoid reminders of cancer?

P: I am not sure.

T: Given the fact that your avoidance could be crucial in keeping your problems going, would you consider monitoring this for a week to see when and how often you have to do this?

P: If you can show me how to do that and you think it might help me

This patient returned to the next session having discovered that she was having to engage in significant effort to avoid reminders of cancer. This was used for discussion of the advantages and disadvantages of avoidance and as a way of trying out alternative strategies to address her urge to avoid unpleasant reminders. Modification of intermediate beliefs about avoidance can be combined with behavioural experiments designed to evaluate the emotional, cognitive and behavioural consequences of engagement with cancer stimuli. Patients should be advised to keep note of the advantages of reversing cognitive and behavioural avoidance. Reversal of cognitive avoidance is essential for patients who are experiencing problems related to intrusive memories, flashbacks and nightmares. Patients often find it easier to consider this if intrusive phenomena are normalised, and therapists may need to help patients to address problematic metacognitions which influence cognitive and behavioural avoidance.

Facilitating Control

Many psychological problems associated with cancer can be minimised if people can control the impact of the disease and treatment on their lives.

The use of Weekly Activity Schedules can be implemented during assessment and linked with intervention in this regard. Forward planning can be used to enable people to pre-empt problems associated with treatment by scheduling activities around treatment days. There may be occasions when a patient has to be in isolation—because of an immuno-compromised state or because of radioactivity (in the case of bracy-therapy). The use of an activity schedule can be helpful and provide the patient with structure to buffer the negative emotions which exposure to these scenarios can cause. Many anti-cancer drugs are associated with side effects such as nausea and fatigue. There is evidence for the effective-ness of cognitive and behavioural strategies in the management of chronic fatigue syndrome and an increased acknowledgement that their application to cancer-related fatigue may be helpful. Patients should be encouraged to keep written records of their fatigue and daily activity levels as these can be used to plan responses to fatigue and to schedule appropriate amounts of rest. The Multidimensional Fatigue Inventory (Smets et al., 1995) can be used to monitor outcome. Patients may have difficulty accepting the need for rest and the limitations which accom-pany a diagnosis, and this can often be addressed by enabling them to set more achievable goals and changing the thoughts which make activity more difficult at times of diminished energy.

The following extract outlines how planning activities were discussed with a patient with metastatic ovarian cancer who was struggling to cope with weakness during a course of chemotherapy:

T: You feel that there is nothing you can do—the chemotherapy takes control over your routine?

P: It seems to get in the way of anything I try to do.

T: Do you remember using the activity diary when we first met?

P: The thing on the grid?

T: Yes.

P: Yes.

T: I wondered if we could use it again—this time, to try to work round the chemotherapy. You know when you have to come for it and now that you have been in twice we could probably work out when you were feeling at your worst and work around it.

P: I see . . . keeping a note of what I do again.

T: The main thing will be to make a plan—keeping a note of what you do will be a good idea though as you can check out how the plan goes.

P: Right.

T: When do you get the chemotherapy again?

P: I come in on Friday morning.

T: What do you think then about beginning to make the plan from Saturday to Thursday? We can meet up again next Friday to see how you got on.

P: Just the idea of doing something to try to break the monotony helps.

T: Good. Let's start with Saturday morning and what you usually like to do on a Saturday.

P: I usually try to get out to Tesco for 8.30—for it opening, to miss the rush.

T: When was the last time that you did that?

P: A month ago.

T: How realistic is it, based on the past two chemo visits, that you will be able to do that on Saturday?

P: Mmm, I would like to be able to get it done . . . but I need to sleep.

T: That's what this planning will be about . . . being realistic about what you can achieve. This way you can feel that you have achieved something. Before you were getting down because you did not achieve anything—mainly because your plan was not sensitive to the temporary changes in your life.

P: I see.

T: Is there another shop that you could go to, or could you go at another time, or day?

Promoting Social Support

For some patients the formulation will outline the negative influence of a lack of a social network or adequate social support. Here the therapist's role is to facilitate changes within the patient's environment. To do this, the patient and therapist must first determine the main reasons why there is diminished social support. The most common reasons for this are hopelessness, procrastination, a lack of opportunity to socialise or anxiety. Diminished support may relate to individual family members feeling threatened as a result of the cancer diagnosis and/or having developed psychological problems which require intervention in their own right. Friends and relatives may avoid patients, resulting in less social support being available. When relatives are uncertain about how best to help the patient, therapists can arrange to provide advice on practical cognitive behavioural management strategies and how to overcome some of the obstacles to providing social support. Significant others may need help to evaluate beliefs about the consequences of expressing negative emotion ('If I talk to her about her cancer then I will make things worse'). The management of communication problems which have been triggered by the cancer is much easier than scenarios in which communication problems are a longstanding feature of the patient's life and cancer is just another example of how it can become manifest.

Patients may have held beliefs about the support they thought they would have received and become depressed when this does not materialise. Support may be withdrawn prematurely and/or be provided when it is not needed and interventions must be implemented in a way which takes account of this. Patients who are making predictions about the unrewarding nature of social interaction can be encouraged to identify and evaluate these thoughts and, if appropriate, evaluate them using a behavioural experiment. Some patients find that they have no idea what they will say to other people who ask about their cancer and may need assistance both in evaluating their predictions about this and developing skills to manage their interactions with others confidently. They may require skills training or role play in relation to things they can say to others. In some cases, cognitive behavioural therapists may arrange hospital admission (or attendance at a daycare facility) for the purposes of enabling people to test out strategies and increase social support.

T: So you have very few contacts with other people at the moment?

P: I suppose so. That's why they want me to go to the day centre.

T: Has that always been the case—that you don't tend to see too many people during the week?

P: No, I used to fill my week without a problem.

T: What sorts of things filled your week that you don't have happening now?

P: I had my visits to the church lunches on a Tuesday, my sister visited on a Wednesday, I did some voluntary work on a Friday and Saturday was always my day for seeing the family.

T: When was the last time that your week had this normal pattern for you?

P: Let me see, must have been about two weeks before the surgery—yes, that would be the last time I had a 'normal' week for me.

T: What would you see as being the main things that have interfered with you being in touch with other people like you used to be?

P: I don't know.

T: Let's look at it another way—what would need to happen for you to have a week which was more like the ones that you used to have?

P: It would need to be for two months' time—that's how long the doctor said it would be before I had fully recovered.

> T: That's certainly one way of looking at it. Can you think of any disadvantages of relying on the passage of time alone?
>
> P: I get very low with no one around.
>
> T: That's what I was thinking too—your depression does seem to relate to having few contacts at the moment. Is there any way that you could have contact with the people from your normal week but not have to go out and about to see them all?
>
> P: I couldn't ask them to all come and see me.
>
> T: Could you ask some of, or even one of them, if they would like to come for a visit?
>
> P: Yes, maybe they are waiting to be asked.

Handling Uncertainty

Some patients can accept the uncertainty associated with the course of their disease. They interpret this as an inevitability which cannot be avoided and are able to keep their thinking focused upon what is known to them, without becoming preoccupied with 'what ifs' and what might be. The way in which cancer services are delivered can worsen problems with uncertainty. Waiting for test results, appointment scheduling arrangements and the way in which information is provided to patients can all be modified with good result to minimise the problems of those struggling with uncertainty. Therapists should consider environmental and situational strategies as first-line intervention strategies. There is a huge variability in the psychosocial correlates of uncertainty—some patients interpret this as a positive reason to 'live for the moment' and others tend to respond to uncertainty with hopelessness and fear. In some cases, the uncertainty is so unbearable that patients would prefer to believe that their predictions are true. They may start to become resigned to the fact that cancer will return and may begin to live their lives according to what they predict will happen. In some cases the experience of uncertainty activates intermediate beliefs about the world and their place within it ('If I don't know what will happen to me, then there is no point in living'). Cognitive intervention strategies for uncertainty begin by enabling patients to understand that it is not the uncertainty which is mediating their problems, but that it is their thoughts and beliefs about uncertainty which are causing difficulty. Life is always full of uncertainties—it is just that most of the time we choose to avoid thinking about them. The following extract illustrates how cognitive interventions can be used to enable patients to build a new way of viewing the uncertainties associated with cancer:

T: The last panic attack was in the clinic?

P: Yes.

T: That was the time that you were having thoughts that you were going to go mad and end up in Gartnavel? (*Note: A local psychiatric hospital*)

P: I couldn't stand not knowing—the uncertainty was unbearable.

T: This is perhaps something else that we could work on by looking at your thoughts . . . your thoughts about uncertainty and your ability to deal with it.

P: I need certainty.

T: What would you like to have certainty about?

P: That the cancer will not come back.

T: You want to be told for certain that the cancer will never return?

P: I know, I know I can't have that . . . that would solve the panic though.

T: What is it about knowing it wouldn't come back that would help you feel less panicky?

P: I would know that I could control things again.

T: What sort of things?

P: Well, I could still work, could still see my children and have some sort of life.

T: Is is that you think that this is not going to happen—being with your children and having some sort of life?

P: When I feel panicky, yes.

T: So, you think about the fact that you cannot be certain about the cancer coming back, this then leads you to feel panicky?

P: I just think . . . I can't deal with the uncertainty, it is going to drive me mad. It will all come back, I know it will.

T: So your awareness of the uncertainty leads you to think things will go out of control—that the cancer will come back. Feeling more in control you think might help you to feel less panicked about it?

P: Yes.

T: Perhaps we could also put together an action plan of all of the things you could do if the cancer were to come back—this might mean that you have less need to keep going over this possibility in your mind.

P: Not just yet, if I can feel more in control then I think I could just about face this.

T: I agree, let's spend our next session on that topic—helping you to feel more in control and able to deal with the certainties in life.

The strengths of the cognitive behavioural model is that it can be applied to many aspects of psychosocial oncology. An example of this is the application of work on schema to understanding sexual dysfunction.

Patients with sexual problems may benefit from a schema-driven intervention aimed at modifying self-concept (with particular reference to sexual self-concept). This may involve addressing behavioural elements of the patient's sexual repertoire, addressing affective components of sexual activity (e.g. minimising embarrassment or anxiety) or imaginally based strategies for tackling arousal. In some circumstances it may be necessary to target spousal behaviours which interfere with optimal sexual functioning.

Having knowledge of positive automatic thoughts can be helpful when there is a need to promote affect closure at the end of a distressing session. Using this information can also be helpful when patients are finding it difficult to shift mental focus away from realistic negative automatic thoughts or when the negative aspects of their cancer experiences are particularly sailent.

SUMMARY AND CONCLUSIONS

Cancer and its treatment are associated with a wide range of psychological problems, many of which can be understood in terms of 'hurdles' that are faced by patients who develop the disease, and cognitive behavioural assessments can be structured around this idea of hurdles. The issues which will be important for patients are very dependent upon the type of cancer, their experiences of cancer, treatment regimes and their prognosis. Fear and anxiety are commonly featured in problem-level formulations and the way in which cancer can intrude on a patient's life frequently encapsulates the reasons for referral to a cognitive behavioural therapist. Interventions need to enable patients to maintain control, manage the pervasive uncertainty which is a part of most cancer patients' experiences, address dysfunctional, behavioural and cognitive avoidance and ensure that patients have the most supportive environment possible. This is an area of CBT practice where therapists must not overlook the importance of assessing, formulating and addressing patients' experiences of realistic thoughts when personal tragedies occur.

Chapter 6

CHRONIC PAIN

INTRODUCTION

More has been written about cognitive behavioural aspects of chronic pain and CBT for chronic pain than any other chronic medical problem (see Jensen et al., 1991; Spence, 1993; Kelly, 1996; Keefe, Jacobs & Edwards, 1997; Tan & Leucht, 1997). CBT has been extensively evaluated and shown to be effective in terms of its impact on a number of bio-psychosocial variables (Morley, Eccleston & Williams, 1999). While there are a number of common components and themes across disorders where chronic pain is a feature, therapists need to tailor their assessment, formulation and interventions to take account of the particular aetiological and phenomenological elements of the chronic pain problem being experienced by the patient. These will vary according to whether patients have arthritis, migraine, back pain and occupational overuse disorders of the upper limbs such as repetitive strain injury.

Chronic pain commonly results in significant psychosocial problems for patients and can begin to dominate almost every aspect of their lifestyle. Patients may become depressed, have fears about their future, report decreased pleasure in their everyday activities and may even feel helpless in the face of continuous pain. This may in turn result in quality of life problems such as impaired ambulatory function, and reduced frequency of socialisation, particularly among older adults (Widner & Zeichner, 1993). Significant role changes can occur within family systems and with regard to occupational functioning. Patients may also have been prescribed analgesic medications which cause problems related to side effects. CBT has become the leading non-medical treatment for chronic pain; indeed, CBT has now become an integral part of most chronic pain management programmes.

This chapter will outline the core components of cognitive behavioural work with those who are experiencing longstanding pain, but will also illustrate when necessary the ways in which these core elements need to be modified for particular presentations.

ASSESSMENT

Patients with chronic pain need to feel understood by those involved in their care. A cognitive behavioural assessment provides therapists with the ideal means of gathering information which will help them to communicate a sound understanding of what it is like to experience chronic pain. Most patients with chronic pain will have no prior experience of this sort of approach to understanding their experiences, and assessment should not only cover the generic areas already outlined but should also gather detail on pain-specific factors. This must involve assessment of the current experiences and patterns of pain sensations and environmental factors that influence pain experience. This important element of cognitive behavioural management is best achieved by the completion of a pain diary.

Pain Diary

Cognitive behavioural assessment should almost always begin with completion of a pain diary which includes information on pain intensity, control over pain and the intake of analgesic medication. This is essential as many of the interventions which are used require patients to use pain intensity changes as triggers to implement coping strategies or as stimuli to begin to evaluate pain-related thoughts. Assessment should cover the bodily locations at which the patient experiences pain and the triggers for these pains. Pain diaries should aim to include at least one psychosocial variable, even if this is only behavioural activity. Most people with chronic pain problems will be using at least one analgesic drug, and details of the dosage and when this is taken should be recorded in diary monitoring. Assessing pain which occurs at multiple sites can involve a substantial proportion of an initial assessment session. The time spent on this is important and is essential in communicating to patients that their pain experiences are important.

T: The knee pain is the one that you get most often after activity?

P: Yes, though sometimes I get pain here in my back too.

T: Knee pain, back pain and pain in you lower legs . . . those are the main areas you said? Do you ever get back or leg pain in relation to activities?

P: I don't think that I do, no.

T: When you get the knee pain, is this usually accompanied by the other pains?

P: Sometimes.

T Would it be fair to say that it is quite difficult to work out if there is any pattern to your pain experiences?

P: Yes, it is all a jumble to me.

T: What about if we get you to complete a pain diary. This way you can note down what you are doing and how bad the knee, back and leg pains are. That way we can analyse the links when you have monitored them in this way.

In some cases, it is useful to construct individualised pain diaries (see Figure 6.1) where patients can provide details on pain at multiple body sites or on other emotional and/or behavioural variables which are unique to their experiences of living with pain. Patients may report that their pain seems to be more difficult to deal with or that it is more severe when they are angry or when they feel tired. Gathering data on these variables means that hypotheses can be generated about the links between them and episodes of pain, and pain diaries should be completed for a period of at least two weeks. Figure 6.1 shows examples of two very different sorts of pain diary.

Day: Mon / Tues / Wed / Thurs / Fri / Sat / Sun (circle one)   Date: ....

Time	Activity	Pain Severity (0 - 10)	Irritability (0 - 10)	What did you do to cope? How effective was it? (0 - 10)

Figure 6.1. Pain diary

Pain diaries may also need to be modified in response to disorder-specific variables such as food intake (in the case of some types of headaches) and stages of menstrual cycle (for some female patients with chronic pain) or in response to environmental factors such as shift patterns at work or to record the presence of a relative or acquaintance. Pain severity ratings are usually taken using a ten-point scale (sometimes represented visually as a visual analogue scale), and most people have no difficulty in understanding how to use this when they have had the anchor points defined (i.e. 0 represents no pain at all and 10 represents the worst pain that you can imagine). The way in which these anchor points are defined will depend on therapist preference and patient characteristics. If the upper anchor point is defined as the worst pain that someone has ever suffered then some patients will use this rating for every pain they experience. In such cases it is useful to define the upper anchor as the worst possible pain that the patient can imagine. Some patients (in diaries and in response to questions) rate their pain severity as maximum intensity for every waking hour of the day. This sort of response to the assessment of pain severity can present problems for therapists. First, this is unlikely to be the case and is usually the physical equivalent of the sort of biased thinking seen with emotional reasoning. In such cases, patients are very distressed by the occurrence of pain and therefore process their overall pain experience as the worst that they could imagine, as if each time they experience it is the worst. Pain is, of course, a physical and psychological experience and patients who rate their pain in this way are obviously communicating something important. The primary aim of the therapist when faced with this sort of response to monitoring is to summarise and empathise with the intense nature of a patient's pain experience. This should be followed by attempts to help the patient to think about any small differences noticed when experiencing the pain. Some patients may find it helpful to define their own pain-rating scale by assigning prior experiences to each anchor and significant points between. An example of this is outlined in Figure 6.2.

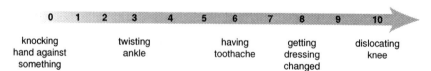

Figure 6.2.   Individualised pain rating scale

Occasionally, separating physical and psychsocial elements of the pain experience does not produce changes in pain rating. Using fluctuations in pain severity helps patients to use changes as the cue for the application of treatment strategies and also helps to demonstrate changes in pain severity ratings following treatment. Therapists can increase the focus on variables that do show fluctuation in diaries (e.g. perceived control or amount of medication taken) or suggest that the rating scale be modified. If a patient records most of her pain severity ratings as 9 or 10 then it is possible to suggest that she should attempt to make further ratings between 9 and 10, which may help her to discriminate some changes in pain severity.

Pain diaries provide a huge amount of data with which many patient and therapist questions can be answered: Are there any times when the pain is absent? If so, when? What is it about this situation/time? How does the pain relate to mood? Are there times when the pain is worse? What might this be due to? Is this happening at other times when the pain is this intense? Patients can be encouraged to look over their diaries, have others look at the diary entries and examine them in detail as therapy progresses. The pain diary is central to the implementation of many treatment strategies such as observational monitoring assignments, behavioural experiments designed to evaluate the impact of a behaviour on pain severity, or as a baseline measure for later comparison at the end of treatment.

T: I wanted to spend some time looking over the pain diary which you completed for today's appointment.

P: It was much easier to do than I thought—sorry if I didn't seem too enthusiastic last time.

T: I remember that you said you thought it was going to be difficult.

P: . . . and here it was easy. That's me all over—making mountains out of mole hills.

T: That is something that we may come back to later today or at a future session.

P: Right.

T: Did you notice any patterns or anything interesting in the pain diary?

P: Well, let's see—no, I suppose well, yes that I do more than I thought I did in a week.

T: That's a good starting point. What parts of the diary stand out as being the parts that demonstrate to you that you do more than you thought that you would do in a week?

P: Here . . . I do more in the mornings than I thought. I am always saying to Jim that I never get anything done because of the pain.

Self-report Measures

It is perhaps not surprising, given the proliferation of literature on cognitive behavioural aspects of chronic pain, that many self-report measures have been designed to assess psychosocial aspects of chronic pain. This section focuses on four commonly used measures.

Pain Coping Strategies Questionnaire

This is a 44-item questionnaire (Rosenstiel & Keefe, 1983) which is predominantly composed of a list of coping responses that patients might use when they are experiencing pain. Respondents are asked to indicate the extent to which they use each strategy (0, 'Never do' to 6, 'Always do that'). The subscales on this measure are Diverting Attention, Reinterpreting the Pain Sensation, Catastrophising, Ignoring Sensations, Praying or Hoping, Coping Self-Statements and Increased Behavioural Activities. Some of the items from this measure are outlined in Table 6.1.

Table 6.1   Sample items from the Pain Coping Strategies Questionnaire (Rosenstiel & Keefe, 1983)

I try to think of something pleasant
It is awful and I feel that it overwhelms me
Although it hurts, I just keep on going
I pretend it is not there
I ignore it
I do something I enjoy, such as watching television or listening to music

Despite the lack of normative data for this measure, it is useful in identifying individual coping strategies for pain. The catastrophising subscale is particularly useful. Identification of catastrophising is important and often pivotal in formulating emotional reactions to pain and needs to be targeted in treatment plans. Individual items or clusters of items can also be used to evaluate changes as treatment progresses. This measure is available as part of the 'Pain and Pain Behaviours' module of Measures in Health Psychology (Weinman et al., 1995).

McGill Melzack Pain Questionnaire

The MMPQ (Melzack, 1975) consists of drawings of the body (one facing forward and one backward) upon which patients are asked to indicate the location of their pain. They are encouraged to choose one descriptive adjective from a group of listed words (though they do not need to choose a word if there is none within a group to describe their pain). This measure can be particularly useful as the first component of an assessment— particularly when patients may be concerned about seeing a psychological therapist. The use of the MMPQ within a cognitive behavioural assessment communicates that the physical aspects of a patient's pain, such as location and the way it is experienced, are important parts of assessment and understanding the patient's experiences. The MMPQ words chosen by patients to describe their pain can also provide a useful introduction to begin the exploration of emotions, thoughts and behaviours associated with pain. Patients can be asked to elaborate on why they have chosen a particular word in preference to one of the others that are included in the group, or asked what other thoughts, feelings or images come to mind when they think of the word they have chosen. The MMPQ can be scored in various ways, further details of which can be obtained in Weinman, Wright and Johnston (1995).

Beliefs About Pain Control Questionnaire

This measure (Brown & Nicassio, 1987) is based on work on the concept of perceived locus of control. It contains items which require patients to endorse their level of agreement according to a six-point Likert scale (1, Strongly disagree to 6, Strongly agree) and provides subscale scores for scales labelled 'internal' (belief that pain is controlled by internal factors), 'powerful doctors' (belief that pain is controlled by doctors) and 'chance' (belief that pain is controlled by chance). Some sample items are outlined in Table 6.2.

Table 6.2 Sample items from Beliefs About Pain Control Questionnaire (Brown & Nicassio, 1987)

If I take good care of myself, I can usually avoid pain
Whenever I am in pain, it is usually because of something I have done or not done
I cannot get any help for my pain unless I go to seek medical help
People who are never in pain are just plain lucky
I am directly responsible for my pain
No matter what I do, if I am going to be in pain, I will be in pain

Pain Stages of Change Questionnaire

This questionnaire (Kerns et al., 1997) can be routinely incorporated into most assessments. Kerns et al. (1997) have applied this model to understanding patient readiness to adopt the sort of self-management approach to chronic pain required for CBT. Baseline scores on the PSCQ can be compared with those obtained after interventions which aim to enable patients to move forward in terms of their readiness to adopt a problem-focused approach to managing pain. This measure has been reproduced in Appendix 3, with the permission of Dr Robert Kerns, for therapists who wish to use this measure in their work with patients experiencing chronic pain.

Illness Representation

The importance of individual illness representations has been highlighted throughout this book. It is particularly important that this be assessed with people experiencing chronic pain, as it is often the main factor in formulations. Assessment of illness representation is particularly important where chronic pain symptoms have arisen as a result of disorders which have (or are perceived by patients to have) uncertain aetiology. It is in these circumstances that patients are most likely to rely upon elements of their illness representation to understand their experiences. The sorts of questions which can help to identify beliefs about pain are outlined in Table 6.3.

Table 6.3   Assessment questions for pain representations

What do you think causes the pain?
What do you think will happen to the pain in the future?
What have you been told about your pain?
How do you explain things when it gets better/worse?
Do you ever think that you might be causing damage to yourself?
What sorts of things have you given up since the pain became a problem?
Are there things that you would like to be able to start again?
What things would you like to be able to do in the future?
What is the main reason that you do not do as much as you used to?

Visits to healthcare staff can provide useful scenarios as the focus for assessments of pain representations, as it is often at these times that they are activated. Many of the experiences of people with pain are understandable in terms of their pain beliefs and representations about the origins of their pain, acceptable ways to express pain and the most appropriate ways of coping. This is why a substantial proportion of the assessment should be devoted to this topic.

T: One of the important things which I want to assess today is the way you think about pain—what you think about its causes, how to control it, that sort of thing.

P: Pain is pain isn't it?

T: In my experience pain can mean a lot of very different things to the people who come to the pain clinic. I don't like to assume that I know how people think about pain or what view they take of it, until I have asked some more questions about pain. Would it be OK if I ask you some more about what pain means to you?

P: I would have thought that pain was pain and that was the end of it.

T: I suppose I am suggesting to you that this might not be the case—that you may have a very unique and personal set of beliefs about pain which we need to assess. Let's start with the causes—what do you see as being the main cause of the pain?

P: The cause?

T: Yes, what things do you think cause the pain?

Pain Behaviours

Assessment of pain behaviours may need careful explanation if patients are to feel able to disclose details about how they react to experiencing pain. Patients may spontaneously report examples of their pain behaviours in response to direct questioning ('What do you do when you experience pain?'). More commonly, this information is obtained by screening for the presence of common pain behaviours such as those outlined in Table 6.4. Behaviours which are related to pain may be positively reinforced by consequences such as the attention of others or the provision of other positive reinforcers such as physical contact or food. Pain behaviours are often negatively reinforced by the avoidance and/or removal of aversive circumstances. An example of this might be when someone in pain grimaces when they move to get an object. This grimace is noticed by a relative who tells the patient to sit back down, gets the object and passes it to the patient.

Table 6.4   Examples of pain behaviours

Sighing	Wearing cervical collars	Bracing
Groaning	Using walking sticks	Complaining
Irregular gait	Limping	Rubbing the affected area

Assessment of pain behaviours can be difficult as some patients interpret therapist's questions as if it is being suggested that they are intentionally looking for sympathy or attention by behaving in a particular manner. Such patient reactions to the assessment process can be informative in themselves (particularly when patients express considerable offence at the suggestion). Such reactions should be followed up at some point as they are likely to result in the disclosure of information about patients' views on how they believe their pain problem is viewed by others in their life. If assessment of pain behaviour is to proceed without resulting in a rupture in the therapeutic alliance, then patients need to have a rationale to understand what they are being asked about and why. Asking first about how people generally tend to behave when in pain serves to reduce the likelihood of adverse patient responses to questioning about their own experiences in this regard. Once this has been done it is possible to begin to address personal experiences by determining whether the information discussed with regard to pain behaviour in general might be relevant to the patient's situation. This is illustrated in the following extract from an assessment session:

> T: I want to spend some time asking you now about what you do when you are in pain. The reason I want to ask you about this is that research has shown that this can have a very important part to play in how you adjust to your life with pain.
>
> P: OK.
>
> T: Before I ask about your own pain problems I want to get you to think about how human beings react to pain in general. Would that be acceptable to you?
>
> P: If you want to . . .
>
> T: As human beings there are a number of behaviours which we use to communicate to other people that we are experiencing pain. . . . Can you think of some of the behaviours which you have seen people use to show they are in pain?
>
> P: What, like screaming and that sort of thing?
>
> T: Well that would be an extreme example of how someone might react when in pain—yes. Can you think of any other things that people do when they are in pain?
>
> P: Moaning and making a face—or sighing a lot.
>
> T: Screaming, moaning and changing facial expression are all good examples. Can you think of any others?
>
> P: No—those are the main ones.
>
> T: Would you say that there are any behaviours that you are more likely to display when you have been experiencing pain?
>
> P: Well I do sigh a lot I suppose . . . and maybe make the odd face now and again—especially when it is really bad.

Relationships and Lifestyle

The reactions of relatives to the patient's pain problems should be determined. Questions such as 'How can other people tell when your pain is bad?', What happens if you don't heed your family's advice to rest or take it easy?' usually provide therapist and patient with recent examples which can be discussed with regard to the responses of others, their thoughts, feelings and responses to this. The impact on patient's relationships in general should be assessed in terms of relationship quality, intimacy and sexual functioning. The impact of pain-related dysfunction on occupational functioning is variable. Some patients struggle to continue working while others finish and have no intention of returning to work. Therapists should attempt to understand the reasoning and decision-making processes that patients have used to arrive at their decisions about work. Factors responsible for the decision to stop working may be related to a global tendency towards avoidance of anything which may exacerbate the pain.

T: Many people who come to the Pain Clinic tell me that they have had to make changes to their working arrangements because of their pain. Is that something that you have had to do?

P: Working is out of the question.

T: What makes you say that?

P: The pain. I can't work if I am in pain, can I?

T: That's something that I am not sure about—I don't know enough about your work, what it involves, how you felt about your work and the sort of pain you experienced at work.

P: I see. I am sorry for snapping—I get sick of people questioning my decision not to go back.

T: It must be annoying. I want to ask you questions about it. I am not questioning your decision. . . . Just trying to make sure I understand the way in which you reached your decision about work.

General Psychological Symptoms

High rates of depression are associated with chronic pain and it is therefore essential that cognitive behavioural assessment determine levels of depressive symptomatology and cognitive behavioural mediators of this. This can be assessed using measures such as the Beck Depression Inventory or Zung Self-Rating Scale for Depression (Zung, 1965). There are some items which, for some patients, may be confounded with their experiences with chronic pain. Pain often interferes with sleep and therapists should aim to determine whether sleep patterns are affected and, if so, the main mediators and moderators of this. This will usually be due to pain which interrupts sleep; preoccupation with the negative effects of pain on daily activity levels; and/or worries about the negative consequences of continued sleep disturbance. Some patients begin to worry that their lack of sleep will make it difficult for them to deal with the pain.

FORMULATION

Problem-level Formulation

The literature on psychological aspects of chronic pain is full of examples of cognitive behavioural moderators and mediators of problems with psychological adjustment. This makes the task of constructing comprehensive and truly evidence-based cognitive behavioural formulation much easier than with most other chronic medical problems. The issue of perceived control is of paramount importance. People with chronic pain problems who have an internal locus of control are less likely to be depressed and generally function better than those who do not. The use of active coping strategies are also associated with better psychosocial adjustment. Cognitive behavioural mediators of the relationship between pain and depressive symptoms such as catastrophic appraisals, helplessness, decreased perceptions of control and perceived interference with instrumental activities often feature in problem-level formulations for chronic pain. Indeed, Maxwell, Gatchel and Mayer (1998) have demonstrated that these represent independent cognitive behavioural dimensions of the chronic pain experience and that, as such, CBT with this group of patients should aim to target all three. It is likely that these will feature in most problem-level formulations. Given that these factors are believed to be independent influences on the links between pain and depression, it is conceivable that some patients will have problem-level formulations which emphasise one dimension but not another. Patients with more negative thoughts in response to pain report more severe pain (Gil et al., 1990). Figure 6.3 outlines the links between

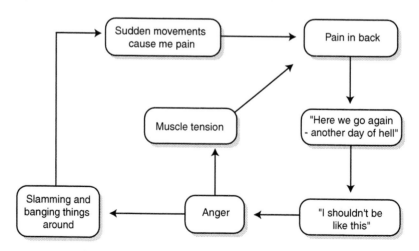

Figure 6.3.   Problem-level formulation (chronic pain)

catastrophising, coping ability, locus of control and affective response to pain. Catastrophising is often associated with increased verbal reporting of pain experiences (Jacobson & Butler, 1995). Patient expectations about pain experiences can also be important in considering pain tolerance and avoidance (Cipher & Fernandez, 1996).

People will often regulate their activity on the basis of the levels of pain they experience. This can be clearly seen when reviewing patient diaries which include the monitoring of activities. Review of activity-level monitoring is one of the easiest ways of collating information for a problem-level formulation relating to patient activities. Patients usually have thoughts about being able to get a lot done when pain severity is lower, and fear of exacerbating pain or causing harm when experiencing mild to moderate pain. Fear of pain or further injury as a result of inappropriate activity or movement is often associated with pain-related avoidance behaviour (Asmundson, 1999). This avoidance of activities at times of increased pain severity and compensatory engagement in activities when experiencing lesser degrees of pain gives rise to the sort of bursts of activity outlined in Figure 6.4. This activity pattern is usually addressed by pacing (see 'Treatment Strategies', below).

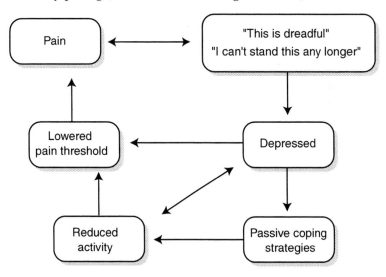

Figure 6.4. Problem-level formulation: linking catastrophising, pain and depression

Pictorial or graphical representation of the relationship between important variables helps patients to appreciate links which might otherwise be difficult to appreciate. They can use them to think about the interactions between dimensions and it provides a shared understanding of these links, a framework to gather data on examples and, perhaps most importantly, a way of conceptualising how changes can be expressed in the form of treatment goals. Two dimensions which can be represented in this way are pain coping strategy focus (active or passive) and mood. The example in Figure 6.5 outlines the horizontal axis representing mood and the vertical axis representing coping strategy focus. Patient monitoring revealed that most of the time passive coping strategies were associated with low mood. The following extract outlines how this graph was then used with a patient to discuss treatment goals.

T: What we have done then is to mark here how you felt and here we have put down whether the strategy that you were using for coping is an active or a passive one.

P: Oh dear, there are a lot in this corner aren't there?

T: There are more here yes, your coping strategies seem to be more passive don't they?

P: Oh dear.

T: You do have some active strategies too. What do you think about the link between your feelings with the active coping strategies and the passive ones?

P: This section is certainly higher—does that mean I am more depressed when I use those ones?

T: Yes, your monitoring has revealed that you seem to be more depressed at times when you have been using passive coping strategies.

P: I need to work on this—we need to get me to have more crosses in this corner.

T: I think so too—we can see if this is accompanied by an improvement in your mood.

Case-level Formulation

Some of the beliefs commonly featured in case-level formulations of chronic pain problems are outlined in Table 6.5. These commonly relate to themes of self-efficacy, control, pain itself and pain management strategies (e.g. medication or psychologically based strategies). Patients may have beliefs which include future-oriented predictions such as becoming confined to a wheelchair. Such future oriented predictions should be included in case-level formulations, with appropriate links to the life experiences and critical incidents which are most relevant to them.

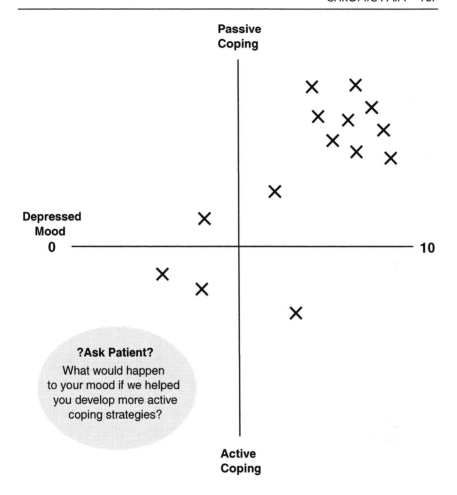

X - mood rating from a diary

Figure 6.5. Graphical representation of mood and coping strategy focus

Table 6.5 Beliefs commonly featured in Case-level formulations for chronic pain

There is nothing I can do to help with the pain
I have no control over pain
If I am in pain then it will interfere with all my plans
Fluctuations in my pain are completely random
It's impossible to understand my pain
Other people think that I am making it up
If I do something when I am in pain, then I may cause harm to myself
If I avoid things which make my pain worse, then this is better for me
Pain medication should only be taken as a last resort

Patients will often have had experiences where (explicitly or implicity) the legitimacy of their symptoms will have been questioned by medical personnel. This is usually the case when there is an absence of structural findings on radiological investigations and for some patients this memory will be a key cognitive mediator at times of pain-related psychological problems. Some people will fear that they are going to be abandoned by medical staff (Livengood, 1996), a feeling that will be particularly problematic for those patients with previous life experiences characterised by substandard care by significant others. The initiation of depressive symptoms can result in increased acknowledgement of negative personal traits (Holzberg, Robinson & Geisser, 1993) and case-level formulations should aim to include this information in longitudinal descriptions of depressive symptoms which become more severe in emphasis.

The pain stages of change model can assist therapists to decide upon the initial focus of CBT—whether patients are ready to commence a trial of CBT or whether they may require treatment targeted at modifying their stage within the stages of change model. Providing patients with a formulation of their experiences which makes reference to stages of change can be helpful in terms of understanding why CBT may not be suitable at the time, and in this way patients can feel that they might be able to return to CBT later. Sometimes patients find it difficult to accept that their pain will not be cured, and this belief can act as a main barrier to change. Referrers find feedback useful, especially on stages of change as this may indicate that a patient is progressing from one stage to the next and that re-referral may be worth considering when this happens.

TREATMENT STRATEGIES

Newshan and Balamuth (1990/91) use what they refer to as the 'big person, small person' concept, which aims to illustrate how intervention can enable someone who feels 'consumed and enveloped by pain' (p. 28) to work towards a position where he or she is bigger than the pain and able to manage it. Patients with chronic pain problems, however, may find it difficult to maintain the same posture for prolonged periods of time and therapists should inform patients that they should feel free to move around during therapy sessions.

Promoting Reconceptualisation

The way in which patients interpret their experiences of painful stimuli influences the levels of pain and distress they experience. However, many patients with chronic pain will not readily accept this suggestion. Education and engagement in CBT requires that patients consider the main emotional, behavioural and physical consequences of how they think of their pain experience. This can be done by discussing situations in which patients experience the same levels of pain but have different emotional reactions, or times when they have had similar pain experiences but behaved differently owing to the presence of others or their situation at that time. Therapists should help patients to think about these things to synthesise this information in a way that moves them from a purely biological model of pain to one that takes account of the range of bio-psychosocial variables which influence the experience of pain.

T: One of the things that we know is important for some people is their thoughts and feelings when they have pain. The way they think and feel can influence how they react to pain.

P: I know it makes me feel so tired when I get sore.

T: This is one of the things that I had in mind. If you were to think about times when you are tired and you have pain, compared with times that you are not as tired and have pain. Can you focus on those two examples in your head?

P: Yes.

T: In which of the two would you find it more difficult to cope with?

P: The one when I am most tired.

T: In the same way that tiredness can lower your threshold for coping with pain—so can your thoughts, feelings and, in some cases, the situation that you are in. Can you think of any times that your mood, your thought pattern or the situation that you are in might have affected your coping ability for pain?

P: When the house is a mess this makes it more difficult to cope with the pain—that's a situation. Is it?

T: What sorts of thoughts do you find that you have when the house is a mess?

P: Usually that no one helps me and that I have to clear up everyone's mess.

T: How do you feel when you think like this?

P: Quite annoyed with the girls and really fed up.

T: Do you think these feelings and your thoughts at the time have any bearing on your experience of pain?

P: I suppose they don't make it easier.

Presentation of information on the gate control theory of pain can be helpful in enabling patients to appreciate the relevance of gaining control over pain by regulating the input messages which may alleviate or exacerbate their pain experiences. The gate control theory can become a shared conceptualisation of pain, which can be used as a rationale by which further interventions can be structured. One way of explaining this is outlined in Table 6.6. Patients can be encouraged to explore links between cognitive behavioural factors and their pain. Therapists should suggest that patients think about the gate control theory as a way of understanding the cognitive behavioural model of chronic pain.

Table 6.6   Explaining the gate control theory of pain

There are sets of nerves which carry information to the spinal cord about sensations such as heat, vibration or touch. So, if you touch the table then the sensation is carried along these sensory nerves to your spinal cord and onward to your brain. It can be helpful to think of these nerve signals as messages which have to pass through a gate before they get to the spinal cord or the brain. A message travels from your finger, along the spinal cord, through a gate and onward to your brain. Pain messages have to travel through a pain gate before they are experienced by you as painful. We know that feelings like tension or fear can make pain seem worse. We think that this is because they keep the 'pain gate' open. We also know that things like relaxation, distraction and activities make pain easier to deal with. This is because they seem to close the gate to pain messages. You may have had the experience of people rubbing an area that is painful and then finding that the pain eases—this is because rubbing sends competing messages through the gate.

This process, what Basler, Jakle and Kroner-Herwig (1996) refer to as a reconceptualisation of pain experience, is essentially one of reframing a person's understanding of pain according to a chronic pain model (as opposed to an acute pain model). Therapists can further help to promote this reconceptualisation by having patients consider the differences between acute and chronic pain.

Patients need to accept that one of the main aims of CBT for chronic pain is to enable them to develop more effective coping strategies. The promotion of cognitive coping skills is associated with more positive experiences of pain (Gil et al., 1996). Patients need to accept a coping model, but this requires acceptance (or at the very least acknowledgement) that complete cure is unlikely. It is, therefore, imperative that patients who harbour ideas about seeking a cure have the opportunity to explore their hopes and beliefs about cure. Indeed, one of the initial goals of CBT may be to help them to accept that a cure is unlikely. This, however, needs to be handled sensitively. Most patients with chronic pain will already have considered the fact that a cure is becoming increasingly unlikely. However, there are some for whom this news will be received as unexpected and devastating.

Assessment will have identified those patients with beliefs about the possibility of cure. The use of guided discovery is often instrumental in enabling people to appreciate the unhelpful and unrealistic nature of their hopes for a complete cure. Eimer (1992) suggests that therapy may need to focus on such beliefs which undermine a patient's responsibility for employing coping and self-management techniques.

T: During our session last week you mentioned that you would accept nothing less than a complete cure. I also noticed that some of the responses on the questionnaires you filled in suggested that you were looking for a cure.

P: Oh yes, I have to get this cured once and for all.

T: That would be something indeed—I know also, from what you have said, how much relief that would bring to you.

P: Bliss!

T: Have any of the medical staff said that they are hoping to be able to cure the pain?

P: No, but that's what they are so good at—Dr Boyd is so good—if anyone can cure this, he can.

T: He is very good at his job, yes. I wondered if it would be OK to spend some time talking about your hopes for cure and how that may relate to what happens during therapy here with me?

P: Yes, I will do anything to get rid of this pain.

T: How long have you been hoping that you will be rid of the pain?

P: Since the accident . . . let me see, that's nearly four years now . . . a long time.

T: And have you always hoped that the pain would be cured as much as you do now?

P: What do you mean?

T: If I had met you six months after the pain started and asked you how much you hoped for a cure would you have been as intent on seeking a cure as you are today, four years later?

P: There are some days when I wonder if it will ever work out but then I see all the latest advances on TV and am sure that one day there will be something for me.

T: What would complete cure from the pain mean for you?

P: Getting rid of the pain.

T: You are really holding out for a cure aren't you?

P: Yes.

T: I'm afraid that that may make my approach to helping you a disappointment.

When patients dismiss psychological variables as largely irrelevant it is best to accept this at the time (after all, this may be true). This provides an ideal opportunity to reinforce the collaborative and empirical stance which characterises CBT. Therapists can suggest that this can certainly be the case for a small proportion of people, but that it is more usual for psychological variables to interact in some way with pain experiences—even if only in terms of the way chronic pain makes them feel about their future. Therapists should beware of the risk of prematurely accepting patient statements about a lack of interaction between psychosocial variables and pain experiences.

Promoting Pain-coping Strategies

Patients usually have their own set of coping strategies for their pain (though they may not recognise them as such). Any attempts to introduce new coping strategies should be preceded by analysis of the effectiveness of existing coping strategies. The decision to use particular coping strategies will often relate to representations of pain and pain control (e.g. a belief that pain can only be alleviated by tablets may result in overuse of medication and underuse of strategies which relate to psychological factors). The introduction of new coping strategies may necessitate the implementation of strategies aimed at belief change initially. The general aim of coping strategy enhancement is to facilitate the implementation of active coping strategies, while simultaneously reducing the use of passive coping. Gil et al. (1996) reported that brief training in cognitive coping skills resulted in increased coping attempts, decreased negative thinking, and lower tendency to report pain during laboratory-induced noxious stimulation. Attempts to enhance pain-coping strategies should always include cognitively based coping strategies. Patients can test out which strategies are most effective for them. The use of analgesic medication should be viewed as a coping strategy, despite the fact that some patients will attempt to convince therapists otherwise. Indeed, coping strategy interventions can be targeted at medication use when it seems from the formulation that medication is being used erratically or contrary to medical advice. Some patients will take too much medication, others will only take this on 'bad days', and others not at all.

Reducing Catastrophising

Miller (1992) has suggested that catastrophising patients are more likely to benefit from self-instruction, whereas non-catastrophisers benefit most from interventions such as attention switching. 'Catastrophisers' benefit from interventions which focus on verbal re-attribution, whereas attention modification strategies such as distraction or attention control training are more relevant for patients who tend not to catastrophise. Patients must first be able to recognise catastrophic cognitions and appreciate the unhelpful nature of these in promoting adjustment to chronic pain. Treatment strategies must be presented in such a way that patients do not feel that their pain experience is being minimised in any way. There is a danger of this when the concept of catastrophising and its management are presented in an oversimplistic manner. The following extracts outline two contrasting attempts by trainees to address catastrophic thinking about pain.

> T: I notice from the Thought Record that you often have the thought 'This is terrible' and when you wake up you often think 'I can't stand another minute of this—this is torture'.
> P: Aye, I think those thoughts a lot—constantly at times.
> T: Is it really true to say that things are 'terrible' and that it is like 'torture'—don't you think that it would be even worse if you were being tortured?
> P: Well, it is really awful you know—day in day out. . . . It feels like torture to me.
> T: I know that's how it feels, but perhaps you need to think if that is how it really is.

In this excerpt the therapist has clearly identified the elements of catastrophising which are most problematic for her patient. However, she has failed to communicate her understanding of how distressing the pain is and the therapeutic alliance is beginning to weaken. In the following example, the therapist acknowledges the catastrophising and enables the patient to think about the consequences of this style of thinking on his emotions, behaviour and ability to tolerate pain. This provides a more solid base from which to suggest that they explore, first, whether there are disadvantages to catastrophising and, second, whether they might develop alternative ways of thinking about it.

> T: I notice from the Thought Record that you often have the thought 'This is terrible' and when you wake up you often think 'I can't stand another minute of this—this is torture'.
> P: Aye, I think those thoughts a lot—constantly at times.
> T: How do you feel when your thoughts are focused upon the terrible and tortuous aspects of being in pain for you?
> P: It is so difficult to stay positive—I despair at times.

> T: So when you think that things are terrible and that it is like torture you notice feelings of despair?
>
> P: Mm.
>
> T: I wonder if we could spend some of the time talking about these thoughts and how they have been making you feel.

Patients may benefit from pain prediction exercises. This involves the completion of pain prediction diaries. Patients are encouraged to plan activities and then predict the level of pain they think will be associated with such activity. 'Catastrophisers' usually overestimate pain severity, but this can be helpful in demonstrating cognitive mechanisms which mediate avoidance and/or reductions in pleasure as a result of anticipatory exacerbations in pain severity.

Contingency Management

Contingency management is indicated when pain behaviours are a predominant feature of a patient's presentation. It is most appropriate when there are no physical findings, when the patient's reports of pain are clearly in excess of physical findings, when there is clearly systematic reinforcement for pain behaviour within the patient's environment or when the behaviour seems to function as the primary factor mediating avoidance of participation in activities. Treatment strategies based purely on contingency management are less appropriate when physical findings account for some elements of a patient's presentation and when there is no evidence of inactivity. It is particularly important to address familial reinforcement of pain behaviour (e.g. making tea contingent upon pain behaviours and/or getting pillows when grimacing), and this may involve individual sessions with family members. Some family members report behavioural patterns which have become so habitual that they need to learn alternatives and try these out in a role-play scenario.

Therapists can invite relatives to individual sessions which aim to help them to develop new ways of responding to their relatives' behavioural expressions of pain. This is illustrated in the following extract from a session:

> T: So we have agreed that some of the responses to George's pain might not always be as helpful as you intend them to be.
>
> P: I am prepared to accept that now, yes.
>
> T: OK, I am pleased about that because I know that your intention is to help him. I know some more effective ways to do this and I would like

to spend some time today helping you to think about how you could put these into practice.

P: This is a bit like what I've seen on TV—teaching parents different ways of responding to their children.

T: Some of what I am going to suggest is probably based on the same ideas to what you have seen. The basic idea is that it is possible to alter other people's behaviour by changing some of the ways in which other people respond to it.

P: What else can I do?

T: Well, given that your main aim is to help him, and keeping in mind that you do not want to do anything that reinforces his pain behaviours or the sick role—what would help?

P: I suppose I could do some of the things that I do already . . . but do I do them when he is not in pain, is that the idea?

T: Exactly so. If you did them when he was not showing pain behaviours then we could see if there was any changes in his ability to cope with pain.

The aims of contingency management are to reduce the frequency of reinforcement of pain behaviours and, by systematically rewarding non-pain behaviours, to increase the frequency of these as responses to pain. Treatment goals are to promote increased physical activity, reduced medication use and the prevention of unnecessary disability.

It is often suggested that ongoing medico-legal involvement is a contraindication for cognitive behavioural interventions for chronic pain problems. There are certainly times when this can compromise response to CBT, especially when ongoing legal involvement is acting as a disincentive to recovery. Some therapists decide that, as a rule, they would rather avoid therapy contracts while patients are still involved in ongoing litigation. However, others decide to assess each case individually before deciding whether the ongoing legal case might compromise responses to treatment (see Chapter 12).

Pacing

Patients need to understand the rationale for this intervention strategy which is essentially 'do what you plan to do, not what you feel like doing'. This intervention strategy is linked to monitoring which has revealed bursts of activity. A graph is drawn with two axes (the x axis is time and the y axis is amount of activity/pain intensity. Patients are asked to provide the therapist with information on their levels of activity on good and bad days. The activity ratings are plotted on the graph for each of the days that the patient is asked to provide information. In addition to determining activity level, therapists should ask patients to rate pain severity for these days. This is entered on the graph as a P value from 0 to 10. When this is plotted on the graph patients are asked to contrast pain and activity on these different days (see Figure 6.6). The following session extract illustrates how this can be used to help patients to set goals to pace their activities:

> T: Sometimes when people have been struggling with pain they find themselves trying to cram in lots of activity when they have less pain but that they pay for it afterwards. I wanted to spend some time looking at your activity levels and how they might relate to the pain you have been telling me about.
>
> P: (*Sees therapist with a graph*) A graph—oh I get it, looking at the links.
>
> T: What was your average pain rating on Monday?
>
> P: Let me see, mostly 3s, a 5 . . . 4 I'd say.
>
> T: And how much did you get done on Monday?
>
> P: Well I really pushed myself as I had so much to do before Bob comes back from the Navy. 8.
>
> T: So here? (*Plots Monday on graph*) What about Tuesday—how much did you get done then?
>
> P: Hardly anything—a 2 I would say.
>
> T: And in terms of the pain on this day what was it?
>
> P: It was an 8 all day.

Patients will hopefully appreciate the fact that they are engaging in bursts of activity and that there is a need to regulate this—i.e. doing less on a 'good day', more on a 'bad day' and thereby sustaining a similar level of activity irrespective of pain experiences (as is indicated by the dotted line on Figure 6.6). This will involve planning activity and setting goals for levels of daily activity. The concept of goal-setting and taking graded steps towards these goals is especially relevant to CBT with this patient population. The analogy of steps on a ladder can be helpful and lead to discussion about progress (taking one rung at a time) and unrealistic expectations about progression (trying to climb three rungs at once when your legs can only reach two rungs in one attempt). CBT for chronic pain is one area of application where therapists should consider having a standing agenda item on the degree of goal attainment.

SUMMARY AND CONCLUSIONS

Chronic pain is the disorder most often associated with CBT applied to chronic medical problems. This is one condition where CBT practice

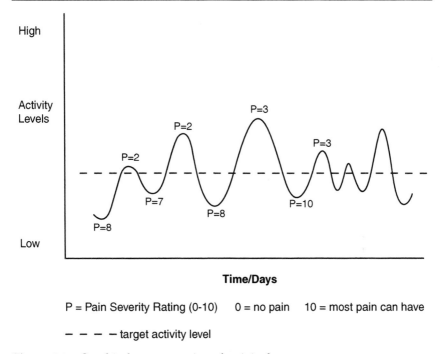

High

Activity
Levels

P=3

P=2

P=3

P=2

P=7

P=10

P=8

P=8

Low

Time/Days

P = Pain Severity Rating (0-10)   0 = no pain   10 = most pain can have

− − − − target activity level

Figure 6.6.   Graphical representation of activity bursts

emphasises the assessment, formulation and intervention with elements of physical symptom experiences. It is most important that patients understand the emphasis within the cognitive behavioural model of chronic pain management on coping and self-management, as this can enable them to gain most benefit from therapeutic strategies designed to help them to develop more effective coping strategies and to feel confident that they can minimise the effects of pain on their daily routine.

Chapter 7

DIABETES

INTRODUCTION

Diabetes is a disease characterised by failure of the pancreas to produce sufficient insulin to support the normal processes involved in the metabolism of food, and this chapter will address the most common elements of psychological problems associated with the disease. These commonly relate to the impact of diabetes on life functioning and the integration of diabetes self-management with premorbid beliefs and lifestyle. The focus will be on cognitive behavioural aspects of adjustment. For a comprehensive overview of generic psychosocial issues relating to diabetes management, treatment and service planning, see Bradley (1998).

A diagnosis of diabetes has major implications for the psychological and social functioning of patients (Wilkinson, 1981) and requires patients to be able to devote significant time and energy to the self-management of the disease. The success with which patients can integrate this with their lifestyles clearly relates to the extent to which diabetes-specific events interact with pre-existing beliefs, thoughts, feelings and behaviours. Diabetes is often associated with the occurrence of psychological problems and psychological disorders, and, unfortunately, these can compromise patients' ability to engage in optimal self-management. This can further exacerbate psychological problems and results in patients becoming trapped in a vicious cycle. The picture can become further complicated by psychological reactions that can have a negative impact on the experience of symptoms of diabetes themselves. This bi-directional influence, where diabetes influences psychological health which, in turn, influences an individual's ability to address self-management demands, is depicted in Figure 7.1 Cognitive behavioural therapists will find it easier to structure their assessment, formulation and treatment when they take account of the psychological impact of diabetes, psychosocial elements of self-management and the interface between them. This chapter will outline the key features of cognitive behavioural assessments of diabetes-related

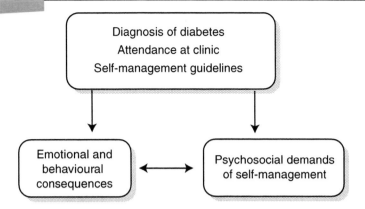

Figure 7.1. Bi-directional nature of psychological aspects of diabetes care

psychological factors, how to formulate patient experiences and plan intervention strategies to take account of these.

For many years the guiding philosophy of diabetes care was that patients modify their lives to fit with the demands and needs of their illness. In recent years this has changed towards enabling patients to fit diabetes into their lives. Most of the intervention strategies within this chapter aim to promote effective self-management of the disease, minimise psychological problems which arise as a direct result of the disease and its consequences, and, more commonly, the subtle and often complex interaction between these factors. The diagnosis of diabetes involves patients having to accept the need for a complete change in lifestyle as well as acknowledgement that diabetes is associated with an increased risk of later physical health problems. Indeed, patients have to live with the knowledge that the risk of developing these later effects is directly related to the success with which they are able to integrate lifestyle changes with premorbid lifestyle. The main areas upon which cognitive behavioural therapists might focus are the stress and daily hassles of living with diabetes, psychopathology in diabetes, the psychological consequences of diabetic crises, and family problems which relate to the diagnosis of diabetes in a family member (Rubin & Peyrot, 1992).

ASSESSMENT

Cognitive behavioural assessments of diabetes are most easily carried out, first, by determining the psychological impact of the diagnosis; second, by focusing upon cognitive and behavioural aspects of self-management; and third, by examining the interaction of pre- or co-existing psychological and social factors with diabetes care.

Patient Interview

Assessment of the psychological impact of diabetes can often be conveniently structured around the chronology of a patient's diabetes. The time at which patients are referred for CBT will obviously determine the extent to which this involves a review of many past events, involving patient ability to recall historical details. Referral some years after initial diagnosis may require therapists to facilitate recall by making frequent summaries. When patients have had diabetes for many years, they may have had prior experiences of diabetic crises or have experienced events which they regard as personally salient and significant in the course of their lives with diabetes ('What events stick out as the most important ones during the time that you have had diabetes'?). Assessment of this is crucial as it may provide information which links the occurrence of these with the development or activation of beliefs about diabetes and its management (essential in constructing a case formulation). For some, these episodes will be the critical incidents which mediated psychological problems that developed as a result. A review of the history of the illness enables the patient and the therapist to understand the main events and how these relate to cognitive and behavioural aspects of life with diabetes. This might include admissions to hospital as a consequence of complications or poor glycaemic control. When patients with a long history of diabetes are referred, assessments should be conducted to focus upon why psychological problems have developed recently and not prior to this.

PSYCHOLOGICAL ASPECTS OF DIABETES

In assessing the impact of diabetes, the therapist and the patient may find it helpful to think about the various domains which make up quality of life. By considering each one it is possible to outline the ways in which the diagnosis has influenced each life domain. Coverage of the physical health domain might involve assessment of pain and discomfort, sleep and rest, energy and fatigue, mobility, activities of daily living, dependence on medicines/aids and work capacity. Further domains include social relationships, where assessment coverage should be factors such as personal relationships, social support and sexual activity. Assessment of the environmental domain comprises financial resources, freedom, physical safety and security, health and social care, accessiblity and quality, home environment, opportunities for acquiring new information and skills, participation in and opportunities for recreation/leisure activities, physical environment and transport.

> T: It is important for me to understand how diabetes has influenced your life up until now. This way we can work out how your thoughts, feelings and coping strategies have been influenced by past events related to the diabetes.
>
> P: OK.
>
> T: If we think of your life as having various domains—physical health, psychological domain, social relationships and an environmental domain, we can take each one so that I can find out how diabetes relates to it.
>
> P: I see.
>
> T: Starting with physical health—how would you say having diabetes has effected your sleep?
>
> P: It hasn't.
>
> T: What about your ability to work?
>
> P: Well that is a different story. I worry about that all the time—since I had to take time off when I was having problems with erratic blood sugar levels.

Diabetes necessitates the need to adhere to a specific self-management regimen. The nature and impact of this was eloquently described by Watts (1980):

> He needs to follow a strict diet, both as far as what he eats and when he eats are concerned. Unless he is a relatively mild diabetic he will need to give himself insulin injections once or possibly twice a day. He will need to correct the insulin, measure the correct dosage and administer it hygienically at the correct time. He will also be asked to test his urine daily, interpret the tests correctly and take appropriate action if the results are not within the acceptable range.

Therapists should ensure that their assessments cover the precise nature of a patient's self-management routine. Patients should be asked about their thoughts and feelings concerning this, and should be encouraged to conduct baseline monitoring of aspects of their self-management routine. This can be introduced after assessment of their patients' understanding of the need for self-management, their feelings and thoughts about this, and its impact on the quality of their lives. The basic structure of a Weekly Activity Schedule can be used to monitor such matters. When screening or when the problem list suggests problems with the integration of self-management with daily routine, patients can use the cells of the Activity Schedule to outline the times when they believe that their diabetes has interfered with their lives in an unacceptable way (see Figure 7.2). Monitoring in this way can also be tailored to include the presence of depressed mood or the occurrence of idiosyncratic elements of patient presentation such as family arguments relating to diabetes.

T: You think there may be times when it is difficult to fit the demands of diabetes within your life?

P: Definitely, yes.

T: That's something that it would be helpful to explore in more detail. I would like to give you a Weekly Activity Diary and show you how to fill it in.

P: I have a diary which I could fill out for you.

T: That will be a help if you are used to filling out a diary—look at this one here. The days of the week are written along the top and each day is divided into hourly segments. The idea is that you fill in what you are doing each day. I am also going to ask you if you can note when you monitor your blood sugar, when you take insulin and, importantly, to mark when aspects of your self-management are a problem.

P: How do I fit all that in the small spaces?

T: You only need a word or two for the activities and the other things can be marked by a B for times when you test your blood sugar, I for insulin and a * for problem times.

P: I would never have thought of that.

T: That way we can look at this in more detail next time—you will also have made an important step forward in applying CBT.

Patients often describe their experiences of diabetes in idiosyncratic terms and sometimes homework assignments can consist of sentence completion methods of assessing cognitions relating to diabetes ('Diabetes is . . .'; 'The worst part about living with diabetes is . . .'). Patients can also be asked to complete the Illness Perception Questionnaire and subsequent assessment sessions can be structured around responses to this measure.

T: As you mentioned, part of your homework from last time was to complete this measure called the Illness Perception Questionnaire. I will look over it while you are filling in this week's Wellbeing Questionnaire. One of the things I want to put on the agenda today is to talk more about how you have answered this. Would that be OK with you?

P: Yes, I hope I have filled it in correctly.

T: It seemed fine to me and has given me material to find out more about your thoughts on diabetes. Was there something else that you wanted to place on the agenda today?

P: I am not sure about how this therapy is going to help me.

T: OK. Let's put that on the agenda. 'How might cognitive behavioural therapy help with your adjustment to diabetes?' I might be able to link that to some of your responses on the questionnaire, so I suggest that we start with that. Was there anything that you wanted to ask me about the questionnaire ?

P: No.

T: You have written here that you disagree with the statement that your illness is not a serious condition. What makes you think that?

Time	Monday	Tuesday	Wednesday	Thursday	Friday	Saturday	Sunday
7 - 8am							
8 - 9am							
9-10am							
10-11am							
11-12noon							
12-1pm							
1-2pm							
2-3pm							
4-5pm							
6-7pm							
7-8pm							
8-9pm							
10-11pm							

For each hour, note your activity and use the following abbreviations to indicate whether you administer insulin or check your blood, or if there is a problem which you want to discuss.

I = insulin administered

B = checked blood glucose

* = problem to discuss

Figure 7.2. Weekly Activity Schedule for diabetes monitoring

Assessment coverage might include discussion of prior life experiences characterised by the need to adhere to or comply with a set of guidelines or recommendations. This is an important element in the assessment of patients for whom adherence to diabetes self-management guidelines is proving to be a problem. Some patients may have had lifelong problems complying with advice or organising themselves to any degree. Those elements of self-management in which patients have more confidence should be assessed. Patients may have had the experience of conquering prior problems and this information will be important in planning certain aspects of CBT targeted at the promotion of self-management. Specific diary monitoring of blood glucose levels, timing of blood glucose monitoring, diabetes symptoms, diet and exercise can help to identify the extent to which there are problems which need to be targeted in treatment. 'In vivo' assessment may be possible for patients who find it difficult to access thoughts and feelings about their self-management. Blood sugar testing and the administration of insulin can be arranged within the session for this purpose. Here, patients are advised that difficulties in providing information on their feelings and thoughts might be easier if they are given help to do this while engaging in self-management behaviours.

Dietary management is an important element of the daily demands of patients. Recommendations on diet for patients with diabetes are less restrictive than was once the case. Patients often have beliefs about the dietary demands of diabetes which are based on experiences of patients who were diagnosed some years ago and/or which relate to a life of 'diabetic' foods ('I will never be able to enjoy my food again'). Many are surprised to find that it will not be the deprived existence which they intially imagined. Schulnt et al. (1999) have suggested that psychosocial assessments should ascertain what, when, where, why and how much a person eats. Premorbid diet and patient's thoughts and feelings about the dietary changes associated with the diagnosis are important as these may become an integral part of later therapy sessions. The role of eating in the patient's life generally can be assessed and, when relevant, monitoring of food intake can be combined with monitoring of variables such as mood or situation. Patients have often already completed food diaries for dieticians.

Significant others may become frustrated by a patient's failures to adhere to self-management recommendations. This can include healthcare professionals and, when this seems to be the case, it is important to elicit information on the cognitive, behavioural and emotional dimensions. The responses of other people can be determined by focusing on one or more discrete examples of situations where their diabetes has become the focus of an interaction. This might be at an out-patient appointment or when someone close observes them administering insulin by injection or comments on their diabetes. In some cases, interview of significant others (including doctors and nurses) can provide crucial information on perceptions about patients.

T: I think you know that Mrs Bogue is attending the CBT clinic for assessment and treatment of her depression.

S: Yes, Dr Smythe told me that he asked for her to be seen.

T: I wanted to find out something of your thoughts and feelings about her—as I know you have been visiting regularly since her husband's accident. (*Patient's husband died in climbing accident*)

S: She is an interesting lady.

T: What do you find most interesting about her?

S: She seems to have a strange way of viewing her diabetes.

T: What precisely do you find strange?

S: The way she thinks that diabetes is something which she can ignore— it is almost as if she doesn't understand what could happen.

T: You find that strange—the fact that she seems to ignore her diabetes. Is that something you have thought when she has been at the clinic?

S: Yes.

T: How do you feel when you think in this way?

S: I know that I get frustrated and I think I am probably a bit short with her if I am really honest. You'll think that I am terrible.

Screening assessment may reveal the presence of sexual complications. Erectile dysfunction is present in up to 50% of men with diabetes. These problems should also be subject to a comprehensive cognitive behavioural assessment. This assessment should cover sexual activity before problems developed, assessment of function, beliefs about the origins and maintaining factors for the problem and a detailed review of a recent problem episode. Patients with diabetes are occasionally referred when medical staff become convinced that they are intentionally manipulating their insulin to produce unhelpful fluctuations in blood sugar levels. The content of assessments of this group of people requires high levels of expertise and sensitive management if therapists are to be able to engage patients and elicit reliable and valid information. However, therapists should not be diverted from assessing this situation in the same manner as they would with someone when these suspicions were not present.

Questionnaires

Wellbeing Questionnaire

The use of assessment measures for symptoms of anxiety and depression in people with diabetes are subject to similar sorts of problems as those patients with cancer or pain. Signs and symptoms of high or low blood sugar levels confound somatic symptoms of anxiety and/or depression. The Wellbeing Questionnaire (Bradley, 1994; Bradley & Gamsu, 1994) is a 22-item questionnaire which assesses patient responses using a four-point Likert scale from 3 (All the time) to 0 (Not at all). There are four subscales: anxiety, depression, energy and positive wellbeing. The questionnaire has benefits in that it includes items to cover issues such as energy and positive wellbeing, which are important for the measurement of progression toward goals. Some of the items from this measure are outlined in Table 7.1.

Table 7.1   Sample items* from the Wellbeing Questionnaire (Bradley, 1994)

I feel that I am useful and needed
I feel downhearted blue
I have been waking up feeling fresh and rested
I have lived the life I wanted to
My daily life has been full of things that were interesting to me
I have felt well adjusted to my life situation

* These items are reproduced here with the permission of Professor Clare Bradley, copyright holder of the W-BQ 22 and W-BQ 12. Those wishing to use one of these instruments should contact Prof. Bradley for permission and updates on the Questionnaires at Health Psychology Research, Department of Psychology, Royal Holloway, University of London, Egham, Surrey, TW20 0EX.

Perceived Control of Diabetes Scale

Bradley (1994) has developed the Perceived Control of Diabetes Scales to assess an individual's beliefs about control of his diabetes. The measure, based on the Multidimensional Health Locus of Control Scale, takes account of the specific needs of people with diabetes. It enables therapists to obtain subscale scores on 'personal control', 'medical control' and 'situational control'. There are versions available for patients with insulin or tablet-treated diabetes, and patients are asked to think about the degree to which hypothesised events are caused and/or controlled by various factors (see Table 7.2 for sample items). This measure is particularly useful in conceptualising patient motivation and self-management behaviour.

FORMULATION

Problem-level Formulation

Problem-level formulations of difficulties with self-management should focus upon those elements of diabetes self-management with which

Table 7.2 Sample items* from Perceived Control of Diabetes Scales (Bradley, 1994)

Imagine that you have successfully avoided the complications of diabetes such as problems with your feet (*Positive Outcome*)

Imagine that for several days you have found high levels of sugar when you tested your blood or urine (*Negative Outcome*)

To what extent was the cause due to something about you?
To what extent was the cause due to the treatment recommended by your doctor?
To what extent was the cause something to do with other people or circumstances?
To what extent was the cause due to chance?
To what extent was the cause controllable by you?
To what extent was the cause controllable by your doctor?
To what extent do you think that you could have foreseen the cause of x?

* These items are reproduced here with the permission of Professor Clare Bradley, copyright holder of the Perceived Control of Diabetes Scales. Those wishing to use one of these instruments should contact Prof. Bradley for permission and updates on the Questionnaires at Health Psychology Research, Department of Psychology, Royal Holloway, University of London, Egham, Surrey, TW20 0EX.

patients have most problems. If patients have problems with all aspects then it may be necessary to construct individual problem-level formulations for dietary advice, exercise, blood glucose monitoring and insulin administration. Self-management problems usually relate to thoughts which minimise the importance of self-management or accentuate the negative aspects of this. Occasionally there will be non-diabetes-related thoughts, feelings, behaviours which compromise the ability to implement self-management and these too must be adequately described at the problem level. Interactions with other people are often influenced by thoughts about being controlled or criticised and can cause problems in a wide variety of situations, each of which can be formulated on an individual basis. These can also be linked in case-level formulations when they can be traced to cross-situational beliefs about how others are involved with the impact of diabetes on their lives ('If people would stop sticking their noses in then I would be fine').

Stress can cause problems with glycaemic control. The hypothesised pathway of this link should be outlined in a problem-level formulation. This may be a direct psychophysiological effect of stress, or it could be the behavioural disruption which is secondary to stress which has disrupted patient ability to manage self-care behaviour. Stressors resulting from other factors can be formulated at the problem level and linked with diabetes in the case-level formulation. Cognitive contributors to stress usually relate to a perceived coping incapacity which (even among patients who have acceptable coping strategies) may paradoxically result in self-management problems which then reinforce perceptions of poor coping. Some examples of problem-level formulation which include these factors are outlined in Figures 7.3 and 7.4).

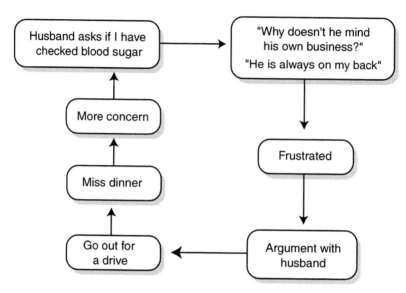

Figure 7.3.   Problem-level formulation (diabetes)

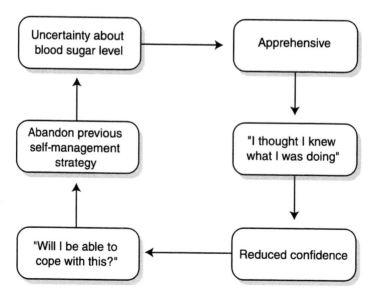

Figure 7.4.   Problem-level formulation (diabetes)

Automatic thoughts relating to themes of acceptance and non-acceptance of diabetes, the course of the disease and opinions on medical advice are often related to problem emotions and behaviours. Patients may find it difficult to accept that the administration of exogenous insulin does not solve or prevent all diabetes-related problems. Acceptance-related thoughts often mediate anger or frustration, but may not necessarily be expressed directly with regard to diabetes. Problem-level formulations can highlight how patients have thoughts which, although unrelated to diabetes, are identical to the predominant themes in their thinking about diabetes.

The concept of 'seemingly irrelevant' decisions can be helpful in considering patient responses which are characterised by unhelpful behaviours such as comfort eating and drinking. This concept was developed in the addictions area where patients would comment upon the fact that they 'just suddenly found themselves in a bar', or on a night out with drug-using friends. Therapist and patients were usually able to identify a subtle sequence of what became known as 'seemingly irrelevant' decisions. It was usually possible to tease out every step towards them being in the situation (e.g. their decision to walk home by a different route just happened to take them past a pub in which they used to drink). This is used in formulation to illustrate that it is rare for behaviours to 'just happen'. More often behaviours represent a chain of events which result in the choice to engage in the behaviour being considered. In the case of diabetes this usually related to situations or behaviours which conflict with the aims of good diabetes self-care.

Formulations of 'comfort' behaviours should outline the nature of the 'comfort', and the thoughts that are associated with positive feelings should be outlined. Might it be due to beliefs that patients have no other pleasures? Is it relief from a negative mood state? Negative feelings or situational problems that such behaviours are designed to alleviate need to be outlined according to the principles of negative reinforcement. Initially patients may describe these occurrences as unexplainable or happening for 'no apparent reason'. Review often leads to the identification of a chain of decision points and facilitative beliefs ('I've had a bad day—I deserve it') each of which increases the likelihood of engaging in a behavioural response which compromises optimal diabetes self-care.

Depressive episodes are often mediated by preoccupation with the losses associated with a diagnosis of diabetes and the impact on patient lifestyles (e.g. loss of enjoyment of food). Patients are often angry and frustrated with their diabetes but this is both triggered by and expressed in relation to factors which do not relate to diabetes. The triggers and mediators should be outlined in the problem-level formulations and the links with beliefs and feelings with diabetes should be specified in the case-level formulation. Angry episodes often link to beliefs and assumptions about acceptance, world views and self-schema. They may also be mediated by beliefs about the diabetes clinical staff and their comments and advice regarding diabetes management. Anxiety and fear reactions usually centre around catastrophic predictions about future diabetes problems (e.g. fears of hypoglycaemia) and the tendency to minimise the ability of patients and the diabetes care team to deal with the predicted problems at some point in the future. Some safety behaviours may serve to minimise the perceived risk of hypoglycaemic episodes and reduce anxiety and panic as a consequence.

Problem-level formulations should almost always aim to outline the links between negative mood states and glycaemic control (via the physiological influences of autonomic hyperarousal, which is a component of moods such as anxiety, panic, frustration and anger). When appropriate this can then be linked with subsequent misperceptions which may occur about the causes of perceived hypoglycaemia. This is crucial for patients who may subsequently be offered Blood Glucose Awareness Training (BGAT; see Gonder-Frederick et al., 2000). The contributors to hypoglycaemic unawareness are varied. Some patients may notice signs and symptoms, recognise them as indicative of low blood sugar and minimise the importance of acting; others may not notice them at all; and, others still will notice them but attribute them to unrelated factors. The way in which hypoglycaemic unawareness is formulated will impact upon the decisions which therapist and patient make about the best ways to intervene. Intervention strategies (aside from BGAT) for misattribution will obviously differ from those used by problems formulated to be the results of inattention.

Case-level Formulation

Case-level formulations should include diabetes-specific problem formulations and specify the way in which these relate to non-diabetes-specific problems. An example of this would be when a patient has discrete problems such as non-optimal adherence to self-management advice as well as frustration with problems meeting deadlines at work. Patients with acceptance-related problems often have premorbid beliefs characterised by an external locus of control. Patients who focus upon advances in biomedical science often have problems assimilating information about the limitations of medical and nursing staff to guarantee a problem-free time with diabetes. An example of this might include: 'If I put my trust in the doctors, then I should have no problems with diabetes'.

Life Experiences

Gran had diabetes "but she died of old age"
No major problems "sailed through life really"
Difficulty accepting diabetes when it was diagnosed
Critical boss

Traits
Optimistic

Formation of Beliefs

I don't need to worry about diabetes
Things generally work out well for me
If something's wrong with my diabetes it's up to the doctors to sort it out
Other people are too stressed by unimportant things

Critical Incidents

Pressure from boss at work

Case-level variables

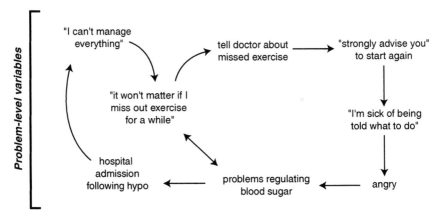

Problem-level variables

"I can't manage everything"

"it won't matter if I miss out exercise for a while"

tell doctor about missed exercise

"strongly advise you" to start again

"I'm sick of being told what to do"

hospital admission following hypo

problems regulating blood sugar

angry

Figure 7.5. Case-level formulation (diabetes)

Diabetes clinical staff may tend to take credit for successes and blame patients for failures. This can cause problems with patients who are already sensitised to criticism, and this should be outlined in the case-level formulation. The nature of pre-existing psychological vulnerabilities to diabetes-related psychosocial morbidity should also be outlined in the case-level formulation as these may relate to perfectionism schema, triggered by the need for vigilance and attention to self-management. Pre-existing fatalistic, pessimistic or optimistic beliefs can moderate the impact of the daily demands of diabetes management as knowledge about diabetes and its management can be one of the key factors which pervade various psychological problems associated with diabetes. Information-processing patterns that are outlined in the problem-level formulation can become generalised, and these should be outlined in the case-level formulation—for example, someone may have a viglilance for diabetes problems that becomes generalised to almost every life situation. Patients may become vigilant not just for fluctuations in blood sugar levels but for all physical symptoms. Patients may also begin to attempt to strive for the same degree of control over relationships, work or other life domains that they exert in controlling their blood sugar. Some patients have a general tendency towards the reporting of negative affect and bodily disturbances and this can often explain many of the components in a case-level formulation (Deary, Clyde & Frier, 1997).

In some cases it is possible to trace problems with adherence to long-standing beliefs about inability to cope or low self confidence (I am helpless; I cannot manage things on my own). Life events and/or other non-diabetes-related problems resulting from these factors can be incorporated into the case-level formulation. The locus of control of patients can have an impact on more than one element of adjustment to diabetes, and can include decisions about preferred method of insulin administration (injection or subcutaneous insulin infusion pump); responses to advice to modify levels of exercise and/or components of dietary pattern and reactions to unanticipated problems or complications with diabetes. Any complications which have occurred with the course and management of diabetes need to be outlined in the case-level formulation, particularly with reference to how these might have influenced intermediate beliefs about diabetes (e.g. There's no point trying with my diabetes as I still get complications). These events should be outlined in terms of whether they are critical incidents.

Dietary restrictions may trigger psychological problems among patients who are already vulnerable to problems by virtue of schemata regarding differences in core elements of self concept such as worth or appearance and assumptions which may link these with weight and eating behaviour. Prior psychological problems (particularly depression) may make some patients vulnerable to problems with self-criticism or reduced motivation. Links with prior procrastinatory beliefs or task-interfering thoughts can be outlined and then linked with current motivational problems. Patients who have become preoccupied by diabetes often report that their lives are 'ruled' by it. This can be outlined in a case-level formulation where the contrast between prior recreational and social activities can act as a trigger to problems such as hopelessness. The sense of being overwhelmed by diabetes can become a self-fulfilling prophecy and case-level formulations should specify the ways in which this may have occurred.

TREATMENT STRATEGIES

Many of the cognitive and behavioural intervention strategies that are used with psychological aspects of diabetes need to be built on a foundation of acceptance that patients have a serious illness which has potentially serious consequences. Patients also need to accept that this is something that they have control over (or can learn to have control over). The seriousness of the diagnosis need not act as a major obstacle to experiencing a good quality of life free from significant physical or mental health problems. Cognitive behavioural treatment strategies seek to enable patients to address discrete psychological problems and maximise their effectiveness regarding the self-management of diabetes. Common treatment goals with this patient group relate to reducing negative mood states, improving elements of self-care and directly or indirectly improving glycaemic control.

Educating and Promoting Acceptance

Problems with acceptance often relate to elements of the diabetes illness representation which are distorted or inaccurate (e.g. 'People with diabetes never have fun'; 'People with diabetes need amputations eventually'). There are a variety of strategies which could be implemented in this scenario. Formulation of acceptance problems usually consists of either an absence of information about diabetes, distorted information about diabetes or an interaction of pre-existing problems which compromise the process of adjustment. Acceptance becomes easier when diabetes becomes associated with more positive representations and greater levels of self-efficacy regarding self-management. If problems with acceptance are confined to patient problems with self-management then addressing them may simultaneously enhance levels of acceptance.

There is evidence from meta-analytic studies that education about the management of diabetes can result in some positive changes in self care and health status. Indeed, many more 'complex' interventions will not succeed if patients do not understand or do not have ongoing access to basic information about diabetes, the rationale for medical advice and the principles of treatment. In saying this, providing basic and general information about the condition in the absence of clinically relevant and personalised information is likely to have limited value. Much of the focus of CBT for diabetes-related problems relates to the medical management of the disease. This presents therapists with many opportunities to provide information. Indeed, it is often easier to personalise the provision of information when it is integrated with other intervention strategies (e.g.

self-management training or CBT of depressive symptoms which are compromising self-care behaviour).

This approach to integrating information provision with the implementation of other cognitive behavioural treatment strategies is illustrated in the following extract from a session where a patient has difficulties accepting that he has an illness that will involve having to regulate his lifestyle for the rest of his life:

T: One of the problems that you were particularly eager to address was your difficulty accepting the diagnosis.

P: I cannot get my head round it all.

T: How have you been feeling when you think about the fact that you have diabetes?

P: Desolate.

T: What have you been thinking when you have been feeling desolate?

P: My whole life is turned upside down, I will never feel confident again—there's no point.

T: That sounds dreadful for you.

P: It has been the worst few weeks of my life, it really has.

T: So many of your difficulties accepting the diabetes relate to thoughts about your life now and predicting that you will never have confidence again.

P: Most of them do, yes.

T: Have there been particular things that you have been told that stick in your mind when you are thinking this way?

P: I find it difficult to understand what is wrong with me—I just know that it is serious.

T: Do you think that not understanding what is wrong has any relationship to your negative thoughts about the impact on your life now and in the future?

P: I don't know what I think.

T: It seems to me that, because you are unsure, you have created all sorts of problems in your head.

P: I suppose I have.

T: How about we arrange to write down some of the thoughts you have had, get you information on diabetes and then look back at the thoughts to see if the information helps you to challenge them?

P: Well, if you think it will help.

T: It might. If it does not then there are other things we can do to help you with the thoughts you have had.

Blood Glucose Awareness

Many patients report uncertainties about the signs and symptoms of blood sugar changes which may require them to implement a response. Patients also vary in their ability to detect the common symptoms of low blood sugar accurately. This variation is usually attributable to inattentiveness, misinterpretation, poor knowledge about diabetes and/or a combination of all of these factors. BGAT has been developed as a psycho-educational intervention to address these factors, and it has many features in common with a cognitive behavioural approach to diabetes care. Therapists can incorporate elements of this into their therapy and/or may wish to implement the BGAT protocol. The incorporation of strategies to promote optimal identification of blood sugar levels (as part of a generic CBT approach) is most likely to be appropriate when this has been compromised by symptoms of depression and/or anxiety.

Therapists should be satisfied that patients understand why blood glucose monitoring is being recommended. This may seem obvious; however, there are some patients who are unable to elaborate on the rationale for monitoring other than reporting that the 'doctor told me to'. There are also patients who may have a basic understanding but little appreciation of how to translate this into action. When screening reveals limited understanding or negative beliefs in this regard, therapists can address this by using treatment strategies such as cost–benefit analyses. These can enhance awareness of the disadvantages of not regularly testing their blood. Cost–benefit analyses should not adopt a purely short-term view of advantages and disadvantages. Short-term disadvantages may need to be weighed against longer term disadvantages. Patients with appreciation and experience of short-term advantages are much more likely to be able to derive maximum benefit when they have experienced (and remembered) a short-term advantage, and therapists may need to draw the patient's attention to this ('I notice that you are less depressed since you started testing your blood sugar more regularly. Have you noticed this?').

Patients should be invited to keep a diary of blood glucose levels (see Figure 7.6). This provides a structure for the recording of symptoms and blood glucose levels. When patients have completed their diary they need to review this with therapists to identify which symptoms were present when their blood sugar was low and which symptoms were not present when their blood sugar was not low. Cox, Gonder-Frederick and Clarke (1996) suggest that patients be encouraged to use the following questions to review times when they have inaccurately estimated their blood sugar levels: 'What subtle cues did I miss?'; 'Why didn't I notice them?'; 'Was I

Date	Time	I	F	E	Symptoms & Performance cues	Est.	Actual	Missed cues	What did I learn? What can I do to improve awareness?

reproduced by permission of Dr. D. Cox (Cox et al., 1993)

List the date and time. I, F and E refer to most recent insulin, food and exercise. Write M, L or U to indicate if you took more, less or usual amounts of insulin, food or exercise. Next, write in cues about blood glucose level (e.g. symptoms, disrupted performance). Then estimate your sugar level. Now take your sugar level. If your sugar level was low and you missed cues, write these down. Think about why this may have happened.

Figure 7.6.   Blood glucose monitoring diary

performing differently from usual?'; Was my insulin, food and exercise different from usual?'. The data that can be gathered with this framework enables patient and therapist to discuss elements such as attributional processes (i.e. 'Which symptoms are attributed to low blood sugar?', 'Why might this be?', 'Where did they learn this as a possible sign of low blood sugar?'). Patients who appreciate the basics of the cognitive behavioural model will find it easier to grasp why monitoring actual blood sugar and estimated blood sugar is so important. Therapists can give examples of patients where monitoring reveals that they had previously been acting on the basis of estimations which they believed to be accurate but which, in fact, turned out to be inaccurate. Patients begin to appreciate that their day-to-day decisions regarding self-management are based on *interpretations* of what is occurring to their blood sugar. These interpretations will vary in their accuracy levels and will be influenced by a range of cognitive, behavioural and situational factors. Accuracy levels tend to vary within and between individuals. Therapists should help patients to improve their accuracy and thereby reduce the frequency of clinically important errors.

Some patients may find that their decisions about the presence of low blood sugar has a very poor relationship with actual physiological variables and that, instead, these decisions have been made primarily on the basis of signs and symptoms which are the result of psychosocial factors. Therapists should aim to help patients to identify the symptoms which are sensitive and specific (i.e. the symptom occurs when blood sugar is low but does not occur when blood sugar is not low). Patients may find some of the ideas easier to appreciate by thinking of the idea of 'false alarms' and 'warning signals'.

T: By getting you to keep a note of the symptoms that you notice and also recording your blood sugar levels, we can begin to work out which symptoms are good signals of low blood sugar and which are not helpful in working out when your blood sugar is low.

P: The doctor said that I should do that on the basis of my blood sugar.

T: Yes, that's right. However, it is not always possible to test your blood sugar, and even when you do there may be changes between times which require your attention.

P: Oh right.

T: Today's session is to help you to think about starting to keep a diary of the times you test your blood sugar, any symptoms that you have, what you predict the blood sugar rating to be, and then the actual rating.

P: I write all that down?

T: Yes. The idea is that when you do this we can work out how accurate your estimates have been and you can slowly build up a picture of what the good signs of blood sugar changes are. If the testing shows that you have missed a cue then you can make a special note to think about this in terms of low or high blood sugar next time that you get it.

Homework assignments should focus on how patients intend to monitor or use internal and external cues as a means of enhancing blood sugar control. Strategies which are useful in enhancing homework adherence are readily applicable to this sort of homework. Examples of this might include discussion of specific dates, times and situations when patients will test blood glucose with a view to completing their self-monitoring diary and/or predicting obstacles which may impede completion of the diary. Therapists could construct experiments where patients use the cues they have learned for one day and not the next. In this way they can compare blood sugar control when using both approaches.

Promoting Self-care Behaviours

Self-care for diabetes involves a range of behaviours such as taking medication, exercising and appropriate dietary management. Self-monitoring of blood glucose is also an integral part of the self-care. Non-compliance with advice on self-management and self-care is often a source of difficulty. Fortunately, problems with compliance often respond to psychological treatments based on cognitive behavioural theory. Many self-care behaviours are straightforward to establish; however, difficulties can occur with their maintenance and generalisation. Motivation to address self-care can be compromised by depressed mood or the occurrence of diabetic complications. When patients have problems with motivation to engage in self-care, therapists should encourage patients to view this as a problem more with action than with motivation. Activity scheduling can be used to enable patients to reconceptualise motivational problems as activity planning problems. The Stages of Change Model can be helpful in helping patients to understand prior unsuccessful attempts to make changes in self-care behaviours.

Therapists should not underestimate the importance and impact of providing reinforcement for progress in establishing, reclaiming or maintaining behavioural responses which will promote adjustment to diabetes or minimise medical complications. Assessments need to focus on what patients would find reinforcing. Some patients may benefit from the construction of self-affirmatory statements when they have made progress. However, for every patient who would respond well to such praise and/or the idea of planning in a treat when they have had success, there will be another who would perceive this as patronising and oversimplistic. Some patients find the suggestion of written flashcards with self-affirmatory statements irrelevant. Others find that this is the crucial factor in enabling them to maintain sufficient motivation to stick at their attempts to make changes in their approach to self-management. Therapists therefore need to determine which patients are most likely to respond to this treatment. In certain cases it may help to involve significant others in this element of treatment—for example, family members can be informed of the behavioural signs to look for and how they might respond to reinforce these. Many attempts to establish new behaviours (and not just those related to diabetes) fail because of a tendency for patients and staff to undermine progress, although this is often done inadvertently.

Positive data logs of the sort used to strengthen core beliefs can be used to chart progress towards the achievement of self-care goals. This can be combined with monitoring the benefits of engagement in new behaviours (in addition to the occurrence of the behaviour itself), and is particularly relevant for exercise. Patients may notice physical and psychological benefits in the early phases of establishing a new behavioural pattern—information which can be reviewed when negative thoughts about lack of progress are impeding further progress. Patients may embark upon attempts to change their self-care behaviours in the belief that occasional lapses will occur. This facilitative belief should be screened for as patients may use this as an excuse or in a way which results in it becoming a self-fulfiling prophecy. Some patients who have had periods that were characterised by good levels of self care behaviour begin to neglect themselves following the development of diabetes-related problems, and this is usually due to thoughts that their prior efforts were pointless. This can usually be addressed by modification of the negative automatic thoughts underlying those elements of self-care that have changed.

Patients sometimes have treatment problems because of the presence of a specific phobia of injections or as a result of a generalised low level of confidence in their ability to perform the constituent components. Some patients may also experience phobic responses to blood. There is good evidence that injection and blood phobias respond to cognitive behaviourally based interventions involving a combination of exposure, education and applied tension. Staff may assume that problems with injections are related to phobic responses when they are in fact mediated by a different set of thoughts. Some patients become concerned about the reactions of others to observation of their administration of insulin and/or experiencing self-critical thoughts about themselves ('I am nothing but a walking pincushion').

SUMMARY AND CONCLUSIONS

Therapists need to be mindful of conducting assessments, constructing formulations and planning treatments so that these take account of the bi-directional influences of psychological aspects of diabetes care provision and patient psychological well-being. In this way assessments, formulations and treatment plans can take account of direct (i.e. diabetes-related) and indirect factors contributing to psychological problems. When patients accept the implications of having diabetes, CBT can be focused upon enabling them to engage in optimal levels of self-care and minimise the chance of compromising their psychological health. Most intervention strategies will succeed when patients have sufficient blood glucose awareness, combined with confidence and competence in a range of self-care behaviours.

Chapter 8

DERMATOLOGY

INTRODUCTION

Despite the wide-ranging psychological consequences which can accompany skin problems, the literature on psychological aspects of dermatology is relatively small. Not surprisingly, the literature on cognitive behavioural approaches to skin problems is even smaller. However, it is possible to make some general recommendations regarding cognitive behavioural assessment, formulation and intervention with the psychological problems associated with skin disorders. This chapter will outline some general principles for working in this area and then outline in detail the way in which cognitive behavioural approaches can be tailored to the assessment, conceptualisation and treatment of itching. It is hoped that therapists will be able to apply the content of this section of the chapter to other types of dermatological symptoms experienced by patients referred for CBT. The chapter ends with coverage of the ways in which CBT may need to be altered when working with patients suffering from some of the common skin complaints who have been referred to dermatologists. Readers wishing a general introduction to the psychological aspects of dermatology are advised to consult Papadopoulous and Bor (1999).

Most psychological disorders among this group of patients relate to the behavioural impact of the condition and/or patient attitudes to appearance (Wessely & Lewis, 1989). Cognitive behavioural therapists are most likely to see patients with skin problems when they develop secondary psychological problems such as anxiety or depression associated with the social consequences of a visible skin problem. Emotions such as embarrassment or anger are often accompanied by visible changes in skin colour; stress has been associated with the course of some skin conditions and some skin problems demand high levels of self care behaviour and/or behavioural control. Dermatologists may also refer patients experiencing particular problems with the management of symptoms like itching and/or when they believe that emotional factors mediate or moderate the severity of skin problems such as psoriasis. The treatment of skin disorders may involve complicated or time-consuming treatments and this can result in psychological problems for some patients. In some cases, patients with obsessive compulsive disorder (OCD) may be referred to dermatologists and/or the skin can become the focus of other psychological problems which can be treated using CBT (e.g. delusional disorders focusing upon the skin). Therapists may need to integrate assessment of disorders like OCD with the assessment of the pertinent cognitive and behavioural dimensions of dermatological aspects of their presentation.

GENERAL ASSESSMENT ISSUES

Interview

Patients should be asked to describe the areas of skin that are affected by their problem. This provides the basis for further detailed assessment of the symptoms at each location and enables therapist and patient to have a common, shared understanding of which body parts are affected by skin problems. In some cases it is also important to know about areas that have not been affected and/or have only a historical link with presenting skin problems. It may be helpful to use body diagrams of the sort which are sometimes used in the management of chronic pain and/or which appear in medical case notes to depict which parts have been injured. The next session extract illustrates how defining the areas affected by skin problems can be helpful in structuring assessment and differentiating areas (which may not always experience identical changes in symptom pattern and severity).

T: Just to check that I understand. This area here at your groin is the one where you have most of the rash, you have described it as a tingling sensation. The same rash is also on the backs of your legs here but instead of a tingling you have a burning feeling. You are also troubled by an itching sensation over both sets of knuckles.

P: You can tell you've done this before.

T: The way you've described your symptoms is very clear and that certainly helps me. Of all of these symptoms, which one is the most upsetting for you?

P: The rash is definitely most annoying.

T: The rash on your groin or on the back of your legs?

P: Oh the back of my legs . . .

T: Do you have the burning sensation all of the time?

P: No.
T: Have you noticed that you get it at particular times of the day?
P: No, I don't know.
T: Are there things that make it better?
P: I think when I am busy the burning is less immediate if you know what I mean.
T: It grabs your attention less?
P: Yes, it is less attention grabbing.

Patient and therapist should devise a rating system to monitor the nature and severity of the skin complaint during the assessment phase of CBT. This will usually consist of rating variables such as redness, flakiness or irritation. In some cases it can be helpful to have the skin condition independently rated by dermatologists and/or specialist nurses in dermatology, and this is particularly useful for patients referred when psychological factors are believed to have a negative impact on the condition of the skin itself. Skin condition can be used as an outcome variable in these cases. It may help when working with hospital in-patients if nursing staff prompt them to make ratings for self-monitoring and/or record their own observations of the skin condition of the patient. Many skin disorders are characterised by exacerbations and periods of remission. Therapists should make sure that they understand the main differences between periods of remission and flare-ups and that they concentrate on assessing cognitive, emotional and behavioural consequences during each type of episode (as there may be important differences). Using a severity scale can help some patients to focus upon what is being asked of them and sometimes a graphical depiction of this enables therapist and patient to appreciate the nature of different experiences in light of various severity conditions.

T: Sometimes skin problems like the one you have are characterised by flare-ups and by times when the skin problems are less severe.
P: That's me too.
T: You have times when it flares up?
P: Yes, last month was horrendous—I nearly scratched myself to death.
T: That must have been when Dr McCrone referred you?
P: Yes, I was at the end of my rope . . .
T: Was last month typical of what happens during a flare up?
P: Yes, fairly typical.
T: Would you be able to take me through a typical bad day last month?
P: Yes, it is there when I wake up and there when I go to bed—and even worse in between.

> T: What is the first thing that you notice when you wake up in the morning?
> P: I feel like there are ants crawling all over the backs of my knees.
> T: Is that the burning sensation?
> P: No it starts with an itching, the burning comes later in the day.
> T: How intense is the itch when you wake up—using the scale I told you about earlier?
> P: It is about a 4.
> T: Do you get this at all when things are not as bad in general as they are now?
> P: Sometimes, at about a 1 or a 2 on the scale though.
> T: Is 4 the most intense itching that you get during a bad spell?
> P: No way, it can go up to an 8. . . . that's more usual.

Common behavioural responses to skin problems are scratching, rubbing (possibly against objects) or behaviours designed to cool the skin. Some patients will have contemplated and/or tried desperate measures to deal with their skin compaints. This may include what has been referred to as 'self-surgery' and/or the application of home-made remedies which paradoxically aggravate their skin condition. Behavioural responses can be assessed using self-report, observations (for ward-based patients) or frequency counts. Complicated rituals may develop over time and therapists should chart the elaboration which may have occurred in these over time. Some patients report that behaviours which they have developed to relieve the unpleasant sensations in their skin become less and less effective as the day, or time, progresses.

A detailed functional analysis of prior treatments and patient response to these can be useful. This often reveals less than optimal adherence to prescribed treatments ('I kept forgetting to put the cream on'). Other contextual influences which may have been operating at the time can be incorporated into formulations when this suggests that non-optimal adherence may have been compromising the effectiveness of a medical intervention. For complicated dermatological presentations it can help if patients can write down the names of skin preparations that they have tried. In rare cases, therapists may be able to work collaboratively with patients and the dermatology team to set up controlled evaluations (along the lines of single-case designs) of the impact of skin preparations on skin condition and other psychosocial variables such as attention toward skin, subjective discomfort, etc. It is unfortunate that some medical staff may still adhere to the once common belief that the absence of organic pathology to account for a skin complaint must mean that it has a psychological origin. This can negatively influence staff behaviour towards patients with skin complaints that are not readily understood by current medical advances.

Assessment of patient feelings and thoughts about staff who suggest this can reveal significant problems with satisfaction with medical care.

When patients have been diagnosed with a skin disorder it is important to assess their current treatment regime from a behavioural perspective (what they have to do, how often, under what circumstances) as concurrent behavioural demands from other elements of their life may interfere with this. The demands of managing their skin problem may interfere with other life domains.

T: What does the treatment involve?

P: I have to apply a cream three times a day.

T: Do you have to apply it this often all the time or are there times when you do things differently?

P: If it is bad I have to apply another cream when things flare up.

T: What would be happening if it was 'bad' like you say?

P: That's when I start to get lumps on the bad bits of skin.

T: Does that happen often?

P: Not that often, thankfully.

T: How does having to apply the cream fit with what you have to do on a day-to-day basis?

P: It is OK if I remember to take the cream with me. When I don't it gets really uncomfortable.

T: Are there any aspects of your life which the skin problem interferes with?

P: It can get really embarrassing if you are out with someone and, you know, you go back to their place. 'Oh by the way, don't get a fright when you see the creamy blotches on my back'—not exactly something to get you in the mood, is it?

Skin disorders are affected by environmental and situational influences such as prevailing temperature, weather conditions and/or humidity. Most patients will be aware of the way in which different environments effect their skin. Most vary in the extent that they can explain the ways in which subtle day-to-day changes in environmental exposure relate to their skin disorder. When patients are exposed to frequent changes and/or therapists are uncertain as to how important environmental variables may be, they can prescribe monitoring of skin symptom variables which takes account of different situations and/or environmental conditions. There are rare occasions when it may be necessary to collaborate with medical colleagues to set up experimental conditions to allow more controlled evaluation of the differential impact of variables such as temperature and humidity on skin.

> T: How is your skin affected by being in situations with differing levels of heat and humidity?
>
> P: My hands can go all blotchy if I start to feel clammy—Dr Myers said that it was something to do with the changes in pigmentation.
>
> T: Do you know that it is going to happen?
>
> P: No, the first that I notice is the purple shades around here. (*Points to hand*)
>
> T: Does this relate to the avoidance that you have been mentioning?
>
> P: I am not sure to tell you the truth.
>
> T: That might be something we could monitor. I just wondered if having this happen to you might generally make you more apprehensive about some situations.
>
> P: It could do, I had never thought of it to be honest—I suppose I am used to it. I don't feel too anxious about it.
>
> T: It may be nothing, the approach I want to take with this problem is to rule nothing out until we have gathered some information from the monitoring diary.

Assessments should aim to gather information regarding patient's beliefs about their skin, skin disease and its management. Many patients have unhelpful beliefs about skin disorders triggered by their diagnoses. Therapists can ask patients about what they thought about skin complaints before their diagnosis and whether any of their beliefs have changed as a result of their experience. Patient beliefs will commonly relate to themes of contagion, cleanliness and the views that other people might have of them because of this.

Patients may engage in what Leary et al. (1998) refer to as 'protective interpersonal strategies'. These commonly involve avoidance of social situations. In addition to the obvious behavioural avoidance which occurs in such scenarios, patients may expose themselves to situations but protect themselves by disengaging from the environment or intentionally diverting their attention from aspects of the situation which distress them. Patients may feel stigmatised. This can be assessed by asking patient about the degree to which they believe others are bothered by their disease, the extent to which they have experienced discrimination as a result of their skin disease and/or the nature and extent of other people avoiding them.

Patients may have encountered situations in which their skin problems have caused them real social problems. Patients do not usually have difficulty generating these examples and therapists will find them a rich source of information on the emotional, cognitive and behavioural aspects of the presenting problems. However, on the rare occasions that this is difficult it can be helpful to screen for the impact of the skin problem on the following interpersonal situations: being at work, bathing or swimming; going out in public; sexual intimacy; kissing or hugging; and shaking hands with other people.

T: Have you found that your skin problems have caused you problems in particular situations?

P: Yes . . . anytime I take my shirt off in the summer

T: What happens?

P: The guys on the building site make jokes like 'here comes lumpy'.

T: Do you find it funny?

P: They are just having a laugh.

T: Do you always think about it like that?

P: I suppose I don't always see the funny side.

T: When you don't see the funny side, what do you tend to think about what they say.

P: I feel like a freak really, like I am some sort of side show at the circus.

T: How does that make you feel?

P: Sometimes I get angry and sometimes I feel quite low about it all.

Patients may experience problems in other areas of their lives which they attribute to be related to their skin problems (but which are in fact related to other factors). Therapists should ask patients if there are areas of their lives which are unaffected by skin problems. This can make it easier to determine the pervasiveness of the impact of skin problems on overall psychosocial adjustment and their quality of life.

Self-report Questionnaires

Fear of Negative Evaluation Scale (FNES)

This measures the level of apprehension at the prospect of being negatively evaluated by other people. The original version (Watson & Friend, 1969) has 30 items and requires that respondents choose True or False for each item. Leary (1983) developed the Brief FNES. This is a 12-item version of the measure which has almost identical psychometric properties to the original scale. Respondents are asked to indicate the extent to which items are characteristic of them using a five-point Likert scale where 1 indicates 'Not at all characteristic of me' and 5 indicates 'Extremely characteristic of me'. The scores on this measure can be linked

Table 8.1   Sample items from Fear of Negative Evaluation Scale
(Watson & Friend, 1969)

I am afraid others will not approve of me
When I am talking to someone, I worry about what they may be thinking of me
I rarely worry about what kind of impression I am making on someone
I am frequently afraid that other people will notice my shortcomings
If I know someone is judging me, it has little effect on me

with the assessment of sensitivity to criticism, levels of social anxiety, and motivation to seek the approval of others. Some of the items from these measures are outlined in Table 8.1

FORMULATION

Problem-level formulation must outline how cognitive behavioural factors might relate to the experience of skin complaints. In most cases this will include how thoughts and images create negative emotional responses, difficulties coping with the presence of a skin complaint and/or result in behavioural responses which exacerbate the problem. Problem-level formulation should specify the extent to which the environment has an influence on the experience of a skin problem and whether this is a direct influence or acts as a setting condition for the influence of another variable. An example of the latter would be when patients are less likely to engage in scratching when among other people. In some cases, it may be appropriate to include emotional factors as the mechanisms underlying the experience of a skin complaint. More usually emotional factors are included as secondary factors which result in worsening a skin problem or cognitive factors which increase the likelihood of behavioural responses which either compromise optimal conditions for skin healing or directly worsen the skin problem.

For patients with comorbid dermatological and psychological disorders, the problem-level formulation should specify the way in which the occurrence of the comorbid disorder relates to the uniquely dermatological components of the patient's problem. Patients with OCD who also have eczema should have a problem-level formulation which outlines the way in which the experience of the skin problem mediates their obsessions, urge to neutralise and compulsive behavioural and cognitive responses. In some cases, the restrictive effect of treatment (e.g. need to avoid activity when wearing creams) might be the mediator for unnecessary avoidance of other situations, and this generalisation of avoidance should be covered in case-level formulation links.

Case-level formulations need to include the nature and extent to which patients have been exposed to others with skin problems. Patients with longstanding skin problems often have early experiences of skin disease and/or problems with appearance which form an integral part of the formulation. Patients who have outdated and unhelpful beliefs about the origins of skin disease should have this included in the case-level component of their formulation as this often influences the way in which patients respond to diagnosis. The progressive social isolation which can occur for patients with visible skin complaints should feature prominently in the contextual components of formulations. In such cases, links need to be made with times when patients become preoccupied with negative thoughts and images, resulting in less sources of information to evaluate their problem thoughts. The reactions of others can be critical incidents for sensitised patients. Patients with high levels of fear of negative evaluation are likely to have problems with a number of situations, and in some cases patients may have attempted self-surgery. These patients are likely to have a lowered threshold to self-injury—possibly as a result of low self-esteem which needs to be given a central role in case formulations. Treatment strategies most commonly involve targeting psychological distress which is a direct consequence of skin disease and skin problems which are affected by behavioural factors or psychophysiological processes. These will be considered in the next section which addresses cognitive behavioural assessment, formulation and treatment of itching.

ITCHING: THE APPLICATION OF CBT

Assessment

Patients should be asked about the presence, nature and frequency of itching and detailed information can be obtained from a review of a recent problematic episode of itching. Diary monitoring of itching is almost essential as this will give details on the key cognitive and emotional factors which moderate itching. This must include, as a minimum, the severity and location of itch and should almost certainly include behavioural responses to itching (see Figure 8.1), which is usually scratching. Therapists should ensure that they understand the way in which patients scratch their itch. This is best assessed by observation and patients will usually be only too willing to demonstrate (especially if they are experiencing itching during the consultation). The primary mediator of scratching is often the urge to scratch as opposed to the itch itself. 'Urge to scratch' should therefore feature in the diaries of patients. Time of day and/or the use of creams should be featured in diaries as itching often varies as a function of these factors. These diaries are best structured on an hour-by-hour basis. Some patients may find it helpful to use a counter to record the number of times they scratch. For some patients, monitoring leads to a reduction in the frequency of scratching, and when this happens it is a useful way of introducing the rationale of displacing scratching with incompatible behaviours (see Interventions below). The types of questions that may be asked to obtain information from the diaries are outlined in Table 8.2.

Complete hourly or when itching begins

Five minutes later

Situation	Itching (0-10)	Urge to scratch (0 - 10)	Response to itching What did you do?	Itching (0 - 10)	Urge to scratch (0 - 10)

Figure 8.1.   Diary monitoring of itching

Table 8.2   Examples of questions used to examine content of itching diary

What situations were you more likely to scratch in?
What situations were you less likely to scratch in?
Are there situations where the itch is more/less severe? Does the diary provide any clues to this?
How does your emotional experience relate to the presence of itching? scratching?
Does the diary help us to work out what might be happening when you get itchy but control the scratching?

In some cases diaries provide data which illustrates that periods of scratching are associated with rebound itchiness soon after the scratching has ceased, and this provides an excellent way for therapist and patient to gather evidence of the disadvantages of scratching and of its potential role as a factor responsible for increasing the overall itch severity and number of problem episodes. Diaries can be the first step in developing situational awareness. This component of diary review may need to be linked to subsequent monitoring, and by this method discoveries from diaries can be verified, and related dimensions can be explored in therapy and related to treatment strategies aimed at breaking the itch–scratch cycle.

T: Are there any other situations in this diary when you notice that you get the same intensity of itch but that you have less urge to scratch?

P: Let me see—here I do. On Tuesday when I was at my friend's house. She knows about the problems I have had with scratching—that's probably why I didn't have the same urge to scratch.

T: So in that situation having someone else who knows about the itching, and the problems which scratching has caused you, meant that you still felt as itchy but had less of an urge to scratch.

P: I suppose it did, yes.

T: Is that something you could pay special attention to next week? It may help you to work out other things which make it less likely that you will scratch.

P: Will I do that with this diary sheet?

T: We could write down here a reminder for what you are going to look out for.

Patients may develop thought control strategies to minimise the likelihood of scratching. The Thought Control Questionnaire (Wells & Davies, 1994) may be helpful in providing information on the strategies which patients have developed to manage their preoccupations with itching and scratching. These should be assessed and beliefs associated with their use elicited. Therapists should look out for patients who tell themselves not to scratch. This strategy is likely to result in greater difficulty to resist the urge to scratch as a result of the rebound effects of thought suppression (Purdon, 1999). The unhelpful role of thought suppression can be demonstrated within sessions by asking patients not to think about scratching. Some patients experience 'itchogenic' imagery, which may take the form of insects crawling over their skin and/or other thematic imagery related to itching. In addition to spontaneously occurring imagery, therapists can use imagery to help patients who have difficulties in expressing themselves to provide details on their experiences. Patients can listen to descriptions of imagery designed to induce itching and therapists can then conduct an assessment of salient dimensions. This strategy can also be used for 'in vivo' practice of treatment strategies to break the itch–scratch cycle.

Therapists should ask their patients if they have ever had any other life experiences characterised by the presence of itching and/or other unpleasant skin sensations. These memories may be triggered by current episodes of itching, as in the case of a patient referred for the treatment of a major depressive disorder which developed in response to an acute exacerbation of a skin complaint.

T: How did you feel when the itching started last week?

P: Sad . . . very low at times.

T: Is there a particular time in your mind that sticks out as being one when you felt very low?

P: Yes, Steven was out and I was in the bathroom. I had just had a bath.

T: Is that when the itching started?

P: Yes.

T: At what point did you start to feel low?

P: Not long after the itch started. (*Starts to cry*)

T: Are you feeling the sadness now?

P: Yes.

T: What is passing through your mind right at this moment?

P: I am . . . I can't . . . I am ashamed.

T: You feel sad and ashamed. . . . Is there something in your mind that makes you feel particuarly ashamed?

P: I had a sexually transmitted disease when I was a student—Euuch . . . I can still see it now. They were crawling about my private parts. I feel so dirty.

T: And every time you get this itch now from the eczema, it reminds you of that time, you get the image—then you think that you are dirty and this makes you feel low.

P: It didn't bother me too much at the time . . . it was a shock of course. Now it all comes back to me.

Formulation

Most formulations contain the itch–scratch cycle as a component (Figure 8.2). The central elements of formulating itching account for the way in which behaviours, thoughts and feelings might relate to increases in itch intensity. They also need to address mediators and moderators of the

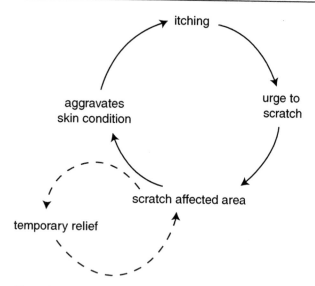

Figure 8.2.   The itch–scratch vicious cycle

urge to scratch, and monitoring diaries usually provide therapist and patient with this information. Case-level variables such as beliefs about skin disease, self-esteem and/or coping ability, can lead to patients having difficulty because of a pervasive view of themselves as worthless people without any ability to tolerate negative feeling and/or cope with problems. In extreme cases, some patients may believe that they are dirty to such an extent that they may wash themselves excessively (causing skin irritation) and/or actually feel as if their skin is dirty at such times. Although this phenomenon is more usually conceptualised as an element of a psychiatric disorder, variants can be seen among patients with less severe psychological symptoms.

Interventions

It is vitally important for therapists to empathise with the irritating and frustrating nature of itching and the overwhelming urge to scratch which patients experience. Therapists who do not do this run the risk of patients dismissing the simplicity of cognitive behavioural interventions for itching on the grounds that therapists do not understand how dreadful their experiences are and how overpowering the urge to scratch can be. It may help to pre-empt such problems by acknowledging this explicitly when CBT is being considered (see Table 8.3).

Any intervention strategy for itching needs to be implemented on the basis of an awareness of the problems that this response causes. Patients

Table 8.3 Empathising with itching and the urge to scratch

Of all the symptoms and problems which patients in my clinics have, I think that itching has to be one of the most annoying and difficult—especially the overwhelming urge to scratch which comes with it. Patients talk of the compelling urge to scratch and of how they know that scratching is something they should avoid. Anyone who has scratched an itch knows that the relief is so instant that it is almost impossible at times to prevent oneself from scratching, not to mention stop when you have started scratching.

need to appreciate that although scratching is associated with short-term gains, there are negative longer term consequences for their experience of skin problems. Some patients will readily accept this while others refuse to acknowledge the longer term associated problems. It is unlikely that patients who espouse such views will engage with interventions to reduce the frequency of scratching, and it is helpful to make sure that such patients can readily recall the unpleasant consequences of scratching. They may be able to recall this in sessions and/or when itch severity is mild. Formulations usually specify how attention is overwhelmed by the urge to scratch when an itch is experienced and it is therefore advisable to have patients write down the disadvantages of scratching on a flashcard. One of the author's patients who used this method of enhancing awarenesss of disadvantages called it her 'scratch card' (Figure 8.3). This method can be used when patients need to be reminded of the problems associated with their scratching, and reading the card at times of urges to scratch can help to suppress the urge to itch by reminding patients of its disadvantages (not to mention the fact that it involves engaging in the incompatible behaviour of picking up the card and reading it). The card can also contain prompts to other aspects of the intervention.

Although my automatic reaction is to scratch, I have discovered the following disadvantages:

1   It only helps for a few minutes
2   When I delay it, the itch and urge subside
3   I am starting to get scars from where I have been bleeding

I can try to:

A   Do something, anything else with my hands
B   Place my hands on itchy area if I need to at first
C   Phone someone — do something to take my mind of it

Figure 8.3. Scratch card

Most interventions involve substituting scratching with other behaviours. Even when therapists have acknowledged the difficulties controlling an automatic urge to scratch, some patients will still perceive these interventions as being oversimplistic and naive responses to their symptoms. The protracted experience of itching provokes a strong need among patients to communicate the extent of their plight and resist any attempts to suggest that there may be alternatives to scratching. It is important to disarm patients in an attempt to engage them in discussion about their need to change scratching. Therapeutic strategies should be presented as a 'no lose' option and patients can be reminded that such strategies will not make their problem any worse.

Agreement with the patient's belief system can sometimes unlock a therapeutic impasse. When therapists 'buy in' to this way of thinking about scratching, most patients will realise that they would be wise to at least attempt to implement the intervention before dismissing it entirely. However, there are some patients for whom it soon becomes clear that, to manage their itching, CBT is unlikely to be an appropriate strategy.

T: It has been dreadful for you. The approach to treating this is to help you begin to do something else with your hands when you get the urge to scratch

P: Don't you think I have tried that already?

T: Have you?

P: Of course.

T: Sorry, I didn't realise that. Tell me about what you did when you tried this . . .

P: Well I tried not to scratch and occupied myself by doing the crossword . . . it was useless . . . I got so annoyed that I just thought 'To damn with it, I don't care I am scratching'.

T: That was a good idea. However, it sounds as if it might have been too much too soon.

P: What do you mean?

T: I wonder if there may be more gradual ways of going from scratching to not scratching.

P: Mm.

T: This might involve first of all keeping your fingers over the area that you want to scratch, when you have confidence that you are able to do this, you could try to keep your hand over an area near to the itchy part . . . and so on, so that you are gradually changing the scratching behaviour.

P: I hadn't thought of that.

T: You can build in things like increasing the time you do this and/or decreasing the time that you scratch.

When it seems difficult for someone to substitute scratching with alternative behaviours, it may help initially for them to work towards reducing the intensity of a subjective itch. Some patients find that they are able to reduce subjective itchiness by creating imaginal representations of their itch and modifying elements of this image. This can be suggested and tried by patients as a potential strategy for reducing itch intensity.

> T: One of the things that can make it easier to break this link between itching and scratching is to work out ways of reducing the itchiness. One way of doing this is to create an image of the image and then change parts of it as a way of reducing the itchiness.
>
> P: An image?
>
> T: Yes. A picture in your mind. Do you get any pictures in your mind of the itch when it comes on?
>
> P: No.
>
> T: Do you think we could work to help you create one that we could change to see if it helps to reduce the itch?
>
> P: I could give it a try.
>
> T: When you get the itch, what sort of sensation is it—scratchy, burning?
>
> P: Just itchy really.
>
> T: Can you think of a picture that might be similar?
>
> P: Mmmm . . . nettles, as if I have just fallen on a huge pile of nettles. I can see a huge bush of nettles.
>
> T: That's a good image. OK, the idea is that we help you to make changes to the parts of the image which are most related to your itchiness and see if that helps to make you feel less itchy. What would you need to change in the image for the itch to become less intense?
>
> P: The nettles would need to be less spikey.
>
> T: How could things change in the image to make that happen?
>
> P: Well, I could cut the spikes off them.

Patients often talk about scratching as a global behavioural response and will almost always mention their difficulty in controlling its initiation and maintenance. Therapists can help patients to break down scratching behaviour into its component parts (see Figure 8.4), and in this way a greater distance can be placed between the itch and the scratch. It also provides therapist and patient with a greater number of possible intervention points.

The central component of CBT for itching is enabling patients to substitute scratching with an alternative behaviour. It is preferable if scratching is replaced with a behaviour that is incompatible with scratching (e.g. playing hand-held game, knitting, typing). This needs to be combined

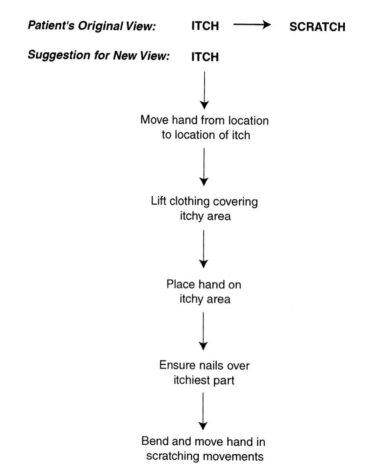

Move hand over affected area and rub

Place hand over affected area rub and keep still for a minute

Place hand over affected area, keep still for a minute and move hand to another part of my body

Place hand on another part of my body and then get on with something else

Figure 8.4.   Graded approach to interruption of itch–scratch vicious cycle

Patient's Original View: ITCH ⟶ SCRATCH

Suggestion for New View: ITCH

Move hand from location
to location of itch

Lift clothing covering
itchy area

Place hand on
itchy area

Ensure nails over
itchiest part

Bend and move hand in
scratching movements

Figure 8.5.   Steps from itching to scratching

with awareness of early warning signs for scratching. The substitution of scratching with alternatives can begin by suggesting that patients place their hands on itchy skin, leave it there for a predetermined period of time, then move their hand to their side. The time period can be lengthened and shortened according to the patient's responses to initial interventions steps. In some cases, initial touching of the skin can be in the form of rubbing or stroking if patients find that the urge to scratch is too overwhelming. The length of time can gradually be reduced within the framework of enabling patients to appreciate that it is possible to gain control over their behavioural responses. This graded approach to breaking the itch–scratch cyle is outlined in Figure 8.4.

Treatment strategies need to address reinforcement which may have previously been contingent upon scratching, and this usually takes the form of social attention (or medical/nursing staff attention). Treatment strategies should emphasise the reinforcement of non-scratching behaviour and patients can complete diaries of non-scratching using the structure of a positive data log. Therapists can ensure that significant others are aware of the need to reinforce incompatible behaviours and that there is a strategy in place to provide patients with reinforcement when data are entered in their positive data logs.

When patient and therapist have decided upon the replacement behavioural response to scratching patients can begin to imagine themselves implementing the alternative response. This can be done in clinic or as homework.

T: Right, we have discussed then that when you get the urge to scratch you are going to try this graded way of breaking the vicious cycle that has built up.

P: Yes, I will honestly try my best.

T: Do you think that there will be any problems with doing this, problems with trying it out?

P: Well, I suppose there might be.

T: What sorts of problems might occur?

P: I might just say 'forget it' at the last minute . . . no, I know that I have already thought of how to respond to these thoughts.

T: I can't remember if you wrote that on the scratch card—did you?

P: Yes, it is there in capitals. (*Laughs*)

T: Do you think it might help if you imagined yourself doing this? . . . That way you can begin to appreciate and imagine what it might be like to try it.

P: I could try.

CBT AND SPECIFIC SKIN DISORDERS

Therapists with experience of the assessment, formulation and treatment of the psychological aspects of itching will find that there are many similarities between this and working with other symptoms of skin disorders. The basic principles are linking emotions, thoughts and behaviours with the experience of, reactions to, and psychological impact of the symptom. There will be enormous variability in the extent to which these factors can be identified between patients. For some, skin problems and their reactions to them will be completely determined by their feelings. For another group of patients, cognitive behavioural assessment will reveal little link between these factors. In these cases, therapists can usually be of most help to patients by strongly reinforcing this in their reports to dermatologists (who may have been wrongly assuming that there were psychological factors in the patient's presentation). There are, of course, times when patients with skin disorders develop social anxiety disorder or depressive disorder and CBT can be implemented without a major need to alter the process or content of therapy to account for skin problems.

It is often difficult for therapists to identify ways in which CBT may be relevant to the problems of patients with skin problems. Patients often assume that a prior unsuccessful medical intervention cannot be implemented again. They tend to think that if it has previously failed to bring relief to dermatological symptoms then this will always be the case. Assessment of context and treatment adherence at the time of previous treatment may open up the possibility of interventions which involve the reimplementation of treatment strategies in combination with cognitive and behavioural strategies.

There are aspects of CBT which can be helpful for some other common skin disorders. Hyperhydrosis is characterised by excessive sweating of the palmar, axillary, facial and anogenital sweat glands. The resultant secretions and associated odour are often sources of anxiety to affected patients. They may become concerned that others will notice that this has occurred and/or the smell which can be produced. Some patients also present with psychophysiologically mediated sweating which is superimposed on an already abnormal sweat response. Assessment should focus upon sweating severity with the aim of differentiating times when emotions or situations result in anxiety-induced sweating. Patients may also have had to deal with the embarrassment of others noticing their wet hands, and this should be featured in formulations. In some cases, sweating is so severe that patients may have to purchase protective footwear and/or dispose of footwear very often. Treatment strategies to promote assertiveness can be helpful. Cognitive behavioural strategies to reduce arousal can help people with sweating which is mediated by this mechanism.

Trichotillomania may present to dermatology clinics. Cognitive behavioural assessments should focus upon antecedents to the urge to pull hair and formulations should emphasise the way in which this is reinforced. This is usually anxiety reduction and, in some cases, environmental reinforcement. Patients can be encouraged to address their anxiety using other strategies and develop competing responses to hair pulling, and therapy may involve verbal reattribution of automatic thoughts that support hair pulling. In some cases, patients are advised to send pulled-out hairs to the therapist; in others, exposure of the affected scalp can sometimes reduce the frequency of hair pulling. Patients can be taught to increase their tolerance to previous antecedents by engaging in behaviours such as running their fingers through their hair. Shirley (1997) outlines the application of some of these strategies in a case study.

SUMMARY AND CONCLUSIONS

Despite the lack of a substantial amount of literature on cognitive behavioural aspects of skin disease, it is possible to offer some guidelines for cognitive behavioural therapists who wish to work with patients who have developed psychological problems as a consequence of having a skin disease. The cognitive behavioural model can usefully be applied to assessing and conceptualising behavioural responses to symptoms such as itching, and is particularly suited to addressing the interpersonal consequences of skin disease. CBT approaches to dermatology emphasise the importance of understanding emotional and behavioural responses to skin problems, conceptualising how these may relate to the nature and course of the skin disease, and linking this with the psychological consequences of the condition.

Chapter 9

SURGICAL PROBLEMS

INTRODUCTION

A substantial number of patients with longstanding physical health problems will have consulted a surgeon at some point during the course of their illness. Many of the medical problems which are outlined in this book often involve assessment by surgeons and/or surgical intervention. Surgical treatments are commonly offered as first-line treatment for breast and colorectal cancers. Patients with serious cardiac pathology undergo cardiovascular surgery such as coronary artery bypass grafting. Orthopaedic surgeons may be involved with the problems of people who have been experiencing chronic pain, and plastic surgeons are commonly involved with the care of patients with disfiguring skin complaints. Patients with chronic medical problems may find themselves in a position where they must address the psychological aspects of adjustment to both their chronic medical problem and the need for surgery. Indeed, some patients find the process of surgery more difficult to cope with than the everyday demands of their medical condition. This chapter is concerned with the generic cognitive and behavioural aspects of the surgical process (as opposed to a detailed examination of the impact of specific surgical procedures). It will focus on the important areas for cognitive behavioural assessments at pre- and post-operative stages and highlight the key concepts in problem- and case-level formulations for patients who have had, or are about to have, surgery. Intervention strategies for preparing patients for surgery will be outlined and the special considerations which need to be addressed in cognitive behavioural work with patients who have been disfigured by surgery will be covered. The pertinent issues relating to cosmetic surgical procedures and transplantation surgery will then be outlined.

ASSESSMENT

The assessment of all surgical patients must seek to address the precise cognitive and behavioural elements of what it means for the patient to be contemplating or experiencing surgery. For some patients this will involve the assessment of their prior experiences of surgery. Have they had surgery which has resulted in successful outcomes? What have been their experiences of post-operative recovery processes and events? It will also involve taking account of the way in which this may have interacted with their experiences of physical ill health and/or prior psychological problems. The nature and complexity of cognitive behavioural assessment of surgical patients depends therefore on the unique nature and history of a patient's individual physical health problems; the nature and history of that person's experience of surgery and surgeons; and the presence or absence of significant psychological morbidity. Much of the information outlined in Chapter 2 on assessment applies to the assessment of patients under the care of the surgical team. The following sections will address elements of cognitive behavioural assessment which relate specifically to the needs and situation of surgical patients.

General Assessment Issues in Surgical Settings

Therapists who work frequently with surgical patients may find it helpful to spend some time observing the surgical procedures that their patients will experience. This can provide invaluable insights into the events which patients will be exposed to before, during and after their surgery. It can help therapists to fully appreciate the patients' surgical experiences and provide a useful source of information for assessing, formulating and treating psychological aspects of adjustment to and problems relating to surgery. Knowledge of what is involved with common types of surgery can also assist with assessment of a patient's surgical history.

Assessing surgical history can provide therapists with a useful framework for eliciting information in relation to key events across the course of a patient's life—with particular reference to physical health problems and especially the patient's surgical management and treatment. This should not only include surgery for chronic medical problems but should also assess details of any surgical admissions for other medical problems. Such an assessment is likely to prove useful for later case formulation and is an ideal vehicle for the exploration of patient representations about surgical process and the interaction of surgical episodes with other significant life events. In the same way that illness representation is often crucial in understanding patient emotional and behavioural responses to illness, cognitive representations of surgery are central to helping patient and therapist to understand the way in which they will approach impending surgery.

T: Mr Jones tells me that you have been in hospital many times before.

P: That's right, I am beginning to lose count now . . . at least ten times in the last six years.

T: I wanted to spend some time asking you about these times in hospital—to focus on how it has affected the way you think about hospital, operations and surgeons.

P: Mmm . . . if you can work that out then you are a better man than me.

T: Well hopefully this is something we can work together. I will help you to focus on what has happened to you and you can help me by trying to tell me more about what it has been like for you.

P: I hope so.

T: When was the first operation that you had here?

P: That would be about seven years ago. It was an exploratory one—to see if I was blocked anywhere. That was in the old ward along the other end.

T: Can you remember how you felt before that operation?

P: It's a long time, but I think I was looking forward to it in a funny sort of way. I wanted to know what was wrong with me.

T: So you viewed it as a way of finding out what was wrong with you?

P: I did.

T: Did that happen?

P: Yes and no.

T: Tell me what was the 'yes' part and in what respect 'no'.

P: He corrected a small twist in the bowel but said that it did not explain all of the problems I had been having.

T: How did you feel about that?

P: Disappointed.

T: Is there anything else about that operation that you remember?

P: No.

T: What was the next operation after that one?

P: The next five operations were all to fix twists and blockages.

T: What was the outcome of all of these operations?

P: They all worked a bit . . . but I was always still left with symptoms.

T: And what did you make of that . . . that each time you were left with symptoms?

P: I started to think that surgery was a waste of time . . . I just went along to please the surgeon.

The main outcomes of the review of patient surgical history should be a chronological description of surgical episodes and information on how experiences have resulted in the formation of beliefs about surgery, surgical outcome and surgeons. Assessment of patient expectations of surgery is important and should be combined with determination of the main sources of information which patients have used in forming their ideas about surgery and the surgical process. These commonly include a combination of friends and relatives, newspapers, the Internet, the ever-increasing number of 'docu-soaps' and medically based documentaries or dramas. Exposure to these sources of information can result in positive surgical beliefs as well as negative or dysfunctional beliefs relating to surgery. The accuracy of patient information about surgery and the way in which information has been processed will influence what they think about surgery.

T: What is your understanding about the operation that you have been advised to have?

P: It is a 'telescopic laparoscotomy removal of the gall bladder'.

T: I am afraid that I am not too good with all the jargon. . . . Tell me what you think that means in basic terms?

P: It is something to do with my gall bladder. The surgeon will not be able to see inside all of me. He will be taking out gall stones and perhaps the gall bladder depending upon what he sees.

T: Where did you learn about that?

P: The surgeon told me and I looked up the Reader's Digest book that my sister has.

T: What else do you know about your operation?

P: That they will use magic stitches, not like the staples I had when I was in ten years ago?

T: What do you know about them?

P: They magically dissolve after a few days.

T: Where did you hear about this?

P: My son said that he had been looking it up in the Internet.

T: So, your understanding is that the surgeon will be removing gall stones and maybe your gall bladder and that he will use dissolving stitches.

P: Mm.

T: What do you know about the length of the operation and your hospital stay?

P: Not a lot.

Assessment of beliefs about surgery enable therapists to ascertain expectations about the purpose and procedural elements of surgery. This can be a crucial component of problem-level formulations where patients hold unrealistic, inaccurate or distorted expectations, perceptions and beliefs about surgery. Surgeons are often afforded special status in the eyes of patients, which is often more marked than the perceptions and feelings that patients have for other doctors and health professionals. This is generally a positive phenomenon used by patients to minimise the psychological impact of uncertainty or other anxieties about surgery. Patients tend to transfer responsibility to the surgeon, focus on the skilled nature of their work and view the surgeon as omnipotent. The negative emotional impact of automatic thoughts can be minimised by these thoughts. Examples might include 'He is a wonderful man, very well respected', 'Mr Smith knows what he is doing—he is in control of everything'. This can be powerful and persist even when surgeons attempt to enable patients to develop a more realistic view of them ('Mr Wilcock said that the operation might not help—he didn't mean that, he justs says that when he does not want to get my hopes up'). Significant problems can occur when conflict arises between the perception of the all-knowing and competent surgeon and the occurrence of post-operative complications or a poor surgical outcome.

Some patients have the opposite view of surgeons as a result of prior bad experiences or personality clashes with their surgeons. Patient perceptions about their surgeons can usually be elicited by asking general questions such as 'How do you feel about Miss Malone?', 'What is your view of Mr Brown as a surgeon?'. Disillusionment and dejection post-operatively can often be traced to pre-operative predictions about surgical outcome, some of which will be linked to views of the surgeon's ability and patient expectations on this basis. Assessments might also include interviews with members of the surgical team to elicit perceptions about patients (and, in some cases, relatives too), but this should be done when therapists think that it may be helpful to involve staff in treatment. Staff beliefs about patients can influence their reactions towards patients (which is particularly relevant when assessing patients and/or patients who have had repeated admissions to the same ward), and beliefs held by staff about patients (e.g. 'She always says it is worse than it really is') can be addressed before they have the opportunity to compromise the integrity of psychological treatment. The assessment of patient beliefs about surgeons is illustrated in the following extract:

T: Which surgeon will be performing your operation?
P: Mr Brownlee.
T: How many times have you met him?
P: Twice, once in the clinic and once this morning.
T: How did you get on with him?
P: OK.
T: How do you feel about him doing the operation?
P: I am pleased. He has been in the local paper—he seems to take an interest in charity work and in raising funds for the clinic here.
T: How does seeing him in the paper relate to your being pleased that he is doing the operation?
P: Well, just that he seems to be respected. He wouldn't be respected if he wasn't good at his job.

There are a minority of patients for whom surgery is an unpleasant reminder of previous trauma in their lives or who tend to interpret elements of their surgical experiences with regard to past trauma. The nature of these experiences may mean that they are not spontaneously reported at assessment. In some cases, patients will disclose this information and will feel that they can provide detail to help therapists assess the way in which it has had an effect on their adjustment. Some therapists decide to include routine screening for prior traumatic events in their assessments of surgical patients.

T: Sometimes surgery can involve experiences which trigger unpleasant memories or reminders of past traumatic or unpleasant events. Is that something which has happened to you at all?
P: It has been a terrible experience . . . it has caused more problems than it has solved.
T: Do you feel able to tell me about what these problems have been?
P: It was when I had that scope thing up inside me . . . (looks away and starts to cry). It is disgusting, I am ashamed.
T: It sounds terrible for you. The test which you had before the operation had triggered some strong feelings—you feel disgusted and ashamed.
P: If I had known that this would have brought it all back to me I would not have had it done in the first place. Now I am in even more pain.
T: What were you thinking as it all came back to you?
P: The picture of him—the bastard. He raped me when I was living with my aunt.

T: The colonoscopy has brought back the memories of being raped by someone when you were a child.
P: My uncle. (*Sobs*)

This session extract illustrates how patients can experience medical and surgical procedures as intrusive and how they might trigger memories or intrusive thoughts which become central to understanding their psychological adjustment and which need to be addressed in CBT.

Pre-operative Assessments

Therapists are commonly asked to assess patients before surgery when it seems that the patient has psychosocial problems which may threaten the course of treatment, recovery and/or rehabilitation. These may not relate to forthcoming surgery and it is imperative that therapists determine the degree to which the prospect of surgery relates to the onset and maintenance of presenting psychosocial problems. Medical and surgical staff may have assumed that problems relate to surgery when in fact the patient's psychological problems are longstanding. In these cases, assessment should focus upon determining the way in which the current surgical episode and past problems have had an impact upon the cognitive, behavioural and emotional components of a patient's adjustment to the prospect of surgery.

T: What have been the main problems for you in recent weeks?
P: The biggest one is that I have been so anxious I can hardly sit still at times.
T: Have you been having the problem since you came into hospital?
P: Yes.
T: And when did the problems start?
P: About three months ago.
T: When did you find out that you were to have this operation?
P: Two weeks ago.
T: Was anything happening three months ago when you first started feeling anxious?
P: My son was told he had a serious heart problem.
T: Is that something that you think about when you are feeling anxious?
P: I can't get him out of my mind, I couldn't bear it if he were to die.
T: So, even before this operation was suggested you have been anxious about your son's health. You notice when you are agitated that your thoughts are focused upon the fact that he may die.

> P: Oh my, it is a mess isn't it?
> T: Is that how you tend to think about it?
> P: Yes.
> T: What exactly do you see as being messy about the situation?
> P: I don't know what will happen to him, I don't know what will happen to me.

Some patients will have been advised that surgery is contingent upon their making changes in their behaviour and/or that the chances of a successful outcome or recovery depend upon their making such lifestyle or behavioural changes. Cognitive behavioural assessments should focus upon the behaviours which need to be modified by asking about their pattern of occurrence in the patient's life. The key determinants of engagement in the behaviour need to be outlined if patient and therapist are to be able to embark upon an intervention designed to address it. Patients also need to be encouraged to take a stepwise view of goal attainment. This idea often needs to be introduced during assessment as a way of engaging patients in discussion about the behaviour to be changed. This is illustrated in the following extract from an assessment session:

> T: You have been told that Mr Cooper will not operate unless you lose some weight. Sister tells me that you have said that you will just forget it as he is asking too much of you.
> P: That's it. There is no way that I can lose two stones.
> T: Has he explained why losing this weight might be helpful to you?
> P: Yes, I don't have a problem with that. I understand that it will reduce the risks of problems after and I will be able to make a better recovery.
> T: You said that Mr Cooper is asking too much of you—I tend to agree with you. It is ever so difficult to feel motivated to lose weight when someone is always reminding you that you have two stones to lose or one stone to go—that sort of thing.
> P: That's what I feel.
> T: I think it would be more reasonable to take an approach where you are being asked to lose one pound. That's all, one pound—and then when you have achieved that we will look at whether you feel able to lose another pound. If we were able to persuade Mr Cooper to help you with that approach would that have any effect on whether you will consider the surgery?
> P: I might feel more like trying.
> T: I do hope so. Can I ask you some more about your weight?
> P: Yes.

> T: What weight are you now?
> P: 16 stone 2 pounds.
> T: Is that your usual weight?
> P: No—it has rocketed since I had the accident and went up when I was put on the antidepressant.
> T: Are there any other things that might have made your weight go up?
> P: I definitely eat too much chocolate.
> T: In general or are there particular times, places or feelings which cause you to eat too much chocolate?

Patients should always be asked to outline their understanding of reasons for surgery ('Tell me what you understand to be the reasons that you need this operation?'). This influences the way in which they process information in the days leading up to the operation. Assessment may reveal significant gaps in knowledge or distortions which need to be addressed as part of a process of pre-operative preparation and/or the treament of psychological problems presenting pre-operatively. Patients should be asked about the way in which the need for surgery was communicated to them as this enables therapists to determine whether patients have assimilated the information and particularly the personal and family implications for the surgical procedure. Satisfaction with pre-operative preparation has consistently been shown to be associated with post-operative psychological morbidity (Johnston & Vogele, 1993). Patients with lower levels of satisfaction are more likely to experience problems with anxiety and depression. In some cases assessments will reveal that there are cognitive and behavioural factors which need to be addressed as a means of enhancing preparation for surgery. There are also clinical scenarios where modification of thoughts about surgery, or behavioural responses to the prospect of surgery, can prevent more serious psychological sequelae. Therapists should be mindful of the need to postpone surgery when assessment indicates longstanding beliefs which are likely to interfere with post-operative recovery. CBT can be offered to address problems at which times the risk for surgery can be reviewed. When medical factors preclude this management option, CBT can be offered post-operatively to minimise psychological complications.

Post-operative Assessments

All of the recommendations that have been made for assessments conducted pre-operatively apply equally to cognitive behavioural assessments carried out following surgery. Therapists need to be mindful of the fact that patient self-report about pre-operative thoughts, feelings, behaviour and experiences will be influenced by emotional status (and physical health) after surgery and the nature of the outcome of surgery. A patient who experiences an unexpected negative outcome may be more negative in his or her recall of pre-operative events than would have been the case if the assessment had been conducted pre-operatively.

T: The nurse tells me that you seemed quite optimistic about your ability to cope after the operation?

P: Did she really? How things change.

T: In what way have things changed?

P: Well I have had the operation now. Things are worse. I am not optimistic about anything.

T: Would you say that she was right in her view that you were optimistic before?

P: I suppose if I think back I was.

T: If I had met with you then and asked you about what you were thinking, what might you have told me?

P: Before the operation?

T: Yes.

P: Well I would have said that it was going to work, that I was looking forward to a better quality of life . . . yes, that's what I kept thinking.

T: Were there specific things that you hoped would happen to give you a better quality of life?

P: I thought about spending less time in bed and being less tired. The idea of gardening really appealed to me.

T: I see.

P: I thought that the aching in my stomach would have gone. . . .

Some people have few overt problems before their surgery but develop problems as a result of the surgery becoming a critical incident in activating prior psychological vulnerabilities or becoming a traumatic stressor. Surgical experiences may feature in the content of intrusive thoughts, images, flashbacks or nightmares. This should be screened for in patients considered to be struggling with trauma associated with surgery. Expectations are important in this regard, and there are a number of these which are so obvious that patients may find it difficult to articulate them (that the nurses will care for them, they will not be allowed to suffer, etc.). Nevertheless, these can be challenged by problems relating to the quality of care delivery. Expectations relating to length of hospital stay, the nature and course of recovery and the relationship of this to the course of their medical problems are all important foci for assessment in this regard. Patients who find that there is a gap between their expectations and actual experience can begin to develop problems related to difficulties accounting for the mismatch between expectation and reality. Patients may, of course, have had unrealistic expectations and sometimes events may have occurred which were genuinely unexpected by the clinical team. In some cases it also emerges that a member of the team has provided the patient with inaccurate information about an aspect of their stay in hospital.

Cognitive behavioural assessments should be implemented in a way that situates the patient's experiences of surgery within the larger context of a patient's recent and more distal life experiences. It is helpful if therapist and patient can understand the extent to which each problem on the problem list is related to the experience of surgery. This will make it easier to produce formulations that take account of important surgical issues and, by implication, interventions which address the key factors as they relate to the current episode of care.

FORMULATION

Problem-level Formulation

Problem-level formulations of the presenting problems of surgical patients should aim to place emphasis on formulating problems specifically related to surgery. There are obviously many patients who will present with problems which do not relate to the surgery per se. It is rare, however, for the prospect of surgery to have no bearing on the frequency, intensity or pattern of a patient's problems. The surgical procedure itself, or elements of patient contact with surgical services, can trigger, exacerbate or influence other symptom experiences. The links between components of the 'unrelated' problem and surgery should be outlined. The example of the patient with concerns about her son's health is formulated at the problem level in Figure 9.1.

Problem-level formulations of surgical problems commonly address issues which are general to all forms of surgery. These include satisfaction with preparation, preoccupation with outcomes, expectations, relationships with staff, being anaesthetised, being separated from loved ones, or survival. In some cases thoughts will relate specifically to the idiosyncratic elements of the procedure being carried out (e.g. a patient with distressing imagery of her heart being stopped during bypass graft surgery). The problem-level formulation of a patient about to undergo cholecystectomy is outlined in Figure 9.2. This patient found it particularly difficult to trust other staff and was dissatisfied with the information that she had been given about her surgery.

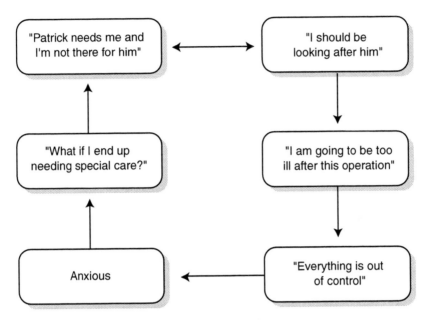

Figure 9.1. Problem-level formulation (surgery)

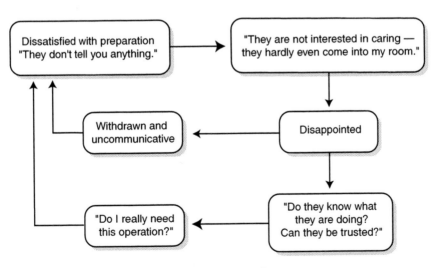

Figure 9.2. Problem-level formulation (surgery)

Case-level Formulation

The essential issue which must be addressed in formulating psychological problems among this patient group is the extent to which presenting problems relate to prior psychological problems, surgery or other current life experiences and life events. Case-level formulations will outline whether psychological problems associated with surgery have triggered a pre-existing vulnerability. Duits et al. (1999), in their study of anxiety and depressive symptoms among patients who have experienced coronary artery bypass graft surgery, found that neuroticism was related to pre- and post-operative anxiety and depression. This trait needs to be outlined in case-level formulations of surgical patients. Problems with surgery may be mediated by factors which are responsible for other problems in a patient's life (e.g. pervasive belief that has no control over anything). The way in which problem-level formulations of medical problems relate to problem-level formulations of surgical issues should be outlined. Assessment material often suggests that there is a link between the timing of surgery and the onset of psychological problems. This should be outlined. What caused the patient problems about having surgery? The specific nature of the surgical procedure may act as an important triggering factor. Why did having major heart surgery trigger depression for this patient? Would this have happened if the patient had had major orthopaedic surgery?

Early experiences of illness, memories of relatives after operations and beliefs about surgeons, control, recovery and hospitals should be considered for inclusion. Access to medical and social support can buffer problems and links are made here. The case-level formulation in Figure 9.3 outlines how a patient awaiting mastectomy surgery experienced problems relating to pre-existing difficulties with panic disorder, memories of her mother's experience of surgery, and her problems with post-operative pain, and outlines how the effects of all of these are worsened by a partner who is critical and does not understand her needs, and a poor social support network.

INTERVENTION STRATEGIES

Preparation for Surgery

Most cognitive behavioural interventions for surgical patients can be conceptualised to be related in some way to the patients' satisfaction with the knowledge and information they have about their surgery. When it has been established that a patient is dissatisfied with some element of the

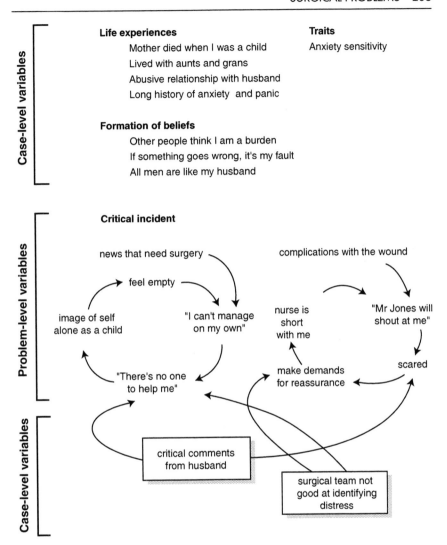

Figure 9.3. Case-level formulation for patient in surgical ward

pre-operative preparation, it becomes necessary to outline both the nature of this dissatisfaction and how it might be addressed. Enhancing satisfaction may be a matter of providing new information, or repeating old information, or presenting it in a new manner or in a way which takes account of factors that are unique to that patient. It may also involve tackling factors which result in a patient perceiving information in a negative way ('Things never work out for me') or behaviours which result in dissatisfaction being more likely ('I can't go to get the information leaflet as I am scared I'll collapse on the way to the doctor's surgery').

Behaviourally and situationally based intervention strategies can be implemented to enhance satisfaction and increase self-efficacy. This might include structured experiences for observational learning, such as watching patient education videos or using discussion with other patients as a way of gathering information. Psychological preparation for surgery can usually be integrated with most cognitive and behavioural strategies which are implemented pre-operatively, and patients should be informed about the physical and psychological benefits of this—particularly if their motivation to enhance satisfaction is in doubt.

T: Research has shown that patients who feel satisfied with what they know about their operations and how they might feel afterwards do much better afterwards. They are less anxious and need less painkilling medication.

P: Really?

T: Yes, that was why I suggested that we put your level of satisfaction with the surgery on our agenda this morning.

P: I am glad you did.

T: I wanted to help you to focus upon what is going to happen and how you might feel—so that you can be prepared.

P: I used to be in the scouts—so I know about being prepared. (Laughs)

T: It will help if you can write down the information that I give you and things you discover today. This way you can refer to it when you get back to the ward. We can also refer to it when we are reviewing how satisfied you are with what you know and whether we need to improve this.

P: OK. Can I borrow a pen?

When therapists (usually in conjunction with other staff) have provided information about the procedural and sensory aspects of surgery, satisfaction needs to be assessed and strategies put in place to enhance this.

T: So you really are quite dissatisfied with it all?

P: Yes.

T: If you were to give your level of satisfaction a score, where 0 is not at all satisfied and 100 is completely satisfied—where would you say that you are?

P: 40.

T: When you are thinking that you have a 40% level of satisfaction, what do you think about?

P: It is OK for them, they have seen this done hundreds of times. I need to know what might go wrong and how they will deal with it. I am sick of the patronising 'Don't worry, Mr Morrison we will take care of that'—I am not a child, you know.

T: But the staff have spoken to you in a way which feels like that.

P: Yes.

T: Are there other things you have been focusing upon relating to this dissatisfaction?

P: I want to know what things will be like when I get home.

T: What would you most like to know about?

P: I don't want to rely on my wife to dress me. Sister said that we would cross that bridge when we came to it. See, put it off again, palm the patient off with a patronising explanation.

T: Does Sister know that you have not been satisfied with your preparation for the operation?

P: Yes, she gave me a leaflet to read.

T: Did that help?

P: I haven't read it.

T: So if I understand you correctly, the main things which are making you dissatisfied with your preparation for the operation are the way in which the staff dismiss your questions and the fact that this means that you have unanswered questions.

P: Exactly.

T: What would need to happen for you to have a higher satisfaction score?

P: They could start treating me with some respect.

T: If you were to write down some of the questions that they have been avoiding, and if I was to work with them to try to answer your questions more honestly, would that go some way to improving the satisfaction score?

Adjunctive CBT

Patients who need to make significant changes to their behaviour and/or who have problems associated with behavioural and cognitive factors which impede their recovery, often benefit from CBT applied as an adjunct to other medical and rehabilitative strategies. The targets of CBT are often problems relating to adherence to advice, difficulties accepting the pace of recovery, problems adopting the role of 'patient', insomnia, loss of appetite or pain. Depressive or anxiety disorders can impede the course of recovery and CBT for them can have a secondary impact on physical recovery. The following extract outlines how CBT might help someone to think about their problems with speed of recovery:

T: Dr Jess says that you have been very frustrated with how things are going.

P: I get so angry with myself.

T: What do you find you get most angry about?

P: I should be able to do more by now.

T: Is that the sort of thing you find you think when you are angry?

P: Yes, it is always focusing on what I should be doing but am not.

T: What make you think that you should be doing these things?

P: I just thought that I would be doing them.

T: And you wanted help today to reduce the number of times when you get angry?

P: If I could, it would be a help—my family are getting annoyed with my moaning.

T: Let's continue with looking at your evidence for the belief that you should be doing more than you are. You say you thought you would be doing them. Anything else which makes you think you should be doing these things?

P: Mmm . . . I always kept fit beforehand.

T: So because you were fit and always thought you would be able to do more you are getting angry for not meeting these standards?

P: Yes.

T: What did Dr Jess say you should be able to do by three weeks?

P: He didn't say.

T: Do you think he would say that you are not doing what you should be doing?

P: I don't know.

T: Is that something you could find out—what he thinks you should be able to do?

P: Yes, I see him next week. I will ask him.

T: What things are you able to do?

P: I can walk to the corner shop . . . but that's nothing. So, I force myself to walk to the park.

T: What else can you do?

P: I have been able to get in and out of the bath myself.

T: Did you think that you would be able to do these things by now?

P: Yes. They are basic.

T: These things that you can do—is there any difference with repeating them. Are they easier to do a second time?

P: I don't know.

T: How would you feel if Dr Jess said that you were doing more than he would expect.

P: It might help a bit.

T: But?

P: I think I will always be frustrated by not being like I was.
T: So it seems that much of your frustration comes from your own thoughts—that you were once fit and that you thought you would be able to do more. Asking Dr Jess will help you to check out what his expectations are, but perhaps we also need to help you pay more attention to what you are doing and help you to pay attention to what you can do and less on what you are having problems doing.
P: I do tend to focus on what I can't do.

It is important to emphasise the importance of a graded approach which emphasises self-efficacy. Patients tend to forget that their bodies have suffered a major assault and that it is often unreasonable to expect to make the progress that they are seeking or to do so within the time frame that they expect. Increasingly, modern society is characterised by a 'quick fix' mentality and patients, particularly those who are used to being in control of their lives, find it difficult to accept the need for rest and recuperation. Appreciating small changes is crucial and therapists should be vigilant for patients who tend to dismiss them. Therapists should build in strategies for enabling their patients to notice small improvements and reward themselves for smaller steps toward greater confidence and recovery. These elements are outlined in the following extract from a ward-based session with a patient who had stopped eating and was depressed following surgery for inflammatory bowel disease:

T: You have been feeling very low since last week?
P: I can't see anything changing. It is all so dreadful. I feel empty.
T: The nurses are worried about your appetite and the fact that you have been refusing food.
P: I know. I can't face it. I haven't the energy to eat what they are giving me.
T: Can we put that on the agenda for today?
P: Yes.
T: Is there anything else that we need to put on the agenda?
P: They are starting to talk about me going home—I can't face it.
T: OK, we need to spend some time helping you with your thoughts about going home.
P: I never thought that surgery could make you feel so bad.
T: Is there any food that you can face?
P: The things that I want to eat don't appear on the menu.
T: Have they ever been on the menu?
P: Once, but I was feeling too low and had no energy to lift the spoon.

T: What about if we were to work on a list of foods that you want to eat, foods that you think could face?

P: What's the point? There isn't any—they won't be on the menu and I can't be bothered.

T: I have been suggesting ways in which we might help you with your eating and it seems that this has triggered more negative thoughts—'There's no point trying, I can't be bothered'.

P: Well it's a fact.

T: I would like to suggest that this is a thought which is part of your depression and which we can try to tackle by making there seem a point in trying and by making eating something that you have energy for. Assuming we can help you to see the point and have more energy to try—what would you like to eat?

P: I like carrot soup . . . all you get here is minestrone.

T: What else do you like to eat?

P: I like pasta.

T: If I could arrange for you to choose what you want to eat each day and we could make sure that each day you are given a manageable amount to eat, would you be willing to try that to see if it is any easier to face and whether you can be bothered eating what they bring?

P: I can't see how it will make a difference.

T: The important thing is not to assume that it won't—trying it is the only sure way of finding out if it will help you with your eating.

SPECIAL CONSIDERATIONS

Many of the problems of surgical patients can be addressed with reference to the issues outlined in the earlier sections of this chapter and by ensuring that mainstream cognitive behavioural strategies are implemented sensitively to take account of the impact of surgery. There are some special clinical scenarios, however, which require the integration of further concepts and principles. Cognitive behavioural formulations need to take account of the unique circumstances of the surgical procedures in question and there may be patient presentations which need sensitive handling. The remainder of this chapter will outline the assessment, formulation and interventions which can be implemented when working with patients who have been disfigured by surgery, patients requesting cosmetic surgical procedures and patients for whom transplantation surgery has been recommended.

DISFIGURING SURGERY

Western culture places great importance on appearance and appearance-based stereotypes. Attractiveness tends to be associated with happiness, success, intelligence, interest and social prowess. It is hardly surprising, therefore, that patients with the experience of a surgically induced change in appearance often develop problems. All surgery alters appearance to some extent—even if this is restricted to the scar which remains after surgery. This objectively minor change in appearance may have the same degree of psychological significance for the patient as the loss of a limb for another person. Indeed, this reflects one of the basic issues when it comes to the assessment and conceptualisation of the psychological aspects of appearance-altering surgery. The psychological impact of surgery which results in unwanted changes in appearance is heavily influenced by the meaning of the appearance change for patients and less so by the extensiveness or objective severity of the change. Medical and nursing staff often refer to post-operative appearance changes as 'body-image problems'. There has been much confusion in the literature and the term is often confused with other constructs such as self-esteem.

Assessment

Body image dimensions are closely linked with feelings about the self and are inextricably linked with social and interpersonal factors. They are sensitive to mood, environmental context and can exert a significant influence on information processing, self-presentation and relationships. Altabe and Thompson (1996) have suggested that a body-image schema exists, consisting of self-evaluative information about one's appearance, and can be assessed using self-report questionnaires or responses to interview questions. Higgins' self-discrepancy theory (Higgins, 1987) has been successfully applied to the study of body image experiences and can be used to structure elements of the pre- or post-operative assessment of patients who have had appearance-altering surgery. This theory has also been used in the development of a separate measure for the assessment of self-ideal discrepancies. The theory states that cognitive self-structures can be conceptualised as a relationship between two self-state representations: acutal and ideal states. It further outlines how these states can be considered from the perspective of self or others. This is a helpful way of structuring assessment of thoughts, beliefs and feelings.

T: It sounds as if you have been quite upset about this since the operation.
P: Yes, it is just dreadful.
T: Did you have an idea how it was going to look ideally?
P: Very much so—I knew there would be scar, that's OK. It is the shape—it all sags just below the scar.

> T: So part of the problem is that the shape of your abdomen below the scar does not match with what your ideal is.
> P: Exactly.
> T: How do you feel when you are aware of this discrepancy.
> P: I am so disappointed.
> T: Do you ever think about the impact of this on other people's views or reactions?
> P: I mostly think about how disappointed I am.
> T: What are your feelings on the perspective of other people and this gap from your ideal?
> P: I won't let Jim see it—I am ashamed to. What on earth will he think?
> T: What do you think he will think?

In addition to direct questioning about the cognitive behavioural aspects of appearance-altering surgery there are some self-report measures which can be used to assess this. Rosen et al. (1991) have suggested that the multifaceted nature of body image requires that it be assessed with measures that tap into its different dimensions and features.

Appearance Schemas Inventory

The Appearance Schemas Inventory (Cash & Labarge, 1996) is a 14-item measure which assesses core beliefs and assumptions about the importance, meaning and impact of beliefs about appearance. These beliefs collectively comprise the body-image schema. This measure can be used as part of a pre-operative assessment when it may be necessary to specify the nature of psychological vulnerability by virtue of negative assumptions which may be triggered by surgery. This measure is reproduced as an appendix to the paper by Cash and Labarge (1996).

Situational Inventory of Body Image Dysphoria

The Situational Inventory of Body Image Dysphoria (Cash, 1994) consists of 48 items. These invite respondents to consider various situations and rate the frequency with which they would experience negative feelings about their appearance in that situation (e.g. 'When my partner sees me undressed', 'When I have my photograph taken'). There are two open-ended items which enable patients to provide information on situations not covered by the preceding items. This measure is particulary helpful for eliciting information on the common behavioural and situational factors relating to negative feelings about appearance. It is likely to be more useful as part of post-operative assessments when patients have left hospital and have been exposed to situations where appearance-related distress may have become manifest.

Body Image Ideals Questionnaire

The Body Image Ideals Questionnaire (Cash & Szymanski, 1995) is used to assess ideal-self discrepancies regarding appearance. It consists of 11 items and invites patients to compare their current experience with regard to 11 physical attributes to their ideal on each attribute ('My ideal facial features are: Exactly as I am, Almost as I am, Fairly unlike me, Very unlike me'). They then rate how important this physical attribute is to them ('How important to you are your ideal facial features? Not important, Somewhat important, Moderately important, Very important'). The physical attributes covered by this measure are height, skin complexion, hair texture and thickness, facial features, muscle tone and definition, body proportions, weight, chest size, physical strength, physical coordination and overall physical appearance. It can be used pre- or postoperatively and is a helpful way of operationalising cognitive vulnerabilities to appearance-changing surgery or outlining the precise nature of problems with self-ideal discrepancies after surgery.

Formulation

White (2000) has outlined a heuristic cognitive behavioural model of body-image dimensions for cancer patients (see Figure 9.4) which can be applied to patients with surgically induced appearance change. The model reflects the fact that there may or may not be a congruence between objective appearance changes and the patient's subjective perceptions regarding the extent and nature of changes in his or her physical appearance. Case-level formulation should specify any significant distortion between the objective reality and patient perception of the nature and severity of appearance changes (e.g. a patient who had experienced minor surgery to remove a small benign lump from her ear, but reported that 40% of her ear had been removed). Perceived changes in appearance will be processed in terms of beliefs about self and appearance. Case-level formulation should also outline the nature of interaction between self schemata and body-image schematic content. These will significantly influence the degree to which a patient has a personal investment in a particular body part and the presence of an actual ideal-self discrepancy.

When links based on Higgins' theory are included, these should outline the nature of the magnitude of self-discrepancy and relate this to the intensity of the affect experienced by the patient as a consequence of awareness of the discrepancy. Cash and Szymanski (1995) have highlighted how investment in discrete physical attributes should be taken into account in considering the psychological impact of appearance. Physical attributes are rarely afforded equal psychological importance.

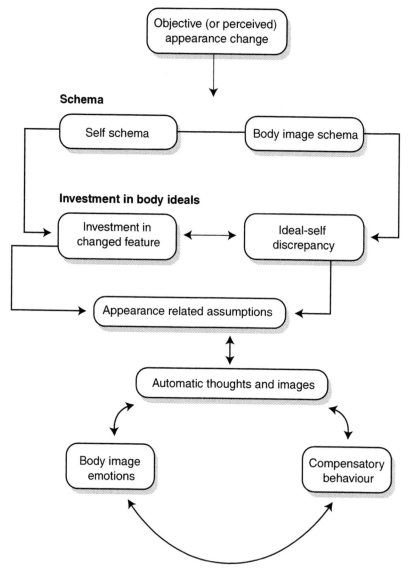

Figure 9.4. Heuristic model of body image dimensions (reproduced, with permission, from White (2000))

Therapists should work with patients to determine how certain attributes become more important to some people or are preferred to other attributes (e.g. the patient who attached more significance to her breasts as a result of childhood teasing about breast size). It has been shown that 'attractive' people receive more social reinforcement for their behaviour, more help from others, encourage more self-disclosure from other people and are believed to be more honest (Burns & Farina, 1992). These interpersonal issues are often encapsulated in the formulation. Social psychological research confirms that 'unattractive' people experience more social anxiety, greater fears of social rejection and a more pronounced external locus of control. Formulations must take account of the visibility of any appearance change and include any attentional biases to the affected body area. Patients who believe themselves to be incomplete may be at particular risk of psychological problems (White & Unwin, 1998).

Intervention Strategies

When patients believe that they are not complete people as a result of changed appearance, they need to be able to appreciate the way in which their interpretations about appearance have changed as a result of surgery. This assumes that they did not believe that they were incomplete before surgery—a fact which therapists should determine before treating compromised physical integrity. Patients tend to link their self-worth entirely in terms of appearance. They need help to separate the changes in appearance from aspects of their life which have not changed.

T: Did you think of yourself as incomplete as a person before you had your leg amputated?

P: No, but I had my leg then.

T: I understand that your thinking tends to focus upon the fact that you had your left leg last week and now that it is gone you see yourself as incomplete. Have I understood you correctly in that before you did not see yourself as an incomplete person?

P: I was complete.

T: Apart from having two legs, what other aspects of you and your life would you say made you a complete person?

P: What do you mean?

T: If I had asked you what made you complete if we met a year ago, what would you have said?

P: What would I have said?

T: Would you only have said I have two legs or would you have listed anything else?

P: Oh I see what you mean. No I would have said that I had a wife, children. . . . Is that what you mean?

T: Is that what you would have seen when thinking about what made you a complete person?

P: Yes.

T What else?

P: My job and I suppose the fact that I had a good set of friends.

T: And you still have these things?

P: It is so difficult to see it like that—I keep focusing on not having my leg.

T: Do you think that that might be the reason you get so depressed—that you tend to see your completeness as a person in terms of only your legs and not in terms of all the things that you used to?

P: It could be part of it.

T: You were saying before that you have avoided friends, that you have not been playing with your children and that you think you will never get back to work.

P: Mm.

T: I wonder what might happen to your feelings of completeness if we could help you to increase how much attention you paid to these things.

The individual contributors to a person's completeness can be represented within a pie chart. When this is done with the factors contributing to completeness before surgically induced change it can help patients to appreciate that their current estimations of the importance of appearance are inflated and that they tend to base their definitions on a narrower range of factors than before. The graphical/pictorial representation on a pie chart helps most to appreciate this change.

Behavioural experiments can be established to help patients to try out new behaviours (or re-establish old behaviours). Some people engage in camouflaging behaviour to hide appearance changes, but these may paradoxically draw more attention to the changed body part. Social support is vital and beliefs which block access to social support can be targeted in treatment. Graded exposure can be used to reverse avoidance related to touching scars, looking at one's reflection in the mirror and having social or intimate contact with other people (see Table 9.1). Behavioural interventions are particularly important in helping patients who have an intellectual acceptance that they are whole or complete but for whom true belief and acceptance requires daily experiences which reinforce this ('What did you do today to reinforce that you are still complete, even though you have one leg?').

Table 9.1   Graded exposure steps: avoidance of scar

Touching the area of the scar through two layers of clothes
Touching the area through one layer of clothes
Wearing a rubber glove and touching the scar
Wearing a thin glove and touching the scar
Washing the scar with a heavily lathered/soapy hand
Touching the scar with my hand (not looking at it)
Touching the scar with my hand

COSMETIC SURGERY

Patients are often referred to clinical psychologists and psychiatrists for opinion regarding their suitability for cosmetic surgery. Comprehensive coverage of the issues which need to be addressed in such assessments are beyond the scope of this book, but therapists working with a cognitive behavioural model are well placed to conduct such assessments as these often involve determination of thoughts about appearance, the need for surgery and behavioural responses to appearance dissatisfaction. The main cognitive behavioural mediators of their desire for surgery should be assessed. In formulating an opinion on the appropriateness of surgery, therapists need to focus on the extent to which patient perceptions of surgical benefits are biased ('If I have a smaller nose then my husband will love me again') or based on limited appreciation of the disadvantages of surgery (e.g. potential for scarring). CBT can also be implemented as an adjunct to referral for cosmetic surgery as patients can be placed on the waiting list for cosmetic surgery while receiving CBT. When patients present with a combination of distorted beliefs and objectively demonstrated appearance changes, this combined approach is particularly appropriate.

TRANSPLANTATION SURGERY

Researchers are beginning to appreciate the psychosocial needs of patients who have experienced transplant surgery (Salmon et al., 1998). Patients awaiting transplantation surgery often experience a pattern of approach and avoidance. They oscillate between a desire to be invited to attend for transplant when a suitable donor organ becomes available, and wishing to avoid this at all costs as they know it will involve a deterioration in their physical health status. Patients will often respond favourably to explanation of these normal and understandable aspects of waiting for a transplant. They can be helped to understand how their feelings about the prospect of a transplant will vary on the basis of whether they interpret it is a sign of potential death or a sign of a potentially improved quality of life. Some people find that the uncertainties associated with being on a transplant list can trigger vulnerabilities to anxiogenic thinking. These can be assessed, formulated and treated according to the cognitive behavioural model of anxiety. Some patients develop guilt following successful transplantation, and this is usually mediated by thoughts that they do not deserve to live when someone else had to die. They may also experience thoughts about the deceased donor and may become preoccupied with concerns relating to the relatives of the deceased donor. Patient thoughts, feelings and behaviours may relate to the organ which has been transplanted. Some experience post-traumatic stress symptoms (Stukas Jr et al., 1999). These can be assessed, formulated and treated according to current cognitive models of trauma.

SUMMARY AND CONCLUSIONS

Surgery tends to be associated with psychological problems which are usually the result of dissatisfaction and/or misinformation. CBT can address obstacles to achieving optimal levels of satisfaction and can be used to treat problems which may compromise the likelihood of achieving a good surgical outcome. Therapy is often implemented post-operatively and should be done in such a way that acknowledges and promotes a graded approach towards building an improved level of physical and psychological health. Appearance-changing surgical procedures often contribute to psychological problems and cognitive behavioural models are well developed to assist with the application of CBT to this area. CBT can also be helpful for conceptualising the reasons for patient requests for cosmetic surgery and for the management of the psychological factors associated with transplantation surgery.

Chapter 10

CARDIAC PROBLEMS

INTRODUCTION

This chapter will outline the way in which cognitive and behavioural approaches can be applied to the issues and problems associated with cardiac problems, their treatment and management. It will cover cognitive and behavioural aspects of the management of patients with cardiac symptoms mediated by psychological factors; cognitive behavioural therapy with patients experiencing pathological cardiac symptoms; cardiac rehabilitation with cardiac patients (including following myocardial infarction and coronary artery bypass graft surgery) and the application of CBT to the psychological problems associated with the use of implanted cardiac defibrillators (ICDs), used for the treatment of cardiac arrythymias. A proportion of patients will present with clinical problems spanning one or more of these areas. It is possible that more than one section of this chapter will be applicable to patients with cardiological problems who are referred for CBT. Therapists will find that they can combine details on assessment, formulation and intervention according to the unique circumstances and experiences of patients.

NON-CARDIAC CHEST PAIN

There are some patients whose cardiac symptomatology is mediated by psychological factors rather than cardiac factors; for example, chest pain, and patients may also experience psychologically mediated palpitations. Patients with chest pain constitute almost half of the new referrals to cardiology clinics (Bass & Mayou, 1995). CBT has been shown to be effective for this group of patients when implemented in both research and general hospital out-patient settings (Mayou et al., 1997). The cognitive behavioural assessment, conceptualisation and management of these symptoms will be outlined in this section. In the most complicated of cases, patients may have symptoms which are mediated by cardiological factors, some by psychological factors and yet others which are the result of a subtle interaction of both factors. Some patients have demonstrable cardiac pathology as the primary mediator of their cardiac symptoms and also secondary exacerbations in their symptoms as a result of psychological moderator variables. The management of this latter group of patients is more complex than patients with no cardiac pathology. However, the principles of their management are similar and will be highlighted in this section. The task of the cognitive behavioural therapist working with patients with cardiac problems is to conduct an assessment which will elucidate the precise ways in which psychological variables might influence symptom experience (even when patients have cardiac problems). Patient and therapist work to discover how patient's life experiences, beliefs, thoughts, emotions and behaviour might be relevant to the understanding of why they experience cardiac symptoms in the absence of cardiac pathology (or in addition to, or in excess of, objective cardiac disease). This information is ultimately linked with the modification of cognitive behavioural mediating factors.

Cognitive behavioural assessment and management of these patients is not possible unless therapists can achieve the crucial first step of engaging patients in a psychosocially focused assessment. This is followed by formulations and interventions which emphasise demonstration of the role of various behavioural and cognitive factors in the mediation and maintenance of their 'non-cardiac' symptoms. These phases—engagement, assessment, formulation, demonstration of key influences and ultimately making changes—will be outlined in the following sections.

Engagement in CBT

Therapists need to begin their work with these patients by focusing on engagement in the assessment process. Patients are likely to have attended the cardiology clinic with the expectation that a medical cause for their symptoms will be identified. The extent to which they have accepted the need for onward referral to a specialist in psychological therapy will vary enormously. There are patients who actively resist any suggestion that their psychological health may relate to their experience of cardiac symptoms. They often attend their appointment with the sole intention of communicating this and convincing the cognitive behavioural therapist that they have been wrongly referred. In some cases, medical and nursing colleagues will have prepared that patient for the referral by addressing concerns and providing an acceptable rationale for the referral. However, some patients may not know that they have been referred to a psychological therapist (e.g. 'I will refer you to my colleague, Dr White, for a second opinion'). The range of ways in which referral is understood makes it vital for the therapist to begin by assessing patient thoughts about referral and implementing strategies which may be necessary to promote engagement in further assessment. Therapists with knowledge and experience of the management of health anxiety, panic disorder and/ or hypochondriasis will often find it easier to work with this group of patients.

Patients should be told that they have been referred to a cognitive behavioural therapist (or, depending upon the work setting of the therapist, their professional background), and therapists should assess patients' reactions to this (either when they were told by the cardiologist or in response to this information at the first assessment).

T: My name is Dr White. I am a clinical psychologist and, as you know, this is the cognitive behaviour therapy clinic for people with chest pain and palpitations.

P: I read about that in the leaflet.

T: About cognitive behavioural therapy?

P: Yes.

T: I wanted to begin by finding out a bit about how you felt when Dr Holmes suggested that you come along to this clinic.

P: Shocked to say the least.

T: You were shocked?

P: Uuh—I sure was.

T: Can you remember any other feelings that you had?

P: I must say I felt a bit scared.

T: What went through your mind when you felt shocked and scared?

P: I suppose that I thought that Dr Holmes didn't think I was a genuine case, I felt like I was getting into trouble.

T: I can see why you would be shocked and scared. You thought that you were not being seen as a genuine case and that you were in the wrong in some way?

P: Yes. I thought he was going to shout at me—stupid really, but that is what I thought.

T: And what do you understand to be the main reasons that you were referred?

P: Dr Holmes said that you had years of expertise in this area. That you could help with my coping and my thinking.

Patients who begin to express their scepticism at the beginning of the appointment should be asked about the decision-making processes which resulted in their decision to attend. They could after all have decided to cancel or not attend, and this often reveals that they did not want to forgo the possibility that attendance may be of some help to them. Patients may express concerns relating to the perceived legitimacy of their symptoms. Patients will often use words like 'imaginary' and/or 'all in my head'. They may also have thoughts that it is being suggested that they have a psychological disorder or a serious mental illness expressed most commonly as 'mad' or 'loopy'. This essentially relates to their interpretation of the mention of psychological factors as meaning there is nothing wrong with them. Therapists should offer an explanation which emphasises that they do not yet have an opinion on the cause of the patient's symptoms as they have not carried out an assessment. The real nature of the patient's symptoms should be emphasised; and it should also be emphasised that although medical staff have not been able to offer an explanation for the patient's symptoms, this does not mean that there is nothing wrong. Emphasis should be placed on the fact that medical staff will have told the patient what his or her problems are *not* caused by, and the task of patient and therapist is to work together to find out what the presenting problems *are* caused by. A statement which explains these elements is outlined in Table 10.1.

Table 10.1   Explaining referral for CBT in non-cardiac chest pain

I know that your chest pains are real. I do not think that they are in your head, that you are mad or that they are in any way imaginary. Dr King has referred you to me as he has been able to tell you what your symptoms are NOT caused by. Unfortunately, he has not been able to find out what they ARE caused by. He thinks that you and I may be able to work on this together. He thinks that your heart is healthy, but because you are still getting very distressing pain I see my task as finding what may be causing this problem for you. I am not saying that we will be able to do this. All I ask is that you accept for now that this is possible for some people in your situation who spend some time examining their pain in detail.

Beginning the Assessment

Once patients have agreed to the principle that it may be possible to work out what contributes to their problems (or, at least, to improve their coping strategies) it is possible to begin the assessment. Patients can be given general information about the importance of cognitive and behavioural factors in understanding emotional and physical reactions, and in this way they will understand why the therapist might ask them about how they think and feel. If therapists can use an example from information the patient has disclosed, this can make it easier to appreciate the applicability of the model. This is outlined in the following session extract:

T: Some of your experiences before you attended the clinic actually illustrate this approach very well.

P: Do they?

T: It seemed from what you were saying that you thought that you were being viewed by Dr Holmes as not being a genuine case. This thought caused you to feel scared as you thought that there was some sort of danger—that Dr Holmes was going to shout at you.

P: I suppose that is what I thought.

T: Did you have any physical sensations when you noticed this shock and fear?

P: What like dizziness or something like that ?—No, I didn't.

T: You didn't have any dizziness or you did not have any sensations?

P: No dizziness. I think my stomach churned—a horrible sicky feeling.

T: So your thoughts about personal threat were accompanied by fear, part of which was that you felt sick and your stomach churned.

P: I see.

T: This shows how your thoughts, feelings and physical sensations can all be connected. That's what I would like to explore with you—to see if this might help us work out what is wrong when you get chest pain.

Therapists can also discuss the physical manifestations of anxiety and general beliefs which link the heart with emotions. An example of this might be the saying 'I almost had a heart attack' when communicating the unexpected fear/shock in a situation. This sort of discussion can help to orient the patient towards the types of questions and concepts that will be used in CBT. This serves to 'normalise' the links between mind and body without stigmatising the patient. When patients remain sceptical about prior statements about CBT for non-cardiac symptoms, it can help periodically to make statements which reinforce alternative interpretations of the reasons for some of the questions which are being asked. One such explanation from a session with a highly sceptical patient is outlined in Table 10.2.

Patients should be asked to focus upon a recent typical episode when they experienced chest pains. Therapists should spend as much time as possible on this. Initially it is helpful to orient patients to the situation as much as possible by having them describe the events leading up to it. In some cases it will help if they can imagine themselves in this situation. ('I wonder if it would help you to close your eyes and imagine yourself in

Table 10.2 Example of reminder to sceptical patient

There are two things which I feel I need to remind you about. First, that when I ask you about what you thought or what you feel, this is not the same thing as saying that the pain is imaginary or all in your head. Second, we need to keep an open mind on what may be happening with the pain that you are describing. Cognitive behavioural therapy is all about trying to see if we can discover an explanation for why you might have the experiences that you describe. You will not be asked to accept observations about your symptoms unless we have gathered evidence for these, perhaps using tasks between appointments.

the situation I am going to ask you about?') Therapists should concentrate on enabling patients to describe their developing awareness of their chest pain (or other cardiac symptom), and this description should be complemented by frequent summaries and questions designed to discover more about thoughts, memories, attentional biases, behaviours and their subsequent effect on cardiac symptoms. The significance of behavioural responses should be assessed. Why has the patient chosen one behavioural response in favour of another? What is it about this behaviour which alleviates their cardiac symptoms? Does this behaviour always work? If not, why not? In some cases, it is possible to enquire about the impact of these repeated episodes on intermediate beliefs about their occurrence and/or the strategies which have been chosen to manage them.

T: Given that thoughts, feelings and behaviours are all linked, I wanted to spend some time asking you about thoughts, feelings and behaviours when you get the chest pains. Would that be OK with you?

P: Yes, fire away.

T: The best way of doing this would be for you to choose a recent example and keep this focused in your mind as I ask you about it. Can you do that?

P: Yesterday—will that do.

T: Yes, great. If you start to tell me about what happened I can help you discover what thoughts, feelings and behavioural reactions you had.

P: It was after my wife went to work, she starts about 2 so it must have been 1-ish. I was in the living room and I felt dreadful.

T: What was the first thing that you noticed?

P: I felt sick.

T: Any other physical sensations?

P: My heart feels all fluttery and then I get the chest pain.

T: How did you feel emotionally when you felt all fluttery?

P: A bit on edge, I suppose.

T: So you were in the living room. Were you sitting down?

P: Yes.
T: In the living room, sitting down and you noticed that you felt sick. This was followed by feeling on edge. What went through your mind as you felt on edge?
P: I was frightened that it was going to happen again.
T: So you felt frightened and on edge . . . what were you thinking yesterday when you felt this way?
P: I worried that I was going to be in on my own.
T: Was there something that you thought would happen when you were in on your own?
P: I know it is silly now, but I thought I was going to die.

Assessment sessions should also focus on patient medical history, family history and exposure to cardiac problems (for example, via the media or extended family). Screening should be carried out for panic disorder, depressive disorders and the presence of health anxiety or symptoms of hypochondriasis. The use of chest pain monitoring diaries is often combined with a later emphasis on demonstrating the role of cognitive and behavioural factors in the maintenance of problems. In this respect, and in common with other 'psychosomatic' symptoms, assessment, formulation and treatment need to be interwoven with the common aim of enabling patients to develop a new framework for the interpretation of their symptoms.

Formulation

Problem-level formulations of cardiac symptoms of non-cardiac origin should outline the nature of the cognitions which relate the experience of a physical symptom to patient thoughts that this is related to cardiac pathology. These usually take the form of anxiogenic misinterpretations of physical sensations such as 'I am having a heart attack' or 'I am going to collapse' and these are often experienced in the form of images. Patients will also report behaviours which they have developed in an attempt to manage their symptoms, which might include the purchase of heart or blood pressure monitoring equipment, palpation of their chest wall or taking aspirin. Problem-level formulation should emphasise the role of behaviours which, although designed to alleviate symptoms, serve to exacerbate them. These are usually linked to thoughts which make these behavioural responses more likely (e.g. 'If I don't sit down then my heart will stop) and which serve to reinforce beliefs about the origins of symptoms that are cardiac in origin. An example of this might include 'It must be my heart because every time I check my heart rate, it is above average'. Imaginal representation of catastrophic outcomes often serve to reinforce patient perceptions about the likelihood of negative cardiac events. Essentially, their images serve to create the illusion that the feared events are actually happening, which inflates their estimates of likelihood.

Patients with cardiac concerns who have diagnoses of panic disorder and/or hypochondriasis tend to notice more cardiac changes and slight increases in breathlessness that other people would not notice. This attentional bias should be outlined when evident in problem-level formulations as it is often a trigger for subsequent anxiogenic thoughts and behavioural responses. In some cases patients have anxiogenic thoughts about the cardiac problems which might be associated with the longer term effects of worry or stress (e.g. 'If I keep worrying then I will have a heart attack'). This type II worry (see Chapter 3) may be a reflection of metacognitions which need to be addressed to minimise recurrence or relapse and, in some cases, to prevent the occurrence of other problems.

Case-level formulations should outline beliefs about the causes and consequences of heart problems (the prior administration of the IPQ can help in this regard) and the incidents which seem to have been pivotal in the formation and activation of these beliefs. Formative events often include the experience of a family member having cardiac problems when the patient was younger or comments made by staff ('Chest pain is always a warning sign Mr Jones'). Triggering events may include the death of a family member as a result of heart disease or when a patient approaches the age at which a family member died of a cardiac disease.

Demonstrating the Role of Cognitive and Behavioural Factors in Symptom Occurrence

Assessment will have revealed cognitive behavioural factors which seem to mediate and moderate the experience of chest pain (or other cardiac symptom). The main emphasis after assessment is the demonstration of their role in the genesis and maintenance of chest pain. This serves to enable patients to construct alternatives to a cardiac-related representation. This need can be made explicit at the start of, and throughout, each intervention stage. Patients can be asked to rate the applicability of cardiac-related explanations (e.g. 'My symptoms are caused by heart disease'; 'Seeing a cardiologist is the best way to deal with my pain') as well as rating cognitive behavioural explanations for their symptoms (e.g. 'My thoughts and behaviours are making me have chest pain'). Therapists

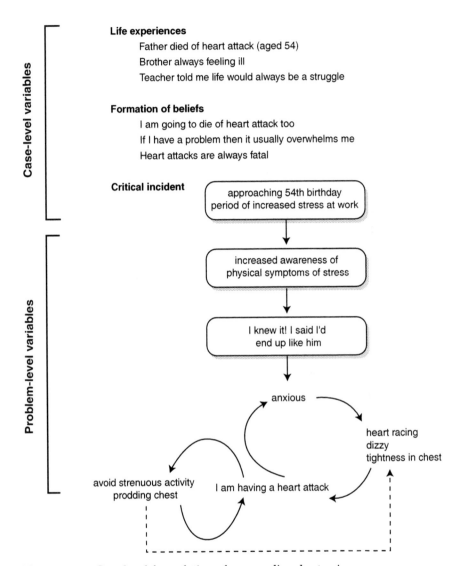

Figure 10.1. Case-level formulation of non-cardiac chest pain

must begin by understanding the evidence base for cardiological representations of symptom experiences. This can be linked to the guiding rationale—the need to gather contradictory evidence for cardiac explanations and confirmatory evidence for non-cardiac-related formulations of problems.

T: It seems from my assessment that most of your experiences are based on the view that your chest pain is caused by a problem with your heart.

P: Well I suppose so, that's just how it seems to me.

T: What I have been starting to suggest is that we work out how you developed this idea and what is keeping it going.

P: Well, I have just always thought that chest pains were symptoms which signalled heart disease—I think most people think that.

T: They can be a sign of heart disease and I can see how you would make the link in this way. Anything else that has resulted in your belief that your chest pains are signs of heart disease?

P: My father and brother both had heart problems—I saw my brother die from a heart attack.

T: Oh dear—how did you feel about having witnessed that?

P: It was awful—I felt helpless.

T: When did that happen to you?

P: Six years ago.

T: I can see why you would believe that chest pain is always a sign of heart disease. However, it may be that there are other factors which explain your chest pain. The idea of this treatment is that we try to explore other explanations of why this might be happening. We also need to look at your evidence why you believe it is heart disease.

P: How do you do that?

T: We will need to work on that together. We need to put our heads together to think about all the reasons why someone may get chest pain. We can then begin to look at each one and see which one is the best explanation for your pains.

P: You mean things like stress?

T: That would be one of the things to put on this list—stress as a cause of chest pain.

P: My sister says indigestion can cause it too—but that is not something I have ever been bothered by.

T: Let's put that down. We should try to think of all the possible reasons.

The most common strategies used in demonstrating cognitive behavioural mediation of cardiac symptoms are those which demonstrate the role of breathing and hyperventilation; the contribution of muscle tension and the role of catastrophic thinking. Patients need to gather evidence on whether these factors relate to their experiences of chest pain, and in this way they can gather evidence for less threatening interpretations for the presence of cardiac symptoms. Enabling patients to appreciate the role of hyperventilation, muscular tension and/or chest wall palpation involves, first, introducing the idea that patient and therapist intend to work together to explore experiences within the session. The role of catastrophic thinking can be demonstrated by using flashcards containing words pertaining to the patients' unique anxiogenic thoughts (collapse, heart attack, pain, crushing). Patients are then encouraged to list the sensations that they attribute to cardiac symptoms and this is used to compare the sensations which they experience during the session as a result of behavioural or cognitive manipulation (though patients are not told that this is going to happen). This can be introduced in the following way:

> T: You will remember that last time we agreed that we need to explore some of the things that might help understand why you have the symptoms that you have had.
> P: Yes.
> T: I wanted to begin by getting you to write down all of the physical symptoms that you get when you are having an episode of chest pain.
> P: Here?
> T: Yes, if you write them down here. Starting with chest pain. What else do you get?
> P: Nausea, light headed . . . oh, and I forgot to say that I feel hot here (*points to forehead*).
> T: Right. . . . I want you to take part in a small experiment now. This will help us to work out whether the way you breathe might relate to these symptoms.

Patients should not engage in an overbreathing demonstration without appropriate medical clearance. The therapist then demonstrates overbreathing and the patient copies the action. Although the patient may be reluctant to continue this as it produces unpleasant sensations, he or she should be encouraged to do so. When this is not possible, therapists can explore the patient's reasons for stopping the experiment, which usually relate to unpleasant sensations and consequent negative predictions about what might happen if he or she were to continue with the experiment. Therapists should not attempt treatment strategies based on symptom induction if they are not confident in their implementation as the strategies often result in the production of distressing physical and emotional symptoms which, if not managed appropriately, may reinforce patient beliefs in serious cardiac pathology (e.g. if the therapist colludes with the cessation of hyperventilation during the session and/or does not challenge the patient's reasons for stopping). These experiments should be presented in a confident manner as patients will interpret overcautiousness on the part of the therapist as evidence that the therapist is also concerned for the integrity of the patient's heart. The role of muscular tension and/or prodding can also be demonstrated within a session. Patients can also begin to appreciate the role of catastrophic thoughts by learning how to identify the automatic thoughts which accompany their experiences of chest pains. Patient discoveries about potential symptom mediators can be used as the first steps in enabling patients to develop more benign interpretations of their chest pains.

Making Changes

When patients have an intellectual understanding of the way in which their breathing, thinking or aspects of their behaviour may relate to their experience of non-cardiac chest pain, they can be encouraged to tackle these factors in their everyday lives. Situations which have been avoided because of previously held beliefs can be confronted using the techniques of graded exposure and/or within the framework of a behavioural experiment. Behaviours which have become habitual because of beliefs about the increased risk of heart problems can be dropped. Anxiogenic thoughts can be evaluated as patients become increasingly aware that their problems are best construed as anxiety symptoms and not as cardiac symptoms. When therapist and patient have identified the main factors which seem to have contributed to perceptions of a cardiac problem (as opposed to an anxiety problem), it is important that further evidence for cardiac risk be elicited and managed. One patient who had successfully identified and modified the thoughts and behaviours which were mediating his chest pain, reported that he still believed (20%) that his pain was an undetected heart complaint. It emerged that this related to the fact that his father had had cardiac problems when aged 53. Although this information had been elicited during the assessment, the therapist had not appreciated that the patient believed that he too would be diagnosed with a heart complaint at that age. Further therapy had significantly reduced the extent to which he believed this to be the case. However, the patient believed that he and his father were similar in so many ways that this must increase the likelihood of them both having heart problems at the same age.

MANAGING ANGINA

Angina results from episodes where insufficient blood flow to the cardiac muscle creates chest pains and shortness of breath, and can often be triggered and exacerbated by stress, emotional extremes and physical exertion. Angina has been shown to be associated with depression, anxiety, neuroticism, type A behaviour and raised levels of somatic awareness. Assessments should emphasise these points, using self-report measures when available. Recent episodes should be reviewed in detail, with particular attention being devoted to the duration of the episode, the reaction of the patient and significant others, as well as their medication use. Activity levels are often implicated as key mediators of problems with physical deconditioning among patients with angina. Inactivity tends to lower the anginal threshold (Lewin, 1997). Many of the concepts which are part of the cognitive behavioural management of chronic pain can be used in the assessment, conceptualisation and management of angina. The use of pain diaries is particularly relevant and help patients and therapists to identify the key influences on their experiences of angina. Problem-level formulations of avoidance of activity often specify the primary mediating role of predictions about worsening chest pain. Case-level formulations should aim to link neuroticism, avoidance and anginal interference with activities. Exercise has been shown to result in significant benefits for patients with angina; however, many patients do not feel able to engage in exercise because of beliefs which promote avoidance related to 'taking it easy'. This is often made more difficult by the fact that misconceptions may be shared by health care staff (Lewin, 1999).

CBT is helpful in enabling patients to modify thoughts and beliefs which block access to exercise, and patients can use graded task assignment and activity scheduling to build exercise into their routine. Patients may avoid returning to work because of overcautiousness, which is usually mainfest as thoughts about overexertion and links with death or an acute cardiac event. Research also suggests that interventions designed to promote relaxation and the management of stress (i.e. perceived coping incapacity) are beneficial. Cognitive mechanisms relating to patient experience of stress can be useful as ways of structuring intervention. Whatever variables are targeted in CBT, angina and activity levels should be monitored as key outcome variables.

CARDIAC REHABILITATION

There are a number of cognitive behavioural strategies which therapists can apply to the process of cardiac rehabilitation (Bennett & Carroll, 1994). In addition to strategies which are specific to rehabilitation (such as the process of risk factor modification), the management of non-cardiac chest pain, other psychologically mediated cardiac symptoms and the cognitive behavioural management of angina often form integral parts of the rehabilitation of patients following a heart attack. Bennett (1993) has summed up the psychological experience of having a myocardial infarction:

A heart attack is a physically devastating event. It is frightening, involving immediate threat to life and loss of control. It can be extremely painful. Sufferers are often surrounded by worried by-standers, rushed dramatically to hospital where they are surrounded by modern medical paraphernalia, monitored by ECG, routinely observed by nurses and given painkilling medications that sedate and confuse.

This experience can act as the trigger which motivates some patients to make significant changes in their lifestyle, and it may be necessary for other patients to help them to think about the advantages of doing so. There are significant data that hypertension, raised serum cholesterol and smoking are risk factors for the presence of coronary heart disease. The presence of more than one risk factor increases the overall risk and thus some patients can be advised to consider focusing on one risk factor as a way of reducing their overall risk. Statistics of this nature can be helpful to some patients embarking upon an intervention to modify their cardiac risk behaviour(s). Cardiac rehabilitation aims to help patients to feel confident in making the lifestyle changes which can reduce their risk of further problems and enhance their quality of life. It may also have a beneficial impact on health service utilisation factors such as re-hospitalisation rates (Black et al., 1998).

Assessment

Patients should be assessed with specific regard to the predominant components of their cardiac illness representation, its relationship to their lifestyle choices premorbidly, and how this might relate to which risk factors to target during rehabilitation. Beliefs about heart disease are central to understanding cardiac-related disability and quality of life (Lewin, 1999). Much of the emphasis of cardiac rehabilitation involves enabling patients to appreciate why lifestyle changes might be advantageous. This is almost impossible if therapists do not first appreciate the extent to which patients' lives involved risk factors for cardiac problems. Assessing the extent to which patients have had the experience of making prior changes in lifestyle (e.g. due to other social or medical factors) may help to identify information which can be used to plan interventions. Patients have varied beliefs regarding the cause of heart disease and vary enormously in the extent to which they understand the functioning and structure of their hearts. Approximatley 40–50% of post-myocardial infarction patients will have problems with anxiety in the months after their admission to hospital, and as many as 20% may still have anxiety-related problems 12 months after the initial cardiac event.

Depression is often more prevalent at discharge from hospital and is now believed to be an independent risk factor for ischaemic heart disease (Hippisley-Cox, Fielding & Pringle, 1998; Hemingway & Marmot, 1999). It is conceivable therefore that the treatment of depressed mood may feature as a distinct component of cardiac rehabilitation for some patients.

T: Some of the nurses may have been talking to you about risk factors for heart disease. Have they?

P: More than once.

T: As I was saying, part of my role as part of the cardiac rehabilitation team is to help you to look at your behaviours and feelings—to see if there are any aspects you might want to change as part of enhancing your quality of life.

P: I would like to change a lot of things, if I could.

T: I thought that it would be best if we started talking about what risk factors you think you have—then we can look at whether you want to think about making any changes.

P: Well, smoking is the biggie—I have tried to give that up.

T: Any other risk factors?

P: I don't do much exercise and I have a stressful job. I think that's about it—what else could there be?

T: Your diet?

P: No, it is OK—the dietician has been in and she says things are OK.

T: What one do you feel that you are most confident to change?

P: Maybe the exercise. . . .

Formulation

Problem-level formulations of problems associated with cardiac rehabilitation commonly focus upon risk behaviours and facilitative beliefs regarding their presence. Formulations should also contain detail on beliefs about motivation to modify them. The Stages of Change Model referred to in Chapter 3 can be used to conceptualise the patient stage with regard to readiness to make changes in risk behaviour. Cognitive Dissonance Theory can be used to conceptualise problems related to patients who minimise the disadvantages of change. The cognitive model of substance misuse (Beck et al., 1993) is particularly useful for the formulation of problems relating to cigarette smoking. Case-level formulations of psychosocial elements of cardiac rehabilitation should outline the critical nature of recent acute cardiac events (e.g. myocardial infarction), the presence of other life events and psychosocial problems which may relate

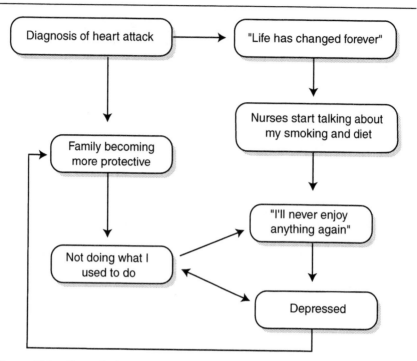

Figure 10.2. Formulating problems during cardiac rehabilitation

to patient strategies for the management of behaviours and feelings resulting from cardiac events. Bennett and Carroll (1994) have noted the lack of cohesion often present in cardiac rehabilitation services. The uncertainty and confusion that this can cause should be outlined in case-level formulations.

Education

Patients may distort or misinterpret statements made by nursing or medical staff regarding their illness and staff advice about the process of rehabilitation. Patients often draw conclusions about the aetiology of heart disease and its treatment based on the statements of staff. These may be factually inaccurate and can become the targets for educational interventions. Common examples of patient misinterpretations include 'If I don't watch what I do then I will surely die'. Inaccurate understanding is also seen in the relatives of patients referred for cardiac rehabilitation. Many of the beliefs of patients and family members relate to the beliefs which link lifestyle factors and the occurrence of future cardiac events. The provision of accurate information early in the course of a patient's cardiac illness trajectory (i.e. during admission or at the first out-patient appointment) can result in belief changes which might be more difficult to achieve months after initial hospital admission. In cases of patients referred many months after the initial event, it may be necessary to combine educational components with behavioural experiments or thought change strategies.

T: One of the things that I noticed during the assessment we did, was that you mentioned that you would have to take it easy now. You were telling me that this was because Sister Brown said to you that you should take things a day at a time and don't overdo it—did I understand you correctly?

P: Yes, that's what she said. Don't overdo it.

T: We talked about your activity diary and you were telling me that your day-to-day routine is largely based on the belief that if you exert yourself when you are tired you are putting too much strain on your heart.

P: That's what I thought she meant by overdo it—yes.

T: Sometimes we find that because of the shock and stress of being in the coronary care unit, patients and relatives misunderstand what the staff have been saying. What do you think that Sister Brown meant by not overdoing it?

P: To rest until I feel like my old self again.

T: Do you think she could have been meaning anything else?

P: I don't think so. Do you?

T: I wonder if she might have meant to do this when you were in hospital. I guess I am not sure if she meant this at home.

Modifying Risk Behaviour

Patients often state that they are motivated to make changes to risk behaviours, often citing the shock which their 'near miss' has produced as the main reason for this. This is often a 'knee jerk' reaction. It is important that all patients who wish to embark upon an intervention designed to modify a risk behaviour spend some time considering the prior function of the behaviour in their lives. They must also consider the reasons why it might be advantageous to them to modify this and the obstacles which might exist to change. Therapists should not take statements about lifestyle changes at face value. Treatment goals should emphasise the reinforcement of small changes. Approaches which consistently remind patients of the need for large changes ('You've got 10 pounds still to lose') can fail because of the demotivating effects inherent in this approach. Risk factor modification should aim to enhance a patient's self-efficacy— something which is often compromised by the shock of a sudden cardiac event. Diary monitoring of risk behaviours, self-efficacy and regular goal-setting will help to keep patients focused upon small changes. This approach to intervention is outlined in the following session extract:

T: We were focusing on how you could cut out some of the cigarettes that you have at coffee break time?

P: Mm . . . you remembered? (Laughs)

T: We thought that this would be a good way of anticipating the problems that you might have when you try to quit for good.

P: It certainly helped me to fill in this sheet that we drew out. I have a lot of disadvantages of stopping smoking written down because of what I did at the coffee breaks.

T: Like what?

P: No one to talk to, feeling on edge, dejected that I have nothing to look forward to at the breaks.

T: I see. So this has been helpful in thinking about helping you to stop— we have discovered some of the factors that are interfering with your confidence and motivation to give up. Using the scale I taught you, how confident are you that you can give up?

P: 25%.

T: And how motivated are you to give up?

P: 40%.

T: It seems like we need to help you to feel more confident and motivated?

P: I think so. If I knew how to deal with all this stuff here I would be able to feel more confident.

CBT AND VENTRICULAR ARRHYTHMIA

Ventricular arrhythmia is a disturbance in the electrical activity of the heart that manifests as an abnormality in heart rate of rhythm. Patients who survive an episode of this problem (it is often fatal) are often treated by having a device implanted into the chest which will deliver an electric shock to the heart in the event of the patient experiencing a further deviation from the normal electrical functioning of the heart. Patients who have survived near death due to this problem often experience psychological responses which respond well to CBT. These are usually characterised by anxiety and/or panic. Patients who have implanted cardiac defibrillators (ICDs) also report problems with anxiety and panic. There is a small but growing literature on the cognitive conceptualisation and management of the problems associated with ventricular arrhythmia (sometimes referred to as ventricular dysrhythmia) (Dunbar & Summerville, 1997).

Assessment

Assessment of patients with ICDs should cover the elements of psychosocial adjustment to serious cardiac problems which have already been outlined. It should also address patient thoughts about the activation of the device and future oriented imagery about this. Patients may have memories of prior life-threatening episodes when serious arrhythmias may have occurred. Some patients with this device may have traumatic recollections of their experiences in resuscitation. They may have experienced shocks from the implanted device—which should be screened for and the cognitive behavioural consequences of activation assessed. Patients who have experienced such activations often report unpleasant memories relating to their experience of a spontaneous shock. Patients who have not experienced activation usually have thoughts and feelings which relate to predictions about how they imagine such activations to be. Patients may be hypervigilant for device activation and therapists should assess the physical signs and sensations that they use to determine their risk status in this regard. Understanding of the need for and functioning of the ICD is important and should be routinely assessed. The time spent thinking about the possibility of device activation may become a target of treatment and certainly provides clues to the significance of the device in understanding overall adjustment.

> T: You spend quite a bit of your time thinking about activation of the device?
> P: Yes, there are very few times when I am not aware that it could go off.
> T: How helpful is that to you?
> P: How helpful?
> T: Yes, how helpful do you think that this is for your quality of life?
> P: Well it is not—no, no way is it helpful.
> T: What are the reasons that you think you spend time thinking about it?
> P: I can't imagine what it will be like.
> T: The unknown. This makes it difficult for you?
> P: Yes, I can't imagine what it would be like to have it happen to me.

T: Would you like to try to imagine what it could be like and, instead of focusing on what might be, using what we know from people where it has happened and your own experieince of heart problems?

P: I could try.

T: What do you think would have to happen before it would go off?

P: I would probably feel a bit unwell at the time. . . .

T: And what would happen then?

P: I have no idea.

T: What do you predict will happen?

P: I just feel that it will be dreadful.

T: Is there something specific that you dread?

P: Well it won't be pleasant. I guess that it is the not knowing I worry about. I don't know what will happen afterwards either.

T: Everyone I have spoken to who has had their device activated has had a different experience. I don't know how you might be affected. Would it help if I arranged for you to meet some of the self help group I know—this way you can ask them about their experiences?

P: I think it might help—but it could make me worse too.

T: What about if you listed all their experiences and then we spent some time helping you think about how you feel and think about them happening to you?

Patients may have beliefs about mechanical, medical devices or technological advances in general ('Technology can't be trusted'). These should be elicited and examples provided of times when these influence psychosocial elements of adjustment to the living with the device. Assessing the patient's experience of and attitudes to using devices such as computers and video recorders often results in information about problems interacting with machinery.

Formulation

Increased levels of distress among patients with serious and recurrent ventricular dysrhythmia has been shown to be associated with pessimistic personality, greater levels of perceived threat and more changes in work status. Problem-level formulations commonly outline patient perceptions of threat and how these relate to psychological symptom occurrence. Problem-focused coping has been shown to be associated with preferable outcomes for those patients with ICDs. Coping style and its relationship to thoughts, feelings and behaviours may be the primary factors mediating difficulties with quality of life. Patients with longstanding tendencies towards self-doubt and suspicion may experience

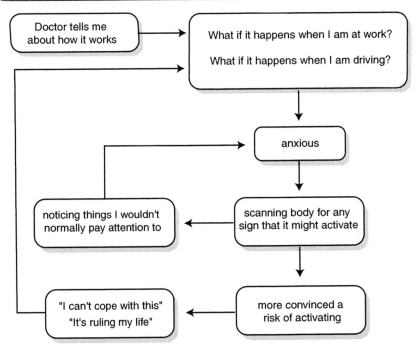

Figure 10.3. Formulation of problems with implantable cardiac defribrillator

automatic thoughts which question the reliability and functioning of the device, and this should be outlined in a formulation. Future oriented imagery may become frozen at the point of shock. Time distortions of this sort are crucial within a formulation as it enables the patient to appreciate why they are always anxious when they think about device activation.

Intervention Strategies

Cognitive behavioural treatments for psychological problems associated with ICDs emphasise the importance of enhancing control and reducing the fear associated with the device and the illness it is designed to manage. Patients need to be able to adjust to the knowledge that their device may activate at any time. Interventions should help patients to understand that the device has been implanted to save their lives, and patients need to explore whether they can work towards viewing it as a source of security (as opposed to a source of threat). Modification of threat representations in favour of those thematically related to security will often result in an improvement in symptoms of anxiety and panic.

The identification of misinterpretations (i.e. 'This is it, I am about to be shocked') can be treated using verbal reattribution strategies which aim to target bias and promote reinterpretation which takes account of the physical manifestations of anxiety and apprehension. Therapists should be careful that they do not dismiss reasonable levels of fear regarding the unpleasant nature of experiencing an unpredictable electrical shock. Patients may benefit from strategies which enable them to differentiate the factors over which they do and do not have control (i.e. no control over when they are shocked but high control over their emotional reactions to shocks). Many patients will have other cardiac problems such as angina, and treatment of this may also result in enhanced confidence in their ability to control fears about the ICD or minimise the anxiety that is triggered by chest pain.

T: The main thoughts that trouble you are your tendency to predict that it is going to activate and also your thoughts that you will not survive if it does go off?

P: Yes, those are the main things that I worry about.

T: Which is the one that you think you need most help with?

P: Definitely my thought that it is going to activate.

T: How many times have you thought this?

P: Hundreds.

T: And of these 100 times how many times has it activated?

P: None.

T: What do you think keeps you thinking that it might activate?

P: I feel so dreadful at the time. . . . I think that it has to happen sometime soon.

T: Is that what you have been told will happen to you before it activates?

P: No—Dr Jones said that you have no warning at all.

T: Do you know what makes it activate?

P: When I have an irregular heart rhythm?

T: Yes. You have had that happen before?

P: Yes, the time I was in A&E. 1998.

T: Looking back on that day, was there any sign that you were not feeling well beforehand?

P: I don't think so.

T: So you have been told that there will be no warning and you don't recall having a warning in 1998. However, you have at least 100 occasions where you are concerned that it will activate because you are getting a warning? I am a bit confused.

P: That sounds cuckoo doesn't it—I wouldn't get a warning sign, would I? Perhaps that's the problem, these are all false alarms—the fact that I think they are warnings means that it can't be that problem. . . . why didn't I think of that?

T: You just did!! (Laughs)

P: (Laughs).

SUMMARY AND CONCLUSIONS

There are many ways in which CBT can contribute to the psychological well-being of people with cardiac problems. These include: the amelioration of chest pain which is non-cardiac in origin; the treatment of anxiety and depression following a myocardial infarction; the modification of behaviours which confer risk for heart disease; and the minimisation of the impact of cardiac symptoms such as angina or treatments such as implantable defibrillators. Formulations are often based on knowledge about heart disease, the regulation of activities, motivation to make lifestyle changes and the role of anxiogenic thinking in the generation of dysfunctional behavioural and physical changes. Some patients have multiple cardiac problems and in such cases interventions consists of a range of CBT strategies.

Part III

PROFESSIONAL PRACTICE AND SERVICE DELIVERY

Chapter 11

PROFESSIONAL ISSUES

INTRODUCTION

There are a wide range of professional issues which face therapists working with people experiencing longstanding medical problems. Some of these are specific to the practice of CBT, others pertain to the practice of psychological therapy with the physically ill and some to the practice of psychotherapy in all settings. Therapists need to ensure that they have arrangements in place for their continuing professional development, supervision and self-care as these are central to ensuring good-quality practice. Most cognitive behavioural therapists would agree that there are times when their practice can be extremely challenging and have the potential to negatively influence their own physical and psychological well-being. The practice of CBT in medical settings brings with it a unique set of challenges as it requires therapists to keep abreast of developments within CBT, health psychology and medicine.

Therapists working in mental health settings are often at an advantage in that many of their colleagues will have an understanding and working knowledge of what CBT is and how it is practically applied to the patients under their care. In physical health settings, medical and nursing staff are much less likely to have this information about or experience of CBT, and it will be unlikely that they will have a basic understanding of the relevance and applicability of CBT to the problems experienced by the patients under their care. However, this can be an advantage insomuch as referrers and clinical colleagues do not have entrenched negative ideas about CBT, cognitive behaviourally oriented therapists or psychological therapy in general. Staff in general hospital settings tend to have greater familiarity with the medical model of illness, which can result in problems with patient acceptance, understanding and/or socialisation to a cognitive behavioural model. Therapists may need to devote proportionally more of their time to working with staff and/or establishing staff training in cognitive and behavioural aspects of physical health problems.

This chapter begins by addressing the training requirements of cognitive behavioural therapists working with the physically ill. It then addresses the ways in which therapists can maintain their professional development, how they might address their supervision needs and what strategies they may need to implement to promote self-care and prevent psychological problems themselves.

TRAINING REQUIREMENTS

Cognitive behavioural therapists who work with the medical problems outlined in this book should be competent in the theory and practice of CBT for the common psychological problems of adulthood. This is usually assumed to be the most prevalent Axis I disorders within the Diagnostic and Statistical Manual of Mental Disorders (American Psychiatric Association). Scott and Moorhead (1998) have outlined a useful framework (see Table 11.1) within which various levels of therapist competency are outlined. Therapists who routinely provide CBT services to patients with chronic medical problems should have at least Level 3 skills within this framework. Ideally, therapist level of skill in the application of CBT should be Level 3 for the application of CBT to common adult psychological problems as well as to the psychological problems and issues faced by the physically ill. It is recognised, however, that there may be a discrepancy betweeen the 'mainstream' skill level and the level of competence required when considering CBT practice in this more specialised area. An example of this might be a therapist who is a competent practitioner of CBT in mainstream adult mental health practice, but an advanced beginner when applying CBT to the psychological problems of people with cancer and/or diabetes (see Table 11.1).

Most therapists will be able to assess, conceptualise and treat psychological disorders among the chronically physically ill when patients present with problems for which their medical problems contribute little to the overall picture. The 'specialist' element of CBT is most applicable to work with patients for whom their medical condition and its management result in the presentation of problems and issues which require therapists to have greater knowledge and skill in tailoring CBT to their physical health needs. CBT services for patients with chronic medical problems should be provided by therapists who are accredited by the British Association for Behavioural and Cognitive Psychotherapies (BABCP). The accreditation criteria are outlined in Table 11.2.

Therapists who are working towards accreditation and/or who wish to enhance their knowledge and skill in the application of CBT to the problems covered in this book need to ensure that they address this ongoing

Table 11.1 CBT levels of skill

Skills level	Clinical behaviour	Training process
Level 1: Novice	Rigid adherence to taught techniques Little overall strategy Poor judgement in choice of target problem	Seminar based teaching Irregular exposure to workshops
Level 2: Advanced beginner	More judgement in choice, but still favours 1–2 techniques Overall strategy still limited All presenting problems given equal importance	More regular workshops Basic supervision Training clinic
Level 3: Competent practitioner	Choice of technique appropriate to identified problem More systematic planning of interventions Structure of therapy follows a standard and routine pattern Sees need for interventions to be part of longer term strategy and case formulation (cannot always achieve this)	Training clinic (a minority will be able to reach this standard in this setting) Regular supervision Post-Qualification Training Course
Level 4: Proficient practitioner	Is guided by the case formulation in choice of target problems and type of interventions Discerns what is most important in communication and more aware of unique needs or characteristics of the person Therapy proceeds smoothly, decision-making is less laboured	Post-Qualification Training Course with post-course maintenance supervision Specialist registrar training post in CBT
Level 5: Expert practitioner	Develops sophisticated and accurate case conceptualisation Focuses on important aspects of problems Uses standard techniques smoothly and is able to repair ruptures in the therapeutic relationship Has intuitive grasp and deep tacit understanding of the individuals problems No longer adheres rigidly to guidelines; able to use technical recommendations flexibly and deviates or goes beyond them when the clinical situation requires this	Continuous experience and practice of CBT (> 4 years) with regular peer supervision and frequent attendance at CPD and training workshops

Reprinted with permission of Scott and Moorhead (1998)

Table 11.2   BABCP accrediation criteria

Applicants must:

- have a relevant professional training to degree level or equivalent;

- have been accountable for their own professional practice to a senior member of their profession for at least two years full time, or equivalent, since professional qualification;

- demonstrate knowledge and understanding of the therapeutic relationship and competence in the development, maintenance and ending of such relationships;

- show evidence of sustained commitment to the theory and practice of Behavioural and/or Cognitive Psychotherapy, which includes continuing professional development;

- have ongoing supervision;

- provide a satisfactory statement of training in the theory and practice of Behavioural and/or Cognitive Psychotherapy related to designated areas of competence;

- adhere to the Guidelines for Good Practice of the British Association for Behavioural and Cognitive Psychotherapies and be willing to be scrutinised in this adherence as required.

need as part of their continuing professional development (CPD) and as they work towards accreditation. All therapists have an obligation to maintain knowledge and skill through CPD. This will include keeping up to date with journals and attending conferences or workshops. These issues are equally relevant to practitioners at all levels of competency as a means of developing, consolidating and maintaining skills. Most cognitive behavioural therapists will be employed on salaries, terms and conditions according to their core professional grouping (e.g. clinical psychology or psychiatry). In most cases this will be appropriate as therapists tend to incorporate skill and knowledge from their profession to the care of patients. There are some situations, however, where two therapists from differing professional groups may be working according to identical job specifications, such as when two cognitive behavioural therapists are working as research therapists in a controlled trial. In these cases, management should certainly consider very carefully the individual tasks and responsibilities of the staff members. When analysis (possibly structured according to some of the systems which exist for the analysis of jobs) reveals that two therapists are performing identical tasks, despite their different professional backgrounds, they should be paid according to what they are employed to do, but the absence of any nationally agreed salary scales for cognitive behavioural therapists can make this a difficult issue.

CONTINUING PROFESSIONAL DEVELOPMENT

Journal Articles

Therapists should regularly review the content of journals in cognitive therapy, behaviour therapy, medicine, surgery, clinical and health psychology. Medically oriented journals occasionally contain articles on CBT and, more often, articles which will help therapists to keep up to date with developments in medicine and surgery. Research published within psychology journals often includes findings which, although not written with CBT in mind, can be helpful in thinking about how it might be applied to the assessment, formulation or treatment of psychological problems. Many of the developments within mainstream CBT can be applied or modified to the problems of people with chronic physical illness, and therapists will want to keep track of the journals in these areas.

Therapists should develop the habit of regularly reviewing the content pages of journals, and some of the journals which are relevant to the needs of cognitive behavioural therapists are outlined in Table 11.3. Some hospital libraries will provide copies of content pages on a routine basis, and technological developments mean that some therapists can take advantage of electronic alerting services. These services e-mail the contents pages of journals in which therapists have expressed an interest. Most of the libraries of larger academic institutions can advise on access to this service and an increasing number of hospital libraries will be able to facilitate access to this service. Some journals also have home pages on the Internet, and therapists without access to the electronic alerting services may be able to obtain contents information in this way. Searching databases such as Medline or PsycLit is another way in which therapists might be able to identify published research. It is also possible to conduct a Medline search, save the search terms, have this electronically repeated at a specific time and have the results e-mailed to you. This service is available at http://www3.infotrieve.com.

Table 11.3 Journals relevant to CBT for chronic medical problems

British Medical Journal	*Psycho-Oncology*
Journal of Psychosomatic Research	*Psychological Medicine*
British Journal of Health Psychology	*Psychosomatic Medicine*
Journal of Clinical Psychology in Medical Settings	*International Journal of Psychiatry in Medicine*
Behavioural and Cognitive Psychotherapy	*Journal of the American Medical Association*
Cognitive Therapy and Research	
Evidence Based Mental Health	*Journal of Behavioral Medicine*
Health Psychology	*Clinical Psychology Review*
Journal of Health Psychology	

Conferences

Attending conferences and workshops provides therapists with useful opportunities to learn about the latest research findings in CBT (often before these findings are published in the journals) and to develop their clinical skills. Conferences and workshops are advertised in some of the journals and via professional organisations such as the BABCP, the International Association for Cognitive Psychotherapy (IACP), the British Psychological Society (BPS) and the Royal College of Psychiatrists. The BABCP website has a section for publicising forthcoming conferences (http://www. babcp.org.uk). Therapists who are having difficulty accessing relevant topics at conferences and workshops could consider inviting someone to present and/or provide a workshop (local BABCP branches might arrange this).

Supervision

Supervision is essential to maintain a safe, effective and good-quality CBT practice. Obtaining specialist supervision for the sorts of problems outlined in this book will not always be possible owing to a shortage of cognitive behavioural therapists with the required levels of expertise. Therapists in these circumstances should aim to complement their supervision in mainstream CBT with reading and attendance at courses on CBT applications with physical health problems. The BABCP register of accredited cognitive and behavioural psychotherapists contains details of therapists with expertise in the application of CBT to physical health problems. It may be possible to arrange telephone supervision and/or keep in touch by e-mail with colleagues who are interested in CBT with this patient population. If a number of local clinicians are interested in CBT with the physically ill, then it may be worth while considering the establishment of a peer supervision group or a special interest group.

Using the Internet

Riley and Veale (1999) have outlined the ways in which the Internet can be of assistance to cognitive behavioural psychotherapists. It is rapidly becoming an invaluable way of keeping abreast of developments within CBT, communicating with colleagues across the world, searching literature, submitting conference papers and journal articles, ordering books and test materials, and finding out about medical conditions experienced by patients. Some websites that may be of interest to cognitive behavioural therapists are outlined in Table 11.4, which includes details on sites that will specifically relate to the application of CBT in medical and surgical settings. There are a number of e-mailing lists (also listed in Table 11.4) which can act as a useful source for information and discussion on professional issues and practice. There are many more of these than would be possible to outline here and therapists should look out for those that are most relevant to their interests and practice. In some cases therapists may even think about establishing their own websites or moderating an e-mailing list.

Table 11.4 Websites and e-mailing lists

Websites

It is obviously impossible to provide an exhaustive list of websites. The best strategy for finding web-based CBT resources is to use a 'meta' search engine (e.g. http://www.dogpile.com; http://www.37.com). The following sites illustrate the range that is available covering journals, professional organisations and interest groups:

http://www.bmj.com
http://www.academyofct.org
http://iacp.asu.edu
http://www.bps.org.uk
http://www.babcp.org.uk
http://www.apa.org
http://www.behavior.net
http://www.ama-assn.org

http://www.health-psych.org
http://www.psychosomatic.org
http://www.ehps.net
http://www.apm.org
http://www.healthanswers.com
http://www.bpos.org.uk
http://www.ipos-aspboa.org/iposnews.htm
http://www.padesky.com
http://www.beckinstitute.org

E-mailing lists

BABCP e-mailing list:
  babcp@mailbase.ac.uk
International Psycho-Oncology Society e-mailing list:
  ipos@listserv.acor.org
Clinical Psychology discussion list:
  clinical-psychologists@listserv.nodak.edu
American Psychological Association, Division of Health Psychology discussion list:
  div38@lists.apa.org
American Psychological Association, Practice Directorate discussion list:
  practice@lists.apa.org
American Psychological Association list for discussions pertaining to clinical psychology:
  Clinapags.lists.apa.org
International Association for Cognitive Psychotherapy discussion list:
  iacp@mailbase.ac.uk

Most of these lists require participants to be members of the organisations which organise the list

---

SELF-CARE

The practice of CBT is demanding. Many of the demands are not unique to CBT practice with physically ill patients as most CBT therapists are used to being repeatedly exposed to the problems experienced by people who have had negative and/or traumatic experiences. Exposure to the negative consequences of physical illness and its treatment can, however, be more difficult if therapists have been unaware of the extent and nature of the sorts of problems experienced as a result of some physical illnesses. It is understandable that clinicians who are not working with illnesses such as cancer or diabetes, and problems like chronic pain or disfigurement, will not always be fully aware of the suffering that these problems can cause. These aspects of working with the physically ill can come as a shock to some and result in increased feelings of personal vulnerability to illness. Therapists who work with people experiencing problems associated with a high mortality rate may find it particularly challenging when more than one patient dies within a short space of time. Difficulties adjusting to these aspects of practice are usually more likely when patients of similar background, personal characteristics or experience die (triggering personal beliefs about potential illness or existential issues) and/or when this occurs at a time of personal change and stress for therapists.

Therapists may wish to think about having a support network of professional colleagues and personal acquaintances who can be contacted in the event of the need for support on the psychological consequences of working with people who are chronically physically ill. This support network can include colleagues or supervisors and in some cases may include therapists who agree to be available to help therapists to think about how they might address psychological problems when they develop. A sample support network is outlined in Table 11.5 as an illustration of the number of people within it and the nature of agreements regarding support (names have been changed). Therapists who develop clinically significant psychological problems can find it difficult to know whom to contact. It is helpful if therapists think about what they might wish to do in the event that they need professional help. Ideally, therapists should contact their GP for referral to an appropriate professional. Therapists should be discouraged from making their own arrangements with colleagues whom they know by virtue of their professional roles.

SUMMARY AND CONCLUSIONS

Cognitive behavioural theory and practice is rapidly changing. Therapists working with chronic medical problems must ensure that they are competent and knowledgeable about cognitive and behavioural practice not only with common psychological disorders but also with the medical problems experienced by their patients. This can be achieved by having a strategy for continuing professional development (which includes

Table 11.5 Sample self-care plan

Professional

Clinical
Fortnightly supervision with Dr D. Jones (Cognitive Therapy)
Fortnightly supervision with Mr G. Hardingham (Clinical Psychology). This
   includes a standing agenda item on effects of work on therapist psychological
   well-being
Three-monthly appraisal with Dr H. Parker (Continuing Professional
   Development/Management)

Research
Monthly supervision with Prof. G. H. McGhee (Research)

Personal

Partner
Close friend
H. Hills (friend who is a clinical psychologist)
Key family members
Certain staff within department

This self-care plan also outlines a number of high-risk events, themes and
psychological signs that may indicate that these high risk situations have
triggered psychological vulnerabilties. It also outlines strategies for the
prevention and amelioration of these problems if they develop.

supervision). The challenges of repeated exposure to the problems of
people with psychological and physical health problems can compromise
the well-being of therapists, and it is for this reason that self-care strategies also need to be incorporated into CBT practice.

Chapter 12

SERVICE PROVISION

INTRODUCTION

Most acute hospital and primary care trusts within the UK National Health Service do not have dedicated CBT services for patients with chronic medical problems. They are more likely to have a range of psychological and psychiatric services which may or may not include therapists skilled in the provision of CBT for the psychological problems and disorders associated with the problems outlined in this book. Cognitive behavioural therapies are likely to be provided as part of existing hospital liaison psychiatry or clinical psychology services and/or through local clinical psychology departments. In some cases these departments will have clinicians who have a defined sessional commitment to particular medical specialties (e.g. a diabetes clinic or a chronic pain service). More usually access to CBT for patients with longstanding physical health problems will be through therapists providing services as part of mainstream mental health services in community clinics and GPs' surgeries. This range of service settings and service configurations means that the provision of CBT services often varies for this patient group, in terms of integration, comprehensiveness and cohesiveness. Nevertheless there are common issues which cognitive behavioural therapists working with the physically ill will need to address regarding service provision. This chapter addresses these common issues and outlines how therapists might take account of them in establishing, enhancing or extending the quality provision of CBT for patients with chronic medical problems.

RANGE OF SERVICES OFFERED

The nature and range of services offered by therapists will be determined by the number of whole-time equivalent cognitive behavioural therapists available to patients with chronic medical problems. The level of training of individual practitioners, their professional affiliations and ability to 'network' with like-minded colleagues will also influence the pattern of service provision. A hospital with one part-time cognitive behavioural therapist will have access to a much more limited range of services than a hospital with two full-time cognitive behavioural therapists. The former hospital may have to accept that the therapist will be unable to concentrate on in-patient work while also managing an out-patient waiting list. The therapists at the other hospital, on the other hand, are more likely to be able to set up their service to combine in-patient and out-patient working and may even have the resources and time to work on staff training, supervision and consultancy. Therapists need to ensure that all potential referrers are aware of the CBT services available within the constraints of the therapist resource. Some of the potential CBT services that might be available are outlined in Table 12.1.

Table 12.1   An example of the range of services offered

- Cognitive behavioural assessment and treatment of psychological problems and disorders associated with chronic medical problems

- Cognitive behaviourally oriented advice to staff on the medical management of patient problems (e.g. where there may be an interaction between emotional and physical factors)

- Consultancy and supervision of staff in basic psychosocial assessments according to a cognitive behavioural model of psychological functioning (e.g. providing specialist nurses with information on ways of eliciting patient thoughts during a nursing assessment)

- Teaching and training on cognitive behavioural models and therapies (e.g provision of a workshop on how to prepare patients for referral to a cognitive behavioural therapist)

- Research into cognitive behavioural factors in chronic medical problems, the effectiveness of CBT and the interface between patients, staff and hospital systems

Patients referred for CBT may have psychological problems which need to be addressed using other forms of psychological therapy (e.g. interpersonal psychotherapy, psychodynamic psychotherapy), medication (e.g. antidepressant medication) or case management. Cognitive behavioural therapists need to ensure that their services are suitably integrated with other mental health and psychological services. This may include hospital-based liaison psychiatric teams, community mental health teams, clinical psychology departments and counselling services. Therapists should also ensure that they have appropriate links with GPs and primary care teams.

Some therapists have found that their CBT work can be focused around specific medical specialties and/or disorders. Common examples of this might include CBT clinics which operate alongside breast cancer clinics or clinics for diabetes. This way of working can have benefits for therapists and medical/nursing colleagues. Staff begin to develop an improved understanding of cognitive behavioural practice, clinic protocols for cognitive behavioural management of psychological disorders may be developed, and staff can begin to provide care which is truly integrated and provided within a biopsychosocial perspective. Staff can arrange for appointments where therapists and medical staff can also conduct joint assessments or therapy sessions which address both medical and psychological variables. There are many ways in which these arrangements can lead to innovative and time-saving strategies. An example of this might be where an anaesthetist has been trained in the socialisation of patients to a basic cognitive behavioural model of chronic pain and can enable patients to begin basic pain severity monitoring to bring to their first appointment for CBT. Cognitive behavioural therapists often find that working in such disorder-specific clinics can increase their knowledge of the medical problems experienced by their patients and can lead to more confident interactions with medical staff and/or advising that colleagues review medical factors previously overlooked.

Clinicians need referral guidelines if the number of inappropriate referrals are to be kept to a minimum. These should outline the types of clinical problems for which there is evidence that CBT is effective. It is also helpful to include advice on which aspects of patient presentation might be contraindications for CBT, or emphasising when particular signs suggest that CBT would be the most suitable form of intervention. Some referrers find it easier if services can be accessed by a referral form. These can be devised in such a way that referrers can provide information according to a forced choice format as well as being able to provide written detail on patient problems. Forms should have a section with prompts about which factors in referral guidelines to consider. An example of a referral form is outlined in Table 12.2.

MANAGING REFERRALS

Therapists will want to ensure that patients have prompt and equitable access for CBT. Most cognitive behavioural therapists will find that their skills are much in demand and those working in out-patient settings will build up a waiting list. The high demand for CBT and the shortage of suitably qualified staff makes this situation inevitable. There are some ways in which this can be avoided. In some cases waiting lists are inappropriate (e.g. palliative medicine services). One way of managing

Table 12.2 Referral form (includes referral guidelines)

Date of referral:
Reason for referral:

Name:
Address:
Unit number:
Date of birth:
In-patient/Out-patient/Day patient (circle one)
Referring clinician:
Specialty:
Diagnosis (medical condition):
Treatment/current management:

Psychological problems (tick those that apply)

Anxiety	Depression	Appearance
Panic	OCD	Adherence to treatment
Post-traumatic stress	Phobia	Coping
Grief	Adjustment	Sexual problem
Marital problem	Anger	Fatigue

Referral criteria

Patient has problems for which there is evidence of effectiveness of CBT (e.g. anxiety disorder, depressive disorder)   YES/NO

Patient accepts that their thinking or behaviour may be relevant to the maintenance of their problems   YES/NO

Patient accepts some responsibility for the process of change and is willing to adopt a self-management approach to their problems   YES/NO

demand is to ensure that referrers are given a 'ration' of appointments. This way they can decide upon whom they will refer, as opposed to referring everyone who might benefit from assessment and treatment. The number of patients who do not attend first appointments can be reduced by sending first appointment letters which provide details of the nature of the referral process and invite patients to 'opt-in' for their appointment. This system is based on the assumption that patients who have no intention of attending can indicate this and/or therapists can re-allocate appointments to patients when people fail to respond to an opt-in referral letter. An example of such an appointment letter is shown in Table 12.3. In addition to the inclusion of a tear-off slip to opt in, the letter outlines what will happen when they attend the CBT clinic. In some cases, it may be helpful to send out information leaflets on CBT (e.g. those produced by the British Association for Behavioural and Cognitive Psychotherapy) or cognitive and behavioural aspects of their problems. Some therapists also include self-report measures and invite patients to complete and return these with their opt-in slip.

Table 12.3 Sample appointment letter (with opt-in slip)

CAW/HAB/34563456

COGNITIVE THERAPY CLINIC
DR C.A. WHITE

12 October 2000

Mrs Belinda Beston
6 The Close
Anytown
Scotland

Dear Mrs Beston

Dr McGhee has asked me to send you an appointment for my clinic at The Anytown Hospital. I have arranged an appointment for you

On: Monday 13 November 2000
At: 10.00 am
At: Out-Patient Suite D, The Anytown Hospital

The purpose of this appointment is to make an assessment to see whether you might benefit from a trial of cognitive therapy. I have included an information leaflet on this form of therapy. The fact that your doctor has referred you to this clinic does not mean that he/she thinks that your problems are 'all in your head' or 'imaginary'. The appointment will last for 50 minutes. I will be interested in hearing about your symptoms, your thoughts and feelings about them and how you have been coping. The purpose of the appointment will be to decide together on whether further appointments might be helpful.

There is a high demand for appointments with me. It would be helpful in our attempts to reduce the number of missed appointments if you could return the tear-off slip below to indicate that you will be attending the appointment. I have enclosed a prepaid envelope for this purpose.

If you do not return this I will assume that you do not wish this appointment. It will be offered to someone else on my waiting list.

Yours sincerely

Dr CRAIG A. WHITE
Chartered Clinical and Health Psychologist

Name: Mrs Brenda Beston
Address: 6 The Close, Anytown, Scotland

I confirm that I will be attending the appointment which I have been offered for Monday 13 November 2000 at 10.00 am

Signature _____   Date: _____

SCREENING ASSESSMENTS

Therapists should ensure that they have established arrangements for the screening and prioritisation of referrals. Screening covers the nature and extent of presenting problems, suitablity for CBT as a treatment approach, and the prioritisation of clinical need. This latter component has featured more in the service specifications of services in recent years. Some service planners and clinicians have begun to realise that it is inappropriate that a patient with a panic disorder of mild severity be asked to wait the same amount of time for treatment as someone with severely disabling depression which has only partially responded to various antidepressant medications. The criteria by which therapists will prioritise patients should be defined and agreed with clinical managers and referring clinicians. Screening systems should be sufficiently flexible that they take account of the fact that patient problems can deteriorate after screening and that this may require a change in priority status as a result. Waiting time guarantees can be tied to priority groups: this may mean that high priority groups will wait no more than two weeks for a treatment appointment, that moderate priority patients will wait no more than eight weeks for a treatment appointment, and that low-priority patient problems might wait for no more than twelve weeks. Table 12.4 outlines an example of the ways in which prioritisation following screeening can be defined.

Table 12.4   Categories for prioritising treatment

High priority

Patients with seriously incapacitating depressive or anxiety symptoms who have poor levels of social support and infrequent access to healthcare services

Patients with significant psychological problems where there is evidence of deteriorating physical health status and/or in need of palliative care

Medium priority

Patients with clinically significant symptoms which have not responded completely to other therapies (e.g. medication, nursing interventions)

Patients with access to ongoing support for their problems (e.g patient who has contact with community psychiatric nurse for supportive counselling and medication review)

Low priority

Patients with one or two circumscribed psychological problems which do not interfere with their everyday psychosocial functioning and who have a range of adequate coping strategies or access to coping strategies

Patients who have had previous periods of cognitive behavioural therapy and present referral is to address residual issues in the form of booster or relapse management issues

Patients should be told about the decisions that have been made on treatment waiting-time priority. In some cases, therapists can provide guidance at the end of a screeening appointment and/or may begin to socialise the patient to the cognitive behavioural model. Some patients can be instructed in self-monitoring and/or introductory reading on the cognitive behavioural approach to their problems.

PROVIDING FEEDBACK TO REFERRERS

Therapists tend to feedback their assessment results and opinions by sending letters to referrers. This will usually be done following screening (when this is a part of the service level agreement), following pre-therapy assessment, part way through therapy and at the completion of therapy. Therapists often complement this with letters at follow-up points and/or when there may be specific issues which need to be communicated during therapy. Letters which communicate the results of assessment are usually structured in such a way that information on timing and location of appointment is followed by a brief description of problems, an outline of relevant history, an opinion on a cognitive behavioural formulation and an action plan. An update letter is usually shorter and includes details of the patient's experience of symptoms, the way in which cognitive behavioural factors have been addressed in therapy, and an opinion on such issues as the maintenance of gains and prevention of future problems. In some cases, letters need to outline the reasons why CBT is inappropriate for certain patients and/or presenting problems. Examples of the sort of information which might be included in these letters are outlined in Tables 12.5, 12.6 and 12.7.

CASE NOTES AND RECORD-KEEPING

Notes kept by cognitive behavioural therapists should not normally form part of the patient's medical notes but should instead form a separate record, the access to which is controlled by the cognitive behavioural therapist (or the service within which the therapist practises). In most cases medical staff are happy to obtain all their information from the letters that they receive, but there are some situations in which it may be necessary to insert an entry into the patient's medical record, and this is particuarly important when therapists are working with patients in an in-patient setting and/or when there have been significant events within sessions which may impinge upon medical management. Examples of such an entry are outlined in Table 12.8.

Table 12.5   Initial assessment letter

CAW/HAB/546499302

COGNITIVE THERAPY CLINIC
DR C A WHITE

DATE ATTENDED: 13 November 2000
DATE DICTATED: 13 November 2000
DATE TYPED: 20 November 2000

Dr Janette White
Department of Haematology
Anytown Hospital
Anytown

Dear Janette

BRENDA BESTON, 6 The Close, Anytown (dob 12.06.40)

Thank you for referring Mrs Beston. She attended my out-patient clinic today for screening assessment. She reported that her main problems in recent weeks have been episodes of sadness and crying, anxiety and panic attacks. The panic attacks have been increasing in severity and seem to be associated with thoughts that she is going to die as a result of her cancer. She experiences intrusive images of her husband and daughter standing at her graveside and described her despair that she could not comfort them. She said they both looked devastated in the image. She became very distressed during the session and had a panic attack in clinic when describing this. Her panic attacks occur almost every day and occur in what seems to her to be a random pattern. She becomes concerned about collapse during each attack and has started to avoid activities which have become associated with the occurrence of panic attacks. The episodes of crying occur after the panic attacks when she is thinking that her life is wasted and that she is useless.

Screening revealed no further symptoms of particular significance. Review of her personal and family history was mostly unremarkable from a psychological perspective. However, she recalls being told by her mother that she became very distressed at the funeral of an aunt when she was 13 years old. Despite the obvious links with her current symptoms, Mrs Beston had not made this link. She clearly has significant problems associated with panic disorder. She is well supported by her GP and one of her daughters has moved back to the family home. She has been taking Seroxat 20mg in the morning, with some effect in that she reports feeling less apprehensive and has been less tearful. I have advised her that she will be placed on the moderate priority waiting list for a trial of cognitive therapy. I suspect that this will target her estimations of the likelihood of dying (which I understand are not as high as she reports), thoughts about her family's reaction to her death, her fears of collapse when panicking, her avoidance of activity and thoughts of uselessness.

I will write again when she attends for cognitive therapy.

Yours sincerely

Dr CRAIG A WHITE
Chartered Clinical and Health Psychologist

Table 12.6   Update letter

CAW/HAB/546499302

COGNITIVE THERAPY CLINIC
DR C A WHITE

DATE ATTENDED: 13 November 2000
DATE DICTATED: 13 November 2000
DATE TYPED: 20 November 2000

Mrs E Symington
Consultant Surgeon
Anytown Hospital
Anytown

Dear Eileen

JOE JEFFRIES, 14 Anytown Street, Anytown

As you know Joe has been attending my cognitive therapy clinic for treatment of his depression and associated problems coping with his longstanding experiences of pain and osteoarthritis. Since I last wrote to you he has attended for a further 3 appointments. He has been making good progress in identifying the thoughts which were underlying his depressive symptoms. He is aware of his tendency to personalise negative events by blaming himself for their occurrence and engages in 'mind-reading' when he tends to make assumptions about what others think of him. He is much more aware of the times when this is happening. He is about to visit family members abroad and the anticipation of this has raised a number of problems which he feels unable to solve. We have agreed a further meeting to review his application of some problem-solving procedures and if he maintains improvements I will suggest moving to 3 month follow-up. He says that he 'feels like a new person' and that he has 'eliminated 90% of the negative feelings I had when I first came'.

I will be in touch again after his next appointment. Please do not hesitate to contact me if you wish further information on his treatment.

Yours sincerely

Dr CRAIG A WHITE
Chartered Clinical and Health Psychologist

Most therapists will have their own method of structuring information in therapy case notes. It can be helpful to try to conduct cognitive behavioural assessments using the same broad assessment headings and to ensure that notes for therapy sessions are made according to a basic framework (see Table 12.9). At a minimum, therapy notes should outline a summary of the topics covered within sessions, treatment strategies

Table 12.7   CBT not appropriate letter

CAW/HAB/546499302

COGNITIVE THERAPY CLINIC
DR C A WHITE

DATE ATTENDED: 13 November 2000
DATE DICTATED: 13 November 2000
DATE TYPED: 20 November 2000

Dr I.T. MacDonald
The Surgery
15 Anytown Mews
Anytown

Dear Ian

MOIRA BROWN, 14 The Cottages, Anyvillage, nr Anytown.

Thanks for referring Miss Brown to the cognitive therapy clinic. She has completed the symptom diaries which you had provided her with and the questionnaire which I sent her with her appointment letter. These revealed that she experiences pain in her limbs almost constantly and that this is associated with a long list of other medical symptoms (which I notice have been extensively investigated). Miss Brown has a marked external locus of control, said that she did not accept any responsibility for changes in the way she coped with symptoms and in fact stated that 'I am quite happy with my life, quite happy to be doing what I am doing'. When I contrasted this statement with her previous statements of the extensive problems that her symptoms have caused, she said that she would prefer to rely on her faith and prayer. We had a long discussion about cognitive behavioural therapy in which I indicated that I would not wish to jeopardise any helpful strategies that she had developed. Indeed, I suggested that we could begin by exploring the helpful aspects of her faith and how this might relate to her experiences.

Unfortunately she did not wish to engage in this line of enquiry. I had to conclude today that she was not currently a suitable candidate for cognitive therapy. Although she completed symptom monitoring, there is little evidence that she is ready to adopt the sort of self-management approach to her problems that cognitive therapy would require. It may be that there are other psychological approaches which would help her. She refused an offer of attendance at my clinical psychology out-patient clinic and an offer of assessment by a colleague.

I have discharged her from this clinic and made no further plans for review.

Yours sincerely

Dr CRAIG A WHITE
Chartered Clinical and Health Psychologist

Table 12.8   Medical records entry

13/12/2000   REVIEW BY DR WHITE

Thank you for referring this lady for assessment. I saw her today on the ward for assessment of her problems and to determine whether a trial of cognitive therapy might be helpful. Her main problems relate to difficulty accepting the diagnosis of diabetes and panic about the possibility of experiencing hypoglycaemia. She is particularly troubled by thoughts of collapse and death. Her past history of panic disorder has made her vulnerable to this problem and the lack of understanding from her family is exacerbating the problem. I have arranged to place her on my waiting list. In the meantime I would recommend that (1) she be encouraged to note any problems which she notices with the day-to-day aspects of living with diabetes and that (2) she complete the panic diary we discussed every day for the next two weeks.

C A White

---

implemented, hypotheses considered by therapists, responses to symptom measures and an action plan for further sessions. In some cases, it may be helpful to record the session agenda and use this to structure note-keeping on sessions.

SERVICE EVALUATION AND MONITORING

CBT clinics should aim, as routine, to collect data for the purposes of monitoring service use and quality. This should certainly include basic service use data such as the waiting times for screening, treatment waiting times, cancellations, non-attendance rates and a breakdown of the specialty of referrers. It is increasingly being recognised that much useful information can be lost if therapists do not collect clinical information on all patients. This can be done by incorporating a broad symptom-based measure such as the Brief Symptom Inventory (Derogatis & Melisatoros, 1983). This can be used to provide service planners with information on the range of problems referred to the service and also information on changes in symptoms at the end of therapy. It is useful for services to collect data on the nature of the medical problems experienced by patients. Psychological services are often commissioned on the basis of medical specialty classifications (e.g. cardiac services or cancer services) and, therefore, being able to provide data on the number of patients with cancer who receive CBT relative to those receiving CBT after a myocardial infarction can make service planning and liaison more productive. This can be structured according to a broad-based classification developed by therapists or in terms of the International Classification of Diseases. The latter strategy requires that therapists obtain reliable information from

Table 12.9 Sample structure for CBT notes

Assessment Sessions
Problem list
Recent example(s) of problems
History
— Problem development
— Medical history
— Family history
— Personal history
— Psychological history
Coping strategies
Relationships and social support
Prior treatments
Patient view of the problem
Preliminary hypotheses
Problem-level formulation
Possible goals for treatment

Treatment Sessions
Agenda
Topics covered (incl. verbatim statements)
Hypotheses generated
Agreed
Plan

Sample Case Note Entry

Agenda
Review and Update, Image of Husband, Pain Coping, Set Homework Topics
Discussed/Strategies Implemented.

Seems that image contains distortions of how husband really was when alive, he says things that are out of character.

Implemented modification of image—hands change from grab to cuddle and he says comforting words.

Has been tending to go back to bed when has pain in lower right of abdomen → this is it, I am on the slippery slope. Suggested evaluating the impact on pain and anxiety of getting up and going to do crossword at this time.
?   Anxiety worse on days when no family members visit
?   Image is easier to dismiss when happens away from family home

Agreed
1   Will practice changing the image of husband daily and when it occurs (monitor in image frequency and nightmares)
2   Will try to resist urge to go to bed and see whether doing the crossword helps with pain and anxiety
3   Will ask at Church if there is someone that can talk to about fear of death

Plan
1   Review in two weeks
2   Repeat administration of Beck Anxiety Inventory
3   More assessment of nature and frequency of contact with family

case notes on diagnosis. In some hospital settings this information is routinely entered onto hospital computer information systems and therapists can access this from these sources.

RESOURCES

The provision of high-quality CBT requires a service which is adequately resourced. Therapists should have the necessary tools to practise CBT and have access to the basic requirements of any psychological therapist (consulting room space, basic office equipment, stationery). There are advantages to ensuring that the secretarial services for cognitive behavioural therapists are situated within the setting where most of the therapy is provided. Therapists need to have access to a basic set of self-report measures, diaries and monitoring resources. Therapists will want to have carbonless paper which ensures that summaries of the session's content can be kept by patient and therapist. They should have a range of information leaflets on CBT, therapy protocols and self-help materials on CBT. Access to at least one audio or video tape-recording machine is essential as therapists will want to make recordings of sessions for themselves and for patients. In some services tape-recording machines which make two recordings simultaneously can be used to ensure that patients can take away recordings of each session. Service budgets should take account of the fact that therapists will require to attend workshops and conferences to maintain their accreditation. Supervision may have to be purchased from external institutions when this cannot be provided locally.

DEVELOPING SERVICES

The recent popularity of CBT and the shortage of qualified therapists will mean that most therapists will be involved at some level on the development of services. The strong evidence base for CBT and the emphasis in the UK National Health Service on clinical governance (and managed care within the US) places CBT in a strong position to argue for the routine provision of CBT for the psychological problems associated with chronic medical problems. Highlighting the evidence base for CBT is unlikely to be sufficient. Service commissioners will have many competing priorities. In some cases, it can be helpful to think about obstacles to service development which are directly related to inaccurate or unhelpful beliefs about CBT ('CBT is not as effective as drug therapies'; 'CBT takes much longer to achieve improvements than drugs'). Service development may take some time and in many respects the Stages of Change Model referred to earlier in this book can be helpful for therapists wishing to think about the readiness of their local service planners to fund developments in the provision of CBT services. Therapists need to ensure that practices which are implemented on the basis of a less effective (including cost-effective) basis are replaced with practices which research has demonstrated to be effective.

THE LEGAL SYSTEM

An increasing number of patients with chronic diseases are becoming involved with the legal system because of claims for compensation relating to accidents, medical negligence and/or criminal injuries compensation. Therapists may be asked to provide opinion on the psychological consequence of an accident and/or event; or may be asked to comment on the progress that patients are making in therapy and/or the likelihood that they will make a recovery from their problems. The decision as to whether it will be appropriate to become involved in such cases is very much a matter for consideration with regard to the patient concerned, the issues being raised and the nature of existing contact with the patient.

The author's general policy for deciding on these factors is that he will provide a full report on any patient with whom he has not had prior contact (subject, of course, to the usual requirements of being within the area of expertise, appropriate, etc.), and will answer specific questions (including those on CBT content and process) for those patients who are currently in the process of being assessed and treated. Most solicitors usually wish details on the main factors predisposing, precipitating and/ or maintaining a psychological problem, and the cognitive behavioural model obviously lends itself well to addressing such questions. Therapists providing legal reports based on cognitive behavioural theory should attempt to link this with empirical findings—something that will make it easier to defend one opinion in light of an expert opinion to the contrary (particularly if it is likely to result in a court appearance). However, therapists should ask solicitors to outline in detail the specific questions that they would like answered in reports. The therapist's role in such cases is to respond to the needs of the legal process and only indirectly to the needs of the patient. Therapists who become involved in medicolegal processes for patients they are already treating may experience a conflict in the roles of therapist and legal expert.

Therapists must not feel obliged to respond to questions that are clinically meaningless and/or are outside the area of their expertise. Copies of all prior evidence, medical and hospital records can be requested and are often useful sources of information on which to formulate hypotheses and/or establish the evidence base for existing hypotheses. Self-report measures must always be completed in the presence of the therapist if these are to be completed as part of a report which will be forwarded to a solicitor. (If this is not done, then it could be argued that the patient had someone else complete the measures.)

SUMMARY AND CONCLUSIONS

Therapists need to ensure that CBT services are fully integrated with medical and mental health care systems. They should have policies and procedures for the processing and management of referrals, particularly prioritisation of the needs of patients referred to for CBT. Therapists need to ensure that they are routinely evaluating the clinical and service level elements of their work and that this is taken account of when commissioning new services. CBT services need to be adequately resourced and therapists should be clear about what is reasonable and appropriate for them to provide as individual practitioners. Developing services is not always as straightforward as one might think. The empirical foundations of CBT and the current climate of evidence-based healthcare should ensure that, in future, more patients with chronic medical problems can gain access to CBT.

Part IV

APPENDICES

Appendix 1

ILLNESS PERCEPTION QUESTIONNAIRE

YOUR VIEWS ABOUT YOUR ILLNESS

Listed below are a number of symptoms that you may or may not have experienced since your illness. Please indicate by circling 'Yes' or 'No', whether you have experienced any of these symptoms since your illness, and whether you believe that these symptoms are related to your illness.

	I have experienced this symptom *since my illness*		This symptom is *related to my illness*	
Pain	Yes	No	Yes	No
Sore throat	Yes	No	Yes	No
Nausea	Yes	No	Yes	No
Breathlessness	Yes	No	Yes	No
Weight loss	Yes	No	Yes	No
Fatigue	Yes	No	Yes	No
Stiff joints	Yes	No	Yes	No
Sore eyes	Yes	No	Yes	No
Wheeziness	Yes	No	Yes	No
Headaches	Yes	No	Yes	No
Upset stomach	Yes	No	Yes	No
Sleep difficulties	Yes	No	Yes	No
Dizziness	Yes	No	Yes	No
Loss of strength	Yes	No	Yes	No

We are interested in your own personal views of how you now see your current illness.

Please indicate how much you agree or disagree with the following statements about your illness by ticking the appropriate box.

	Views about your illness	Strongly disagree	Disagree	Neither agree nor disagree	Agree	Strongly agree
IP1	My illness will last a short time					
IP2	My illness is likely to be permanent rather than temporary					
IP3	My illness will last for a long time					
IP4*	This illness will pass quickly					
IP5*	I expect to have this illness for the rest of my life					
IP6	My illness is a serious condition					
IP7	My illness has major consequences on my life					
IP8	My illness is easy to live with					
IP9	My illness does not have much effect on my life					
IP10	My illness strongly affects the way others see me					
IP11	My illness has serious financial consequences					
IP12	My illness strongly affects the way I see myself as a person					
IP13*	My illness causes difficulties for those who are close to me					
IP14*	My illness has a negative impact on me					
IP15*	My illness is not a problem for me					
IP16*	My illness doesn't bother me much					
IP17	There is a lot which I can do to control my symptoms					

	Views about your illness	Strongly disagree	Disagree	Neither agree nor disagree	Agree	Strongly agree
IP18	What I do can determine whether my illness gets better or worse					
IP19	Recovery from my illness is largely dependent on chance or fate					
IP20*	The course of my illness depends on me					
IP21*	Nothing I do will affect my illness					
IP22*	I have the power to influence my illness					
IP23*	My actions will have no affect on the outcome of my illness					
IP24*	My symptoms are beyond my control					
IP25*	My symptoms will be around whatever I do					
IP26	My illness will improve in time					
IP27	There is very little that can be done to improve my illness					
IP28*	My treatment will be effective in curing my illness					
IP29*	The negative effects of my illness can be prevented (avoided) by my treatment					
IP30*	My treatment can control my illness					
IP31*	There is nothing which can help my condition					
IP32	The symptoms of my condition are puzzling to me					
IP33	My illness is a mystery to me					
IP34*	I don't understand my illness					

	Views about your illness	Strongly disagree	Disagree	Neither agree nor disagree	Agree	Strongly agree
IP35*	My illness doesn't make any sense to me					
IP36*	I have a clear picture or understanding of my condition					
IP37	The symptoms of my illness change a great deal from day to day					
IP38*	My symptoms come and go in cycles					
IP39*	My illness is very unpredictable					
IP40*	My illness condition is present all the time					
IP41*	I go through cycles in which my illness gets better and worse					
IP42*	I experience my illness symptoms pretty much all of the time					
IP43*	The symptoms of my illness are distressing to me					
IP44	I get depressed when I think about my illness					
IP45*	When I think about my illness I get upset					
IP46*	My illness makes me feel angry					
IP47*	My illness does not worry me					
IP48*	Having this illness makes me feel anxious					
IP49*	I worry a lot about my illness					
IP50*	My illness makes me feel afraid					

CAUSES OF MY ILLNESS

We are interested in what YOU consider may have been the cause of your illness. As people are very different, there is no correct answer for this question. We are most interested in your own views about the factors that caused your illness rather than what others, including doctors or family, may have suggested to you. Below is a list of possible causes for your illness. Please indicate how much you agree or disagree that they were causes for you by ticking the appropriate box.

	Views about your illness	Strongly disagree	Disagree	Neither agree nor disagree	Agree	Strongly agree
C1	Stress or worry					
C2	Hereditary—it runs in my family					
C3	A germ or virus					
C4	Diet or eating habits					
C5	Chance or bad luck					
C6	Poor medical care in my past					
C7	Pollution in the environment					
C8	My own behaviour					
C9	My mental attitude, e.g. thinking about life negatively					
C10	Family problems or worries caused my illness					
C11*	Overwork					
C12*	My emotional state, e.g. feeling down, lonely, anxious, empty					
C13*	Ageing					
C14*	Alcohol					
C15*	Smoking					
C16*	Accident or injury					
C17*	My personality					
C18*	Altered immunity					

In the table below, please list in rank-order the three most important factors that you now believe caused *YOUR illness*. You may use any of the items from the box above, or you may have additional ideas of your own.

The most important causes for me:

1. _____

2. _____

3. _____

Items for IPQ–R Subscales

1. Identity (sum of yes-rated symptoms in column 2 on p. 1)
2. Timeline (acute/chronic) items IP1–IP5
3. Consequences items IP6–IP16
4. Personal control items IP17–1P25
5. Treatment control items IP26–IP31
6. Illness coherence items IP32–IP36
7. Timeline cyclical IP37–IP42
8. Emotional representations IP43–50
9. Causes C1–C17

This measure has been reproduced with the permission of Professor John Weinman.

Appendix 2

CANCER BEHAVIOR INVENTORY (VERSION 2.0)

This questionnaire contains many things that a person might do when receiving treatment for cancer. We are interested in your judgement of how confident you are that you can accomplish those things. Make sure your ratings accurately reflect your **confidence whether or not** you have done it in the past. So, your ratings reflect **your confidence** that you can do these things now (or in the near future).

Please read each numbered item. Then rate that item on how confident you are that you can accomplish that behaviour. Circle a number on the scale. If you circle a '1' you would be stating that you are not at all confident that you can accomplish that behaviour. If you circle a '9' you would be stating that you are totally confident that you can accomplish that behaviour. Numbers in the middle of the scale indicate that you are moderately confident that you can accomplish that behaviour.

Please rate **all** items. If you are not sure about an item please rate it as best you can.

		Not at all confident			Moderately confident			Totally confident		
1	Maintaining independence	1	2	3	4	5	6	7	8	9
2	Maintaining a positive attitude	1	2	3	4	5	6	7	8	9
3	Accepting that I have cancer	1	2	3	4	5	6	7	8	9
4	Maintaining work activity	1	2	3	4	5	6	7	8	9
5	Asking nurses questions	1	2	3	4	5	6	7	8	9

		Not at all confident			Moderately confident			Totally confident		
6	Remaining relaxed throughout treatments and not allowing scary thoughts to upset me	1	2	3	4	5	6	7	8	9
7	Seeking support from people and groups outside the family	1	2	3	4	5	6	7	8	9
8	Maintaining a daily routine	1	2	3	4	5	6	7	8	9
9	Asking staff questions	1	2	3	4	5	6	7	8	9
10	Coping with hair loss	1	2	3	4	5	6	7	8	9
11	Using denial	1	2	3	4	5	6	7	8	9
12	Remaining relaxed throughout treatment (chemotherapy, radiation)	1	2	3	4	5	6	7	8	9
13	Coping with physical changes	1	2	3	4	5	6	7	8	9
14	Ignoring things that cannot be dealt with	1	2	3	4	5	6	7	8	9
15	Actively participating in treatment decisions	1	2	3	4	5	6	7	8	9
16	Sharing feelings of concern	1	2	3	4	5	6	7	8	9
17	Remaining relaxed while waiting at least one hour for my appointment	1	2	3	4	5	6	7	8	9
18	Expressing personal feelings of anger or hostility	1	2	3	4	5	6	7	8	9
19	Seeking information about cancer or cancer treatments	1	2	3	4	5	6	7	8	9
20	Expressing negative feelings about cancer	1	2	3	4	5	6	7	8	9
21	Keeping busy with activities	1	2	3	4	5	6	7	8	9
22	Finding an escape	1	2	3	4	5	6	7	8	9

		Not at all confident			Moderately confident			Totally confident		
23	Reducing any anxiety associated with getting my blood drawn	1	2	3	4	5	6	7	8	9
24	Maintaining a sense of humour	1	2	3	4	5	6	7	8	9
25	Accepting physical changes or limitations caused by cancer treatment	1	2	3	4	5	6	7	8	9
26	Seeking consolation	1	2	3	4	5	6	7	8	9
27	Reducing any nausea associated with treatment (chemotherapy/radiation)	1	2	3	4	5	6	7	8	9
28	Maintaining hope	1	2	3	4	5	6	7	8	9
29	Asking doctors questions	1	2	3	4	5	6	7	8	9
30	Doing something, anything	1	2	3	4	5	6	7	8	9
31	Managing pain	1	2	3	4	5	6	7	8	9
32	Managing nausea and vomiting	1	2	3	4	5	6	7	8	9
33	Controlling my negative feelings about cancer	1	2	3	4	5	6	7	8	9

The CBI is scored by summing the patient's scores across all 33 items to obtain a total score. It can also be score by factor as follows:

Maintenance of activity and independence
        Items 1, 4, 8, 21 and 30

Coping with treatment-related side effects
        Items 10, 13, 25, 31 and 32

Accepting cancer/maintaining a positive attitude
        Items 2, 3, 24, 28 and 33

Seeking and understanding medical information
        Items 15, 5, 9, 19 and 29

Affective regulation
        Items 11, 14, 18, 20 and 22

Seeking support
        Items 7, 16 and 26

Stress management for medical appointments
        Items 6, 12, 17, 23 and 27

Comparisons can be made across factors (divide the summed score by the number of items in each scale). A short form of this measure is also available. If you intend to use this measure in a research study then Dr Merluzzi would appreciate the data relating to the use of this measure for psychometric purposes. The Cancer Behavior Inventory is reproduced here with the permission of Dr Tom Merluzzi. Further information on the development of the measure can be obtained from Merluzzi and Martinez-Sanchez (1997). Also see http:// www.nd.edu/~tmerluzz

PAIN STAGES OF CHANGE QUESTIONNAIRE

This questionnaire is to help us to better understand the way you view your pain problem. Each statement describes how you *may* feel about this particular problem. Please indicate the extent to which you tend to agree or disagree with each statement. In each example, please make your choice based on *how you feel right now*, not how you have felt in the past or how you would like to feel.

Circle the response that best describes how much you agree or disagree with each statement

1 = Strongly disagree; 2 = Disagree; 3 = Undecided or unsure; 4 = Agree; 5 = Strongly agree

1.	I have been thinking that the way I cope with my pain could improve	1	2	3	4	5
2.	I am developing new ways to cope with my pain	1	2	3	4	5
3.	I have learned some good ways to keep my pain problem from interfering with my life	1	2	3	4	5
4.	When my pain flares up, I find myself automatically using coping strategies that have worked in the past, such as relaxation exercise or mental distraction technique	1	2	3	4	5
5.	I am using some strategies that help me better deal with my pain problem on a day-to-day basis	1	2	3	4	5
6.	I have started to come up with strategies to help myself control my pain	1	2	3	4	5
7.	I have recently realised that there is no medical cure for my pain condition, so I want to learn some ways to cope with it	1	2	3	4	5

8. Even if my pain doesn't go away, I am ready to start changing how I deal with it   1   2   3   4   5

9. I realise now that it's time for me to come up with a better plan to cope with my pain problem   1   2   3   4   5

10. I use what I have learned to help keep my pain under control   1   2   3   4   5

11. I have tried everything that people have recommended to manage my pain and nothing helps   1   2   3   4   5

12. My pain is a medical problem and I should be dealing with physicians about it   1   2   3   4   5

13. I am currently using some suggestions people have about how to live with my pain problem   1   2   3   4   5

14. I am beginning to wonder if I need to get some help to develop skills for dealing with my pain   1   2   3   4   5

15. I have recently figured out that it's up to me to deal better with my pain   1   2   3   4   5

16. I have recently figured out that it's up to me to learn to live with my pain, but I don't see why I should have to   1   2   3   4   5

17. I have incorporated strategies for dealing with my pain into my everyday life   1   2   3   4   5

18. I have made a lot of progress in coping with my pain   1   2   3   4   5

19. I have recently come to the conclusion that it's time for me to change how I cope with pain   1   2   3   4   5

20. I'm getting help learning some strategies for coping better with my pain   1   2   3   4   5

21. I'm starting to wonder whether it's up to me to manage my pain rather than relying on physicians   1   2   3   4   5

22. I still think despite what doctors tell me, there must be some surgical procedure or medication that would get rid of my pain   1   2   3   4   5

23. I have been thinking that doctors can only help so much in managing my pain and that the rest is up to me   1   2   3   4   5

24. The best thing I can do is find a doctor who can figure out how to get rid of my pain once and for all   1   2   3   4   5

25. Why can't someone just do something to take away my pain?   1   2   3   4   5

26. I am learning to help myself control my pain without doctors	1	2	3	4	5
27. I am testing out some coping skills to manage my pain better	1	2	3	4	5
28. I have been wondering if there is something I could do to manage my pain better	1	2	3	4	5
29. All of this talk about how to cope better is a waste of my time	1	2	3	4	5
30. I am learning ways to control my pain other than with medications or surgery	1	2	3	4	5

Scoring of The Pain States of Change Questionnaire

PRECONTEMPLATION: Sum (11, 12, 16, 22, 24, 25, 29)/7
CONTEMPLATION: Sum (1, 7, 8, 9, 14, 15, 19, 21, 23, 28)/10
ACTION: Sum (2, 6, 20, 26, 27, 30)/6
MAINTENANCE: Sum (3, 4, 5, 10, 13, 17, 18)/7

To account for sporadic missing data, sums should be divided by the number of non-missing items. Any scale with more than 25% of its items missing should be considered missing.

This measure has been reproduced by permission of Dr R Kerns. More information on this measure can be found in Kerns et al. (1997).

REFERENCES

Affleck, G., Tennen, H., Pfeiffer, C., & Fifield, J. (1987). Appraisals of control and predictability in adapting to a chronic disease. *Journal of Personality and Social Psychology, 53*(2), 273–279.

Alford, B. A., & Beck, A. T. (1994). Cognitive therapy of delusional beliefs. *Behaviour Research and Therapy, 32*(3), 369–380.

Altabe, M., & Thompson, J. K. (1996). Body image: a cognitive self schema construct? *Cognitive Therapy and Research, 20*(2), 171–193.

Andersen, B. L., Woods, X. A., & Copeland, L. J. (1997). Sexual self schema and sexual morbidity among gynaecologic cancer survivors. *Journal of Consulting and Clinical Psychology, 65*(2), 221–229.

Andersen, B.L., Cyranowski, J.C., & Espindle, D. (1999). Men's sexual self schema. *Journal of Personality and Social Psychology, 76*, 645–661.

Antonucci, D. O., Thomas, M., & Danton, W. G. (1997). A cost-effectiveness of cognitive behavior therapy and Fluoxetine (Prozac) in the treatment of depression. *Behaviour Therapy, 28*, 187–210.

Arai, Y., Kawakita, M., Hida, S., Terachi, T., Okada, Y., & Yoshida, O. (1996). Psychological aspects in long term survivors of testicular cancer. *The Journal of Urology, 155*, 574–578.

Asmundson, G. J. G. (1999). Beyond pain: the role of fear and avoidance in chronicity. *Clinical Psychology Review, 19*(1), 97–119.

BABCP (2000). *BABCP News.* British Association for Behavioural and Cognitive Psychotherapies.

Baider, L., & De-Nour, A. K. (1997). Psychological distress and intrusive thoughts in cancer patients. *Journal of Nervous and Mental Disease, 185*(5), 346–348.

Barton, S. (2000). New possibilities in cognitive therapy for depression. *Behavioural and Cognitive Psychotherapy, 28*(1), 1–4.

Basler, H., Jakle, C., & Kroner-Herwig, B. (1996). Cognitive-behavioural therapy for chronic headache at German pain centres. *International Journal of Rehabilitation and Health, 2*(4), 235–252.

Bass, C., & Mayou, R. A. (1995). Chest pain and palpitations In R. A. Mayou & M. Sharpe (Eds), *Treatment of Functional Somatic Symptoms* (pp. 328–252). Oxford: Oxford University Press.

Beck, A.T. (1976). *Cognitive Therapy and the Emotional Disorders.* New York: Penguin.

Beck, A. T., Rush, A. J., Shaw, B. F., & Emery, G. (1979). *Cognitive Therapy of Depression.* New York: Guilford Press.

Beck, A. T. (1991). Cognitive therapy: A 30-year perspective. *American Psychologist* (April), 368–375.

Beck, A. T., Wright, F. D., Newman, C. F., & Liese, B. S. (1993). *Cognitive Therapy of Substance Abuse.* New York: Guilford Press.

Beck, A. T., Guth, D., Steer, R. A., & Ball, R. (1997). Screening for major depression disorders in medical inpatients with the Beck Depression inventory for primary care. *Behaviour Research and Therapy, 35*(8), 785–791.

Beck, J. S. (1995). *Cognitive Therapy: Basics and Beyond*. New York: Guilford Press.

Bennett, P. (1993). *Counselling for Heart Diease*. Leicester: BPS Books.

Bennett, P., & Carroll, D. (1994). Cognitive-behavioural interventions in cardiac rehabilitation. *Journal of Psychosomatic Research, 38*(3), 169–182.

Black, J. L., Allison, T. G., Williams, D. E., Rummans, T. A., & Gau, G. T. (1998). Effect of intervention for psychological distress on rehospitalisation rates in cardiac rehabilitation patients. *Psychosomatics, 39* (March–April), 134–143.

Blackburn, I. M., & Twaddle, V. (1996). *Cognitive Therapy in Action: A Practitioners Casebook*. Souvenir Press: A Condor Book.

Blackburn. I.M. (1998) Cognitive therapy. In A. S. Bellack & M. Hersen (Eds), *Comprehensive Clinical Psychology* (Vol. 6: *Adults: Clinical Formulation and Treatment*, pp. 51–84): Elsevier Science.

Blenkiron, P. (1999). Who is suitable for cognitive behavioural therapy? *Journal of the Royal Society of Medicine, 92*(May).

Boc, B. J., Borger, S. C., Taylor, S., Fuentes, K., & Ross, L. M. (1999). Anxiety sensitivity and the five-factor model of personality. *Behaviour Research and Therapy, 37*, 633–641.

Bottomley, A. (1996). Group cognitive behavioural therapy: an intervention for cancer patients. *International Journal of Palliative Nursing, 2*(3), 131–137.

Bradley, C. (1994). *Handbook of Psychology and Diabetes. A Guide to Psychological Measurement in Diabetes Research and Practice*. Harwood Academic Publishers.

Bradley, C., & Gamsu, D. S. C. (1994). *Guidelines for Encouraging Psychological Wellbeing*. Report of a Working Group of the World Health Organisation Regional Office for Europe & International Diabetes Federation, European Region, St Vincent Declaration Action Programme for Diabetes. *Diabetic Medicine, 11*, 510–516.

Bradley, C. (1998). Diabetes mellitus. In A. S. Bellack & M. Hersen (Eds), *Comprehensive Clinical Psychology*. Elsevier Science.

Brewin, C., Watson, M., McCarthy, S., Hyman, P., & Dayson, D. (1998a). Memory processes and the course of anxiety and depression in cancer patients. *Psychological Medicine, 28*, 219–224.

Brewin, C. R., & Power, M. J. (1999). Integrating psychological therapies: Processes of meaning transformation. *British Journal of Medical Psychology, 72*, 143–157.

Brewin, C. R., Watson, M., McCarthy, S., Hyman, P., & Dayson, D. (1998b). Intrusive memories and depression in cancer patients. *Behaviour Research and Therapy, 36*, 1131–1142.

Brown, G. K., & Nicassio, P. M. (1987). The development of a questionnaire for the assessment of active and passive coping strategies in chronic pain patients. *Pain, 31*, 53–65.

Buick, D. L. (1997). Illness representations and breast cancer: Coping with radiation and chemotherapy. In K. J. Petrie & J. A. Weinman (Eds), *Perceptions of Health and Illness*: Harwood Academic Publishers.

Burns, L. G., & Farina, A. (1992). The role of physical attractiveness in adjustment. *Genetic, Social and General Psychology, 118*, 157–194.

Butler, G. (1998). Formulation. In P. Salkovskis (Ed.), *Comprehensive Clinical Psychology* (Vol. 6: *Adults: Clinical formulation and treatment*). Oxford, England: Pergamon/Elsevier Science Ltd.

Butler, G., Fennell, M., Robson, P., & Gelder, M. (1991). Comparison of behavior therapy and cognitive behavior therapy in the treatment of generalised anxiety disorder. *Journal of Consulting and Clinical Psychology, 59*, 167–175.

Cameron, L. D., Leventhal, H., & Love, R. R. (1998). Trait anxiety, symptom perceptions, and illness-related responses among women with breast cancer in remission during a tamoxifen clinical trial. *Health Psychology, 17*(5), 459–469.

Cash, T. F. (1994). The situational inventory of body image dysphoria: Contextual assessment of a negative body image. *The Behavior Therapist, 17*, 133–134.

Cash, T. F., & Labarge, A. S. (1996). Development of the Appearance Schemas Inventory: A new cognitive body-image assessment. *Cognitive Therapy and Research, 20*(1), 37–50.

Cash, T. F., & Szymanski, M. L. (1995). The Development and Validation of the Body-Image Ideals Questionnaire. *Journal of Personality Assessment, 64*(3), 466–477.

Cassel, E. J. (1982). The nature and suffering and the goals of medicine. *The New England Journal of Medicine, 306*(11), 639–645.

Cassileth, B. R., Lusk, E. J., Strouse, T. B., Miller, D. S., Brown, L. L., Cross, P. A., & Tenaglia, A. N. (1984). Psychosocial status in chronic illness: A comparitive analysis of six diagnostic groups. *The New England Journal of Medicine, 311*, 506–511.

Cella, D. F., Mahon, S. M., & Donovan, M. I. (1990). Cancer recurrence as a traumatic event. *Behavioral Medicine, 16*(1), 15–22.

Cella, D. F., & Tross, S. (1986). Psychological adjustment to survival from Hodgkin's disease. *Journal of Consulting and Clinical Psychology, 54*(5), 616–622

Chambless, D. L. (1998). Updated on empirically validated therapies II. *The Clinical Psychologist, 51*, 3–16.

Cipher, D. J., & Fernandez, E. (1996). Expectancy variables predicting tolerance and avoidance of pain in chronic patients. *Behavioural Research Therapy, 35*(5), 437–444.

Clark, D. A., Cook, A., & Snow, D. (1998). Depressive symptom differences in hospitalised, medically ill, depressed psychiatric inpatients and nonmedical controls. *Journal of Abnormal Psychology, 107*(1), 38–48.

Clark, D. M., & Fairburn, C. G. (Eds) (1997). *Science and Practice of Cognitive Behaviour Therapy*. Oxford University Press.

Clark, D. M., Salkovskis, P. M., Hackmann A., Wells, A., Fennell, M., Ludgate, J., Ahmad, S., Richards, H. C., & Gelder, M. (1998). Two psychological treatments for hypochondriasis: A randomised controlled trial. *British Journal of Psychiatry, 173*, 218–225.

Clark, D. M. (1999). Anxiety disorders: Why they persist and how to treat them. *Behaviour Research and Therapy, 37*, S5–S27.

Coates, A., Abraham, S., Kaye, S. B., Sowerbutts, T., Frewin, C., Rox, R. M., & Tattersal, M. H. N. (1983). On the receiving end—Patient perception of the side effects of cancer chemotherapy. *European Journal of Cancer and Clinical Oncology, 19*(2), 203–208.

Cox, D. J., Gonder-Frederick, L., & Clarke, W. L. (1996). Helping patients reduce severe hypoglycaemia. In B. J. Anderson and R. R. Rubin (Eds), *Practical Psychology for Diabetes Clinicians*. Alexandria: American Diabetes Association.

Cull, A., Anderson, E. D. C., Campbell, S., Mackay, J., Smyth, E., & Steel, M. (1999). The impact of genetic counselling about breast cancer risk on women's risk perceptions and levels of distress. *British Journal of Cancer, 79*(3/4), 501–508.

Curbow, B., Somerfield, M., Legro, M., & Sonnega, J. (1990). Self-concept and cancer in adults: Theoretical and methodological issues. *Social Sciences and Medicine, 31*(2), 115–128.

Curbow, B., & Somerfield, M. (1991). Use of the Rosenberg self-esteem scale with adult cancer patients. *Journal of Psychosocial Oncology, 9*(2), 113–131.

Cyranowski, J. C., & Andersen, B. L. (1998). Schemas, sexuality, and romantic attachment. *Journal of Personality and Social Psychology, 74*, 1364–1379.

Davidson, K. M. and Tyrer, P. (1996). Cognitive therapy for antisocial and borderline personality disorders: Single case study series. *British Journal of Clinical Psychology, 35*, 413–429.

Davidson, K. (2000). *Cognitive Therapy for Personality Disorders.* Butterworth Heinemann.

Deary, I. J., Clyde, Z., & Frier, B. M. (1997). Constructs and models in health psychology: The case of personality and illness reporting in diabetes mellitus. *British Journal of Medicine, 36*–53.

Derogatis, L. R., & Melisatoros, N. (1983). The Brief Symptom Inventory: An introductory report. *Psychological Medicine, 13,* 595–605.

DeRubeis, R. J., & Crits-Cristoph, P. (1998). Empirically supported individual and group psychological treatments for adult mental disorders. *Journal of Consulting and Clinical Psychology, 66,* 37–52.

Devins, G. M., Binik, Y. M., Hollomby, D. J., Barre, P. E., & Guttmann, R. D. (1981). Helplessness and depression in end-stage renal disease. *Journal of Abnormal Psychology, 90*(6), 531–545.

Dobson, K. S. (1989). A meta-analysis of the efficacy of cognitive therapy for depression. *Journal of Consulting and Clinical Psychology, 57*(3), 414–419.

Duits, A. A., Duivenvoorden, H. J., Boeke, S., Taams, M. A., Mochtar, B., Krauss, X. H., Passchier, J., & Erdman, R. A. M. (1999). A structural modelling analysis of anxiety and depression in patients undergoing coronary artery bypass graft surgery: A model generating approach. *Journal of Psychosomatic Research, 46*(2), 187–200.

Dunbar, S. B., & Summerville, J. G. (1997). Cognitive therapy for ventricular dysrhythmia patients. *Journal of Cardiovascular Nursing, 12*(1), 33–44.

Dunkel-Schetter, C., Feinstein, L. G., Taylor, S. E., & Falke, R. L. (1992). Patterns of coping with cancer. *Health Psychology, 11*(2), 79–87.

Dunmore, E., Clark, D. M., & Ehlers, A. (1999). Cognitive factors involved in the onset and maintenance of posttraumatic stress disorder (PTSD) after physical or sexual assault. *Behaviour Research and Therapy, 37,* 809–829.

Eimer, B. N. (1992). The treatment of chronic pain. In A. Freeman & F. M. Dattilio (Eds), *Comprehensive Casebook of Cognitive Therapy* (pp. 361–372). New York: Plenum Press.

Ell, K., Nishimoto, R., Morvay, T., Mantell, J., & Hamovitch, M. (1989). A longitudinal analysis of psychological adaptation among survivors of cancer. *Cancer, 63,* 406–413.

Enright, S. J. (1997). Cognitive behaviour therapy—clinical applications. *British Medical Journal, 314,* 1811–1816.

Epping-Jordan, J. E., Compas, B. E., Osowiecki, D. M., Oppedisano, G., Gergardt, C., Primo, K., & Krag, D. N. (1999). Psychological adjustment in breast cancer: Processes of emotional distress. *Health Psychology, 18*(4), 315–326.

Fawzy, F. I., Cousins, N., Fawzy, N., Kemeny, M. E., Elashoff, R., & Morton, D. (1990). A structured psychiatric intervention for cancer patients. *Archives of General Psychiatry, 47,* 720–725.

Faulkener, A., & Maguire, P. (1994). *Talking to Cancer Patients and Their Relatives.* Oxford: Oxford University Press.

Fennell, M. J. V. (1997). Low self esteem: A cognitive perspective. *Behavioural and Cognitive Psychotherapy, 25*(1), 1–25.

Fife, B. L. (1994). The conceptualization of meaning in illness. *Social Science and Medicine, 38*(2), 309–316.

Fife, B. L. (1995). The measurement of meaning in illness. *Social Science and Medicine, 40*(8), 1021–1028.

Freeman, A. (1987). Cognitive therapy: An overview. In A. Freeman & V. B. Greenwood (Eds), *Cognitive Therapy: Applications in Psychiatric and Medical Settings.* Human Sciences Press Inc.

Friedman, R., Sobel, D., Myers, P., Caudill, M., & Benson, H. (1995). Behavioural medicine, clinical health psychology, and cost offset. *Health Psychology, 14*(6), 509–518.

Frost, R. O., & Hartl, T. L. (1996). A cognitive-behavioural model of compulsive hoarding. *Behaviour Research and Therapy, 34*(4), 341–350.

Gelder, M. (1997). The scientific foundations of cognitive behaviour therapy. In D. M. Clark and C. G. Fairburn (Eds), *Science and Practice of Cognitive Behaviour Therapy*. Oxford: Oxford University Press.

Gil, K. M., Williams, D. A., Keefe, F. J., & Beckham, J. C. (1990). The relationship of negative thoughts to pain and psychological distress. *Behavior Therapy, 21,* 349–362.

Gil, K. M., Wilson, J. J., Abrams, M. A., Orringer, E., Clark, W. C., & Janal, M. N. (1996). Effects of cognitive coping skills training on coping strategies and experimental pain sensitivity in African American adults with sickle cell disease. *Health Psychology, 15,* 3–10.

Gilbar, O., & De-Nour, K. (1989). Adjustment to illness and dropout of chemotherapy. *Journal of Psychosomatic Research, 33*(1), 1–5.

Glasgow, R. E., Fisher, E. B., Anderson, B. J., LaGreca, A., Marrero, D., Johnson, S. B., Rubin, R. R., & Cox, D. J. (1999). Behavioral science in diabetes: Contributions and opportunities. *Diabetes Care, 22*(5), 832–843.

Gonder-Frederick, L., Cox, D., Clarke, W., & Julian, D. (2000). Blood Glucose Awareness Training. In F. J. Snoek & T. C. Skinner (Eds), *Psychology in Diabetes Care*. New York: John Wiley & Sons Ltd.

Greene, B., & Blanchard, E. B. (1994). Cognitive therapy for irritable bowel syndrome. *Journal of Consulting and Clinical Psychology, 62*(3), 576–582.

Greer, S., Moorey, S., Baruch, J. D. R., Watson, M., Robertson, B. M., Mason, A., Rowden, L., Law, M. G., & Bliss, J. M. (1992). Adjuvant psychological therapy for patients with cancer: A prospective randomised trial. *British Medical Journal, 304,* 675–680.

Guthrie, E. (1996). Emotional disorder in chronic illness: Psychotherapeutic interventions. *British Journal of Psychiatry, 168,* 265–273.

Hackmann, A. (1998). Working with Images in Clinical Psychology. In A. S. Bellack & M. Hersen (Eds), *Comprehensive Clinical Psychology.* (Vol. 6, *Adults: Clinical Formulation and Treatment*, pp. 301–318). Elsevier Science.

Haddock, G., Tarrier, N., Spaulding, W., Yusupoff, L., Kinney, C., & McCarthy, E. (1998). Individual cognitive behaviour therapy in the treatment of hallucinations and delusions: A review. *Clinical Psychology Review, 18,* 821–838.

Hay, P. J., & Bacaltchuk, J. (1999). Psychotherapy for bulimia and bingeing. *Cochrane Database of Systematic Reviews, 4.*

Heidrich, S. M., Forsthoff, C. A., & Ward, S. E. (1994). Psychological adjustment in adults with cancer: The self as mediator. *Health Psychology, 13*(4), 346–353.

Heijmans, M. (1999). The role of patients' illness representations in coping and functioning with Addison's disease. *British Journal of Health Psychology, 4,* 137–149.

Heijmans, M., & de Ridder, D. (1998). Assessing illness representations of chronic illness: Explorations of their disease-specific nature. *Journal of Behavioural Medicine, 21*(5), 485–503.

Helgeson, V. S. (1992). Moderators of the relation between perceived control and adjustment to chronic illness. *Journal of Personality and Social Psychology, 63*(4), 656–666.

Hemingway, H., & Marmot, M. (1999). Psychosocial factors in the aetiology and prognosis of coronary heart disease: systematic review of prospective cohort studies. *British Medical Journal, 318* (May), 1460–1467.

Higgins, E. T. (1987). Self discrepancy: A theory relating self and affect. *Psychological Review, 94,* 319–340.

Hippisley-Cox, J., Fielding, K., & Pringle, M. (1998). Depression as a risk factor for ischaemic heart disease in men: population based case-control study. *British Medical Journal, 316* (June), 1714–1719.

Holland, J. C., Kash, K. M., Passik, K. M., Gronert, M. K., Sison, A., Lederberg, M., Russak, S. M., Baider, L., & Fox, B. (1998). A brief spiritual beliefs inventory for use in quality of life research in life-threatening illness. *Psycho-Oncology, 7,* 460–469.

Holland, J. C., Passik, S., Kash, K. M., Russak, S. M., Gronert, M. K., Sison, A., Lederberg, M., Fox, B., & Baider, L. (1999). The role of religious and spiritual beliefs in coping with malignant melanoma. *Psycho-Oncology, 8,* 14–26.

Holman, H., & Lorig, K. (2000). Patients as partners in managing chronic disease. *British Medical Journal, 320,* 526–527.

Holzberg, A. D., Robinson, M. E., & Geisser, M. E. (1993). The relationship of cognitive distortion to depression in chronic pain: The role of ambiguity and desirability in self-ratings. *The Clinical Journal of Pain, 9,* 202–206.

Hopwood, P. (1997). Psychological issues in cancer genetics: Current research and future priorities. *Patient Education and Counselling, 32,* 19–31.

Ingram, R. E., & Smith, T. W. (1984). Depression and internal versus external focus of attention. *Cognitive Therapy and Research, 8,* 139–152.

Jacobson, P. B., & Butler, R. W. (1995). Relation of cognitive coping and catastrophizing to acute pain and analgesic use following breast cancer surgery. *Journal of Behavioural Medicine, 19*(1), 17–29.

Janoff-Bulman, R. (1989). Assumptive worlds and the stress of traumatic events: Applications of the schema construct. *Social Cognition, 7*(2), 113–136.

Jensen, M. P., Turner, J. A., Romano, J. M., & Karoly, P. (1991). Coping with chronic pain: A critical review of the literature. *Pain, 47,* 249–283.

Johnston, M., & Vogele, C. (1993). Benefits of psychological preparation for surgery: A meta-analysis. *Annals of Behavioral Medicine, 15*(4), 245–256.

Johnston, M., Morrison, V., MacWalter, R., & Partridge, C. (1999). Perceived control, coping and recovery from disability following stroke. *Psychology and Health, 14,* 181–192.

Jones, C., Cormac, I., Mota, J., & Campbell C. (1999). Cognitive behaviour therapy for schizophrenia. *Cochrane Database of Systematic Reviews,* 4.

Katz, M. R., Rodin, G., & Devins, D. (1995). Self esteem and cancer. *Canadian Journal of Psychiatry, 40,* 608–615.

Keefe, F. J., Jacobs, M., & Edwards, C. (1997). Persistent pain: Cognitive-behavioural approaches to assessment and treatment. *Seminars in Anesthesia, 16*(2), 117–126.

Kelly, J. F. (1996). Cognitive-behavioural approaches to the management of chronic pain. *Pain Digest, 6,* 359–363.

Kerns, R. D., Rosenberg, R., Jamison, R. N., Caudill, M. A., & Haythornthwaite, J. (1997). Readiness to adopt a self-management approach to chronic pain: The pain stages of change questionnaire (PSOCQ). *Pain, 72,* 227–234.

Kissane, D. W., Bloch, S., Miach, P., Smith, G. C., Seddon, A., & Keks, N. (1997). Cognitive-existential group therapy for patients with primary breast cancer—techniques and themes. *Psycho-Oncology, 6,* 25–33.

Lacroix, J. M., Martin, B., Avendano, M., & Goldstein, R. (1991). Symptom schemata in chronic respiratory patients. *Health Psychology, 10*(4), 268–273.

Lazarus, A. A., & Lazarus, C. N. (1991). *Multimodal Life History Questionnaire.* Champaign, Illinois: Research Press.

Leahy, R. (1996). *Cognitive Therapy: Basic Principles and Applications.* Jason Aronson Inc.

Leary, M. R. (1983). A brief version of the Fear of Negative Evaluation Scale. *Personality and Social Psychology Bulletin, 9*(3), 371–375.

Leary, M. R., Rapp, S. R., Herbst, K. C., Exum, M. L., & Feldman, S. R. (1998). Interpersonal concerns and psychological difficulties of psoriasis patients:

Effects of disease severity and fear of negative evaluation. *Health Psychology,* *17*(6), 530–536.

Ledanowski, L. M., Gebing, T. A., Anthony, J. L., & O'Brien, W. H. (1997). Meta-analysis of cognitive behavioral treatment studies for bulimia. *Clinical Psychology Review, 17,* 703–718.

Lee-Jones, C., Humphris, G., Dixon, R., & Bebbington Hatcher, M. (1997). Fear of cancer recurrence—A literature review and proposed cognitive formulation to explain exacerbation of recurrence fears. *Psycho-Oncology, 6,* 95–105.

Lepore, S. J., & Helgeson, V. S. (1998). Social constraints, intrusive thoughts and mental health after prostate cancer. *Journal of Social and Clinical Psychology, 17*(1), 89–106.

Leventhal, H., Diefenbach, M., & Leventhal, E. A. (1992). Illness cognition: Using common sense to understand treatment adherence and affect in cognition interactions. *Cognitive Therapy and Research, 16*(2), 143–163.

Lewin, B. (1997). The Psychological and Behavioural Management of Angina. *Journal of Psychosomatic Research, 43*(5), 453–462.

Lewin, B., Cay, E. L., Todd, I., Soryal, I., Goodfield, N., Bloomfield, P., & Elton, R. (1995). The angina management programme: A rehabilitation treatment. *British Journal of Cardiology* (September), 221–226.

Lewin, R. J. P. (1999). Improving quality of life in patients with angina. *Heart, 82,* 654–655.

Livengood, J. M. (1996). Psychological techniques for chronic pain management. *Pain Digest, 6,* 77–82.

McCaul, K. D., Sandgren, A. K., King, B., O'Donnell, S., Bransetter, A., & Foreman, G. (1999). Coping and adjustment to breast cancer. *Psycho-Oncology, 8,* 230–236.

McDaniel, M., & Schlager, M. (1990). Discovery learning and transfer of problem solving skills. *Cognition and Instruction, 7,* 129–159.

Magaletta, P. R., & Oliver, J. M. (1999). The hope construct, will, and ways: Their relations with self-efficacy, optimism, and general well-being. *Journal of Clinical Psychology, 55*(5), 539–551.

Manne, S. L. (1999). Intrusive thoughts and psychological distress among cancer patients: The role of spouse avoidance and criticism. *Journal of Consulting and Clinical Psychology, 67*(4), 539–546.

Manson, H., Manderino, M. A., & Johnson, M. H. (1993). Chemotherapy: Thoughts and images of patients with cancer. *Oncology Nursing Forum, 20*(3), 527–532.

Maxwell, T. D., Gatchel, R. J., & Mayer, T. G. (1998). Cognitive predictors of depression in chronic low back pain: Toward an inclusive model. *Journal of Behavioural Medicine, 21*(2), 131–143.

Mayou, R. A., Bryant, B. M., Sanders, D., Bass, C., Klimes, I., & Forfar, C. (1997). A controlled trial of cognitive behavioural therapy for non-cardiac chest pain. *Psychological Medicine, 27,* 1021–1031.

Melzack, R. (1975). The McGill Pain Questionnaire: Major properties and scoring methods. *Pain, 1,* 277–299.

Merluzzi, T. V., & Martinez-Sanchez, M. A. M. (1997). Assessment of self efficacy and coping with cancer: Development and validation of the cancer behaviour inventory. *Health Psychology, 16*(2), 163–170.

Meyer, T. J., & Mark, M. M. (1995). Effects of psychosocial interventions with adult cancer patients: A meta-analysis of randomized experiments. *Health Psychology, 14*(2), 101–108.

Miller, L. (1992). Psychotherapy of the chronic pain patient: II. Treatment principles and practices. *Psychotherapy in Private Practice, 11*(1), 69–82.

Milne, D. L., Baker, C., Blackburn, I. M., James, I., & Reichelt, K. (1999). Effectiveness of cognitive therapy training. *Journal of Behaviour Therapy and Experimental Psychiatry, 30,* 81–92.

Montgomery, C. (1999). Psycho-oncology: A coming of age. *Psychiatric Bulletin, 23,* 431–435.

Moorey, S. (1996). When bad things happen to rational people: Cognitive therapy in adverse circumstances. In P. Salkovskis (Ed.), *Frontiers of Cognitive Therapy* (pp. 450–469) New York: Guilford Press.

Moorey, S., Greer, S., Bliss, J., & Law, M. (1998). A comparison of adjuvant psychological therapy and supportive counselling in patients with cancer. *Psycho-Oncology, 7,* 218–228.

Morley, S., Eccleston, C., & Williams, A. (1999). Systematic review and meta analysis of randomised controlled trials of cognitive behaviour therapy and behaviour therapy for chronic pain in adults, excluding headache. *Pain, 80,* 1–13.

Murphy, H., Dickens, C., Creed, F., & Bernstein, R. (1999). Depression, illness perception and coping with rheumatoid arthritis. *Journal of Psychosomatic Research, 46*(2), 155–164.

Nelson, T. O., Stuart, R. B., Howard, C., & Crowley, M. (1999). Metacognition and clinical psychology: A preliminary framework for research and practice. *Clinical Psychology and Psychotherapy, 6,* 73–79.

Newshan, G., & Balamuth, R. (1990/91). Use of imagery in a chronic pain outpatient group. *Imagination, Cognition and Personality, 10*(1), 25–38.

Nordin, K., Berglund, G., Terje, I., & Glimelius, B. (1999). The mental adjustment to cancer scale—A psychometric analysis and the concept of coping. *Psycho-Oncology, 8,* 250–259.

O'Connor, A. P., Wicker, C. A., & Germino, B. B. (1990). Understanding the cancer patient's search for meaning. *Cancer Nursing, 13*(3), 167–175.

Osborne, R. H., Elsworth, G. R., Kissane, D. W., Burke, S. A., & Hopper, J. L. (1999). The Mental Adjustment to Cancer (MAC) Scale: Replication and refinement in 632 breast cancer patients. *Psychological Medicine, 29,* 1335–1345.

Overholser, J. C. (1993). Elements of the socratic method: 1. Systematic questioning. *Psychotherapy, 30* (Spring).

Padesky, C. A. (1993). Socratic Questioning: Changing minds or guiding discovery? *Behavioural and Cognitive Therapies* (September).

Padesky, C. A. (1993). Schema as self-prejudice. *International Cognitive Therapy Newsletter,* Vol. 5/6, 16–17.

Papadopoulous, L., & Bor, R. (1999). *Psychological Approaches to Dermatology.* Leicester: BPS Books.

Papageorgiou, C., & Wells, A. (1998). Effects of attention training on hypochondriasis: a brief case series. *Psychological Medicine, 28,* 193-200.

Papageorgiou, C., & Wells, A. (1999). Process and meta-cognitive dimensions of depressive and anxious thoughts and relationships with emotional intensity. *Clinical Psychology and Psychotherapy, 6,* 156–162.

Parle, M., Jones, M., & Maguire, P. (1996). Maladaptive coping and affective disorders among cancer patients. *Psychological Medicine, 26,* 735–744.

Pauli, P., Wiedemann, G., Dengler, W., Blaumann-Benninghoff, G., & Kuhlkamp, V. (1999). Anxiety in Patients with an automatic implantable cardioverter defibrillator: What differentiates them from panic patients? *Psychosomatic Medicine, 6* (January/February), 69–76.

Penninx, B. W. J. H., van Tilburg, T., Boeke, A. J. P., Deeg, D. J. H., Kriegsman, D. M. K., & van Eijk, J. T. M. (1998). Effects of Social Support and personal coping resources on depressive symptoms: Different for various chronic diseases? *Health Psychology, 17*(6), 551–558.

Petrie, K. J., Weinman, J., Sharpe, N., & Buckley, J. (1996). Roles of patients' view of their illness in predicting return to work and functioning after myocardial infarction: longitudinal study. *British Medical Journal, 312,* 1191–1194.

Prat, L. A., Ford, D. E., Crum, R. M., Armenain, H. K., Gallo, J. J., & Eaton, W. W. (1996). Depression, Psychotropic medication and risk of myocardial infarction. Prospective data fom the Baltimore ECA follow up. *Circulation, 94*(12), 3123–3129.

Price, J. R., & Cooper, J. (1999). Cognitive behaviour therapy for chronic fatigue syndrome in adults. *Cochrane Database of Systematic Reviews, 4.*

Prochaska, J.O., & diClemente, C. C. (1986). Toward a comprehensive model of change. In W. R. Miller & N. Heather (Eds), *Treating Addictive Behaviours: Processes of Change.* Applied Clinical Psychology (pp. 3–27). New York: Plenum Press.

Prohaska, T. R., Keller, M. L., Leventhal, E. A., & Leventhal, H. (1987). Impact of symptoms and aging attribution on emotions and coping. *Health Psychology, 6*(6), 495–514.

Purdon, C. (1999). Thought suppression and psychopathology. *Behaviour Research and Therapy, 37,* 1029–1054.

Rachman, S. (1998). Progress toward a cognitive clinical psychology. *Journal of Psychosomatic Research, 45*(5), 387–389.

Reynolds, M., & Wells, A. (1999). The Thought Control Questionnaire—Psychometric properties in a clinical sample, and relationships with PTSD and depression. *Psychological Medicine, 29,* 1089–1099.

Rosen, J. C., Srebnik, D., Saltzberg, E., & Wendt, S. (1991). Development of Body Image Avoidance Questionnaire. *Journal of Consulting and Clinical Psychology, 3*(1), 32–37.

Rosenetiel, A. K., & Keefe, F. J. (1983). The use of coping strategies in chronic low back pain patients: Relationship to patient characteristics and current adjustment. *Pain, 17,* 33–44.

Rubin, R. R., & Peyrot, M. (1992). Psychosocial problems and interventions in diabetes. A review of the literature. *Diabetes Care, 15*(11), 1640–1657.

Rudy, T. E., Kerns, R. D., & Turk, D. C. (1988). Chronic pain and depression: Toward a cognitive-behavioural mediation model. *Pain, 35,* 129–140.

Safran, J., & Segal, Z. (1996). *Interpersonal Process in Cognitive Therapy.* Jason Aronson Inc.

Salkovskis, P. M. (1989). Somatic problems. In K. Hawton, P. M. Salkovskis, J. Kirk & D. M. Clark (Eds), *Cognitive Behaviour Therapy for Psychiatric Problems.* Oxford: Oxford University Press.

Salkovskis, P. M. (1999). Understanding and treating OCD. *Behaviour Research and Therapy, 37* (Suppl. 1): S29–S52.

Salkovskis, P. M., & Rimes, K. A. (1997). Predictive genetic testing: Psychological factors. *Journal of Psychosomatic Research, 43,* 477–487.

Salmon, P., Mikhail, G., Stanford, C., Zialinsk, S., & Pepper, J. R. (1998). Psychological adjustment after cardiac transplantation. *Journal of Psychosomatic Research, 45*(5), 449–458.

Scandlyn, J. (2000). When AIDS became a chronic disease. *Western Journal of Medicine, 172,* 130–133.

Schmidt, N. B., Joiner, T. E., Young, J. E., & Telch, M. J. (1995). The Schema Questionnaire: Investigation of psychometric properties and the hierarchical structure of a measure of maladaptive schemas. *Cognitive Therapy and Research, 19*(3), 295–321.

Schnoll, R. A., Harlow, L. L., Brandt, U., & Stolbach, L. L. (1998). Using two factor structures of the Mental Adjustment to Cancer (MAC) Scale for assessing adaptation to breast cancer. *Psycho-Oncology, 7,* 424–435.

Scott, J. (1996). Cognitive therapy for clients with bipolar disorder. *Cognitive and Behavioral Practice, 3,* 29–51.

Scott, J., & Moorhead, S. (1998). Cognitive therapy training for psychiatrists. *Advances in Psychiatric Treatment, 4,* 3–9.

Shaw, B. F., Olmsted, M., Dobson, K. S., Sotsky, S. M., Elkin, I., Yamaguchi, J., Vallis, T. M., Lowery, A., & Watkins, J. T. (1999). Therapist competence ratings in relation to clinical outcome in cognitive therapy of depression. *Journal of Consulting and Clinical Psychology, 67*(6), 837–846.

Shirley, E. (1997). Treatment of hair pulling. *Beck Institute Newsletter,* October.

Smets, E. M. A., Garssen, B., Bonke, B., & de Haes, J. C. J. M. (1995). The multidimensional fatigue inventory (MFI) psychometric qualities of an instrument to assess fatigue. *Journal of Psychosomatic Research, 39*(5), 315–325.

Smith, M. Y., Redd, W. H., Peyser, C., & Vogl, D. (1999). Post traumatic stress disorder in cancer: A review. *Psycho-Oncology, 8*(6), 521–537.

Spence, S. H. (1993). Role of cognitive therapy in the management of chronic pain. *Behaviour Change, 10*(4), 228–236.

Stukas Jr, A. A., Dew, M. A., Switzer, G. E., DiMartini, A., Kormos, R. L., & Griffith, B. P. (1999). PTSD in heart transplant recipients and their primary family caregivers. *Psychosomatics, 40*(3), 212–221.

Szymanski, M. L., & Cash, T. F. (1995). Body-image disturbances and self-discrepancy theory: Expansion of the body-image ideals questionnaire. *Journal of Social and Clinical Psychology, 14*(2), 134–146.

Tan, S., & Leucht, C. A. (1997). Cognitive behavioural therapy for clinical pain control. *International Journal of Clinical and Experimental Hypnosis, 45*(4), 396–416.

Tarrier, N., Yusupoff, L., Kinney, C., McCarthy, E., Gledhill, A., Haddock, G., & Morris, J. (1999). Randomised controlled trial of intensive cognitive behaviour therapy for patients with schizophrenia. *British Medical Journal, 317,* 303–307.

Taylor, S. E. (1983). Adjustment to threatening events: A theory of cognitive adaptation. *American Psychologist* (November), 1161–1173.

Thompson, S. C., Sobolew-Shubin, A., Galbraith, M. E., Schwankovsky, L., & Cruzen, D. (1993). Maintaining perceptions of control: Finding perceived control in low-control circumstances. *Journal of Personality and Social Psychology, 64*(2), 293–304.

Turner, J., & Kelly, B. (2000). Emotional dimensions of chronic disease. *Western Journal of Medicine, 172,* 124–128.

Wallston, K. A., Wallston, B. S., & De Vellis, R. (1978). Development of the Multidimensional Health Locus of Control (MHLC) Scales. *Health Education Monographs, 6* (Spring).

Wallston, K. A., Stein, M. J., & Smith, C. A. (1994). Form C of the MHLC Scales: A condition specific measure of locus of control. *Journal of Personality Assessment, 63*(3), 534–553.

Warwick, H. M. C., Clark, D. M., Cobb, A. M., & Salkovskis, P. M. (1996). A controlled trial of cognitive-behavioural treatment of hypochondriasis. *British Journal of Psychiatry, 169,* 189–195.

Watson, D., & Friend, R. (1969). Measurement of social-evaluative anxiety. *Journal of Consulting and Clinical Psychology, 33*(4), 448–457.

Watson, L. M., dos Santos, M., Greer, S., Baruch, J., & Bliss, J. (1994). The Mini-MAC: Further development of the Mental Adjustment to Cancer Scale. *Journal of Psychosocial Oncology, 12*(3).

Watson, M., Greer, S., Young, J., Inayat, Q., Burgess, C., & Robertson, B. (1988). Development of a questionnaire measure of adjustment to cancer: The MAC scale. *Psychological Medicine, 18,* 203–209.

Watts, F. N. (1980). Behavioural aspects of the management of diabetes mellitus: Education, self-care and metabolic control. *Behaviour Research and Therapy, 18,* 171–180.

Weinman, J., Wright, S., & Johnston, M. (1995). *Measures in Health Psychology: A Users Portfolio.* Windsor: NFER Nelson.

Weinman, J., Petrie, K. J., Moss-Morris, R., & Horne, R. (1996). The illness perception questionnaire: A new method for assessing the cognitive representation of illness. *Psychology and Health, 11,* 431–455.

Weishaar, M. E. (1993). *Aaron T Beck.* Sage Publications.

Weiss, D. S., & Marmar, C. R. (1996). The Impact of Events Scale—Revised. In J. P. Wilson and T. M. Keane (Eds), *Assessing Psychological Trauma and PTSD* (pp. 399–411). New York: Guilford Press.

Wells, A. (1985). Relationship between private self consciousness and anxiety scores in threatening situations. *Psychological Reports, 57,* 1063–1066.

Wells, A., & Davies, M. T. (1994). The Thought Control Questionnaire: A measure of individual differences in the control of unwanted thoughts. *Behaviour Research and Therapy, 32,* 871–878.

Wells, A. (1997). *Cognitive Therapy of Anxiety Disorders.* Chichester: John Wiley & Sons.

Wells, A. (2000). *Emotional Disorders and Metacognition. Innovative Cognitive Therapy.* Chichester: John Wiley & Sons.

Wessely, S. C., & Lewis, G. H. (1989). The classification of psychiatric morbidity in attenders at a dermatology clinic. *British Journal of Psychiatry, 155,* 686–691.

White, C. A. (2000). Body image dimensions and cancer: A heuristic cognitive behavioural model. *Psycho-Oncology, 7,* 2.

White, C. A., & Unwin, J. C. (1998). Post-operative adjustment to surgery resulting in the formation of a stoma: The importance of stoma related cognitions. *British Journal of Health Psychology, 3,* 85–93.

Widner, S., & Zeichner, A. (1993). Psychological interventions for the elderly chronic pain patient. *Clinical Gerontologist, 13*(4), 3–18.

Wilkinson, D. G. (1981). Psychiatric aspects of diabetes mellitus. *British Journal of Psychiatry, 138,* 1–9.

Yurek, D., Farrar, W., & Andersen, B.L. (in press). Breast cancer surgery: Comparing surgical groups and determining individual differences in post-operative sexuality and body change stress. *Journal of Consulting and Clinical Psychology.*

Zigmond, A. S., & Snaith, R. P. (1983). The hospital anxiety and depression scale. *Acta Psychiatrica Scandinavica, 67,* 361–370.

Zung, W. W. S. (1965). A self rating scale for depression. *Archives of General Psychiatry, 12,* 63–70.

INDEX

Note. Page references in *italics* refer to figures; those in **bold** refer to tables.

Index compiled by Annette Musker

The Wiley Series in

CLINICAL PSYCHOLOGY

Martin Herbert, Eric Emerson, Chris Hatton, Jo Bromley and Amanda Caine (Editors)	Clinical Child Psychology (second edition) Clinical Psychology and People with Intellectual Disabilities
J. Mark G. Williams, Fraser N. Watts, Colin MacLeod and Andrew Mathews	Cognitive Psychology and Emotional Disorders (second edition)
Phil Mollon	Multiple Selves, Multiple Voices: Working with Trauma, Violation and Dissociataion
Paul Chadwick, Max Birchwood and Peter Trower	Cognitive Therapy for Delusions, Voices and Paranoia
Peter Sturmey	Functional Analysis in Clinical Psychology
Frank Tallis	Obsessive Compulsive Disorder: A Cognitive and Neuropsychological Perspective
David Fowler, Philippa Garety and Elizabeth Kuipers	Cognitive Behaviour Therapy for Psychosis: Theory and Practice
Robert S.P. Jones, Peter G. Walsh and Peter Sturmey	Stereotyped Movement Disorders
D. Colin Drummond, Stephen T. Tiffany, Steven Glautier and Bob Remington (Editors)	Addictive Behaviour: Cue Exposure Theory and Practice
Carlo Perris, Willem A. Arrindell and Martin Eisemann (Editors)	Parenting and Psychopathology
Chris Barker, Nancy Pistrang and Robert Elliott	Research Methods in Clinical and Counselling Psychology
Graham C.L. Davey and Frank Tallis (Editors)	Worrying: Perspectives on Theory, Assessment and Treatment
Paul Dickens	Quality and Excellence in Human Services